KRISHNAMURTI:
His Life and Death

KRISHNAMURTI:
His Life and Death

MARY LUTYENS

St. Martin's Press
New York

Library of Congress Cataloging-in-Publication Data

Lutyens, Mary.
    Krishnamurti, his life and death / Mary Lutyens.
        p.   cm.
    ISBN 0-312-05455-6
    1. Krishnamurti, J. (Jiddu), 1895-   . I. Title.
    B5134.K754L86   1991
    181'.4—dc20   90-49169
                                                                        CIP

First published in Great Britain by John Murray Limited.

First U.S. Edition: April 1991
10 9 8 7 6 5 4 3 2 1

Contents

CONTENTS

Illustrations

(For thirty years Krishnamurti would rarely allow himself to be photographed, hence the lack of pictures of him in middle age.)

I am deeply grateful to Mark Edwards for giving me copies of his photographs, published by courtesy of the Krishnamurti Educational Trust Ltd who own the copyright.

Acknowledgements

I wish to apologise to Krishnamurti's many friends who have not been mentioned in this book. I hope they will understand that in compressing his life into one volume much extraneous detail has had to be omitted, though nothing, I hope, essential to his development.

For giving me permission to quote from their writings, my deep gratitude is due to David Bohm, Mary Cadogan, Mark Edwards, Pupul Jayakar, Dr Parchure, the late Doris Pratt, Vanda Scaravelli and especially to Scott Forbes and Mary Zimbalist. I should also like to thank Ray McCoy for promptly sending me from the Brockwood Centre anything I asked for in the way of books, video tapes and cassettes, and Radha Burnier for giving me a copy of Nitya's long letter to Mrs Besant from the Theosophical Archives at Adyar describing the beginning of 'the process'.

Without the friendship and generosity of the late B. Shiva Rao, I could never have attempted to write Krishnamurti's biography in the first place.

Introduction

Krishnamurti requested several times that there should be no authoritative interpretation of his teaching, although he encouraged those interested in it to discuss it among themselves. This present book, therefore, makes no attempt to explain or evaluate the teaching which is available in dozens of books, cassettes, audio and video tapes. Its aim, rather, is to try to discover the source of the revelation on which the teaching is based, to illuminate the nature of a most remarkable human being, to trace the course of his development and see his long life in perspective. This it is difficult to do in three detailed volumes separated by a space of years – eight years in the case of the first and second volumes.

After the first volume, *The Years of Awakening*, was published I was asked whether I believed in the happenings I had recorded. My reply was that I certainly believed in them until 1928 – that is, until I was twenty – with the exception of the crazy events in Holland in 1925. Subsequently, my attitude to them changed in accordance with Krishnamurti's own.

I cannot remember a time when I did not know Krishnamurti. This was because my mother had befriended him when he first came to England in 1911, a bewildered young man of seventeen, seeming much younger than his age, who, two years before, had been chosen by the leaders of the Theosophical Society in India as the vehicle for the coming messiah. My mother had joined the Theosophical Society in 1910, before I was three years old, and I was brought up on its tenets which were outwardly very simple: a belief in the brotherhood of man and the equality of all religions. Instead of 'Our Father which art in heaven . . .', I was taught to recite every morning: 'I am a link in the golden chain of love that stretches round the world and I promise to keep my link bright and strong.' There was, however, an esoteric heart to Theosophy of which I did not become fully aware until I was about thirteen. This esoteric core and the founding of the Society will be described in the first chapter of this book.

Theosophy was to cause a breach between my parents which widened as the years went by, yet, ironically, it was through my father that my mother discovered Theosophy. In 1909 my father, Edwin Lutyens, had received a commission from a French banker, Guillaume Mallet, to build a house for him at Varengeville on the coast of Normandy, not far from Dieppe. On my father's return from his first visit to the site he told my mother that the Mallets were Theosophists. When she asked him what that meant he said he did not know but that they had a secret cupboard of books which they always kept locked. This intrigued my mother and when she accompanied my father on his next visit to Varengeville she persuaded Madame Mallet to give her a short outline of Theosophical beliefs. What struck her most was the normality of the Mallets, the lack of crankiness in them which she would have associated with a 'quack' religion. Their only eccentricity was that they were strict vegetarians. At Christmas, Madame Mallet sent my mother the *London Lectures* of 1907 by Mrs Annie Besant,* President of the Theosophical Society, which filled her with such 'absorbed interest and delight', according to her autobiography,† that at moments she became 'so excited' that she could hardly restrain herself 'from shouting with joy'. It seemed to open up to her new vistas of spiritual understanding.

My mother was ripe for conversion. After thirteen years of marriage to an increasingly ambitious, successful architect, who, although loving her passionately, was so absorbed in his work that he had no time to give her or their five children any companionship, she was desperately searching for some satisfying occupation to stimulate her emotional and

---

*Mrs Besant, born in 1847, had been married to a clergyman, Frank Besant. After the birth of two children she lost her faith and had the courage to tell her husband. He divorced her and was given custody of the children although she fought hard in the Courts, conducting her own defence, to keep them. She then became a declared atheist and a social reformer, a colleague of Charles Bradlaugh and a close friend of Bernard Shaw. She was converted to Theosophy in 1889 when W. T. Stead asked her to review *The Secret Doctrine* by Madame Blavatsky, one of the founders of the Theosophical Society.

†*Candles in the Sun* (Hart-Davis, 1957).

intellectual needs. Housewifery, and ordinary social life bored her intensely and her children were cared for by a perfect nanny. She had become an ardent supporter of the Womens' Suffrage movement (but was never a militant for fear of going to prison and being forcibly fed); she had read a great deal of sociology and joined an organisation called the Moral Education League, concerned with the State-regulation of prostitution for which she wrote pamphlets and attended conferences in many parts of England. As part of this work she became a weekly visitor to the Lock Hospital for the treatment of venereal disease where she read Dickens to the patients. (She had a superb gift for reading aloud.) She also organized evening discussions at our house in Bloomsbury Square to consider such questions as heredity versus environment. But, unlike so many of her contemporaries, she was not interested in spiritualism,* nor, at that stage of her life, in occultism or Indian mysticism which had drawn so many Westerners to the East since their Christian faith had been undermined by Darwin.

Being of a very devotional nature, an ardent Christian in youth with a strong sense of her closeness to Jesus, the Theosophical belief in the near coming of the messiah, and the need to prepare the world for this stupendous event, satisfied every aspect of my mother's being. After joining the Society early in 1910 all her energies went into the movement; she took lessons in public speaking so that she could travel about giving lectures on Theosophy (she became an accomplished public speaker). She also started a new Theosophical Lodge† with Dr Haden Guest (later Lord Guest), also a recent convert, 'intended to unite all those who wished to give practical effect to the Theosophical tenets of brotherhood.'

In the summer of 1910 Mrs Besant came to England from India and my mother went to hear her lecture at the Fabian Society on 'An Ideal Form of Government'. Bernard Shaw and Sidney Webb were on the platform. 'I got quite a shock when I first saw her,' my mother wrote. 'She looked so unlike anyone I had ever seen before. She was dressed in flowing white robes of a most feminine character, while her fine

---

*Spiritualism – that is, the belief that the dead can communicate with the living, especially through mediums – was still one of the most burningly controversial questions of the day. The Society for Psychical Research had been founded in England in 1882 to investigate the evidence. Interest in all forms of the supernatural was widespread.

†The Society was divided into Lodges. There were Lodges in all the big towns in England and Scotland, and many in Europe, which arranged meetings and lecture tours.

massive head with its short white curls looked entirely masculine. She was sixty-three but showed not the slightest sign of decreasing vigour. She had the most amazing vitality of anyone I have ever met.'

A few weeks later my mother heard her speak again at a hall in Kingsway on 'The Coming Christ', and afterwards found the courage to approach her and ask her to lunch. She accepted. The only other person present at the lunch was my father.

Mrs Besant asked on arrival if she might remove her hat, shaking out her short white curls when she did so which my mother later found to be characteristic of her. My mother remembered thinking that she had eyes like a tiger, of a curious shade of brown, which seemed to look right through her and penetrate her inmost thoughts. My father, at this first meeting, liked Mrs Besant and was impressed by her, especially when she asked him before she left to design the new English Theosophical Headquarters in Tavistock Square (now occupied by the British Medical Association). It was only gradually that he came to resent her influence over my mother.

In 1929, at the age of thirty-four, Krishnamurti severed himself from the Theosophical Society, after a spiritual experience that completely changed his life, and renounced his role of coming messiah to travel the world as a teacher with his own religious philosophy, unattached to any orthodox religion or sect. The single object of his teaching was to set men free from all the cages which divide man from man, such as race, religion, nationality, class and tradition, and thereby bring about a transformation in the human psyche.

There has been no diminution of interest in Krishnamurti's teaching since his death in February 1986, three months before his ninety-first birthday. Indeed, his reputation is spreading. The reason why he is not even better known is that he never sought personal publicity. People heard of him through word of mouth or from accidentally coming across one of his books.

While Krishnamurti was being proclaimed by the Theosophical Society, money and gifts of land and property were showered on him by its members. When he resigned from the Society and denied his role, he returned these gifts to the donors and began his new life without knowing whether he would have any followers or any money beyond an annuity of £500. As it happened, he attracted a new following from a wider and far more interesting world, and money appeared as if by magic for most of the projects he set his heart on. He would say for the rest of his life, 'Do a thing, and if it is right the money will come in.'

Krishnamurti refused to be anyone's guru. He did not want people to follow him blindly and obediently. He deplored the cult of gurudom and transcendental meditation brought from India to the West. Especially, he did not want disciples who might create another religion around him, build up a hierarchy and assume authority. All he claimed for his teaching was that it held up a mirror in which people could see themselves exactly as they were inwardly and outwardly, and if they did not like what they saw *change themselves*.

Krishnamurti's special interest was in the education of children before their minds became rigid with the prejudices of the society in which they had been born. The seven schools he founded and which bear his name – five in India, one in England and one in California – still flourish. His oldest school, Rishi Valley, founded in the early 1930s between Madras and Bangalore, now has 340 students, a third of them girls, and a reputation for being one of the best schools in India. His English school in Hampshire, the smallest, has only sixty pupils, but of twenty-four nationalities and an equal number of boys and girls.

A large Krishnamurti Centre for adults was opened soon after his death, close to the English school though quite separate from it. The conception of this Centre, and the building of it was one of Krishnamurti's chief concerns in the last two years of his life.* Three smaller adult centres have now been built in India. Krishnamurti also established three Foundations in the 1960s – in England, India and California, and a subsidiary one in Puerto Rico – of a purely administrative nature, each with its board of trustees. There are also asociated committees in twenty-one countries.

Krishnamurti had dozens of friends in as many countries as there are these committees, in every walk of life from queens to Buddhist monks. In the early days Bernard Shaw, Leopold Stokowski and Antoine Bourdelle, the sculptor, had been among his greatest admirers, and, later, Aldous Huxley, Jawaharlal Nehru and Pablo Casals were among his friends. More recently, he made friends with Mrs Gandhi, Professor Maurice Wilkins, winner of a Nobel prize for medicine, Dr David Bohm, the physicist, Rupert Sheldrake, the biologist, and Terence Stamp, the actor, and he came to know some of the well-known people who interviewed him or held discussions with him, including Dr Jonas Salk and the Dalai Lama. Krishnamurti undoubtedly helped in building a bridge between science and religion.

---

* Photographs of this Centre appear in the Prince of Wales's book, *A Vision of Britain* (Doubleday, 1989).

The audiences for Krishnamurti's talks were not large, varying between 1,000 and 5,000 in his last twenty years according to the size of the hall or tent in which he spoke. What was his attraction for those who came to hear him? It was remarkable how few hippies there were among them, although the majority were young. His audiences for the most part consisted of well-behaved, cleanly dressed people, as many men as women, who listened to him seriously and intently even though he had no gift of oratory. His teaching was not intended to bring comfort but to shake people into awareness of the dangerous state of the world for which every individual was responsible since, according to him, every individual *was* the world in microcosm.

Part of Krishnamurti's attraction was no doubt his appearance. Except as a young boy he had been extraordinarily beautiful, and even in old age he retained great beauty of figure, bone structure and carriage. But more than this, there was a personal magnetism that drew people to him. He could speak publicly with sternness, sometimes almost fierceness, but with people individually or in small groups there was a sense of great warmth and affection. Although he did not like being touched himself, he would, when sitting talking to someone, frequently lean forward to put a hand on his or her arm or knee, and he liked to hold tightly the hand of a friend or someone who came to him for help. Above all, when he was not talking seriously, he loved to laugh and joke and exchange silly stories. His loud, deep laugh was infectiously endearing.

The fact that there is a sustained, or even growing, interest in Krishnamurti since his death shows, I think, not only that some of this personal magnetism comes over in his cassettes and video tapes but that his teaching has a message for today which people desperately want. Although one may not agree with many of the things he said, his sincerity cannot be doubted.

KRISHNAMURTI:
His Life and Death

1

'What of the boy Krishna?'

The most remarkable thing about Krishnamurti's life was that the prophecies made about him in his youth were fulfilled, yet in a very different way from what had been expected. For an understanding of his development it is essential to have at least a slight knowledge of the Theosophical mysticism that nurtured him. The Theosophical Society, whose object was 'to form the nucleus of a Universal Brotherhood of Humanity', was founded in America in 1875 by that extraordinary Russian mystic, clairvoyante and miracle worker, Madame Helena Petrovna Blavatsky, and Colonel Henry Steel Olcott, a veteran of the American Civil War who was deeply interested in spiritualism and also claimed clairvoyance. This odd couple, who remained close 'chums', as Olcott put it, for the rest of their lives, adopted as their occult creed so many of the ancient traditions of the East that, in 1882, they moved their headquarters to a large compound at Adyar, a suburb south of Madras, a most beautiful spot where the Adyar river joins the Bay of Bengal, with one of the largest banyan trees in India and a mile of river frontage stretching to an empty, sandy beach. There the International Headquarters of the Society has remained ever since, with more houses built and more land acquired, and from there the movement soon spread all over the world.

To become a member of the Society it was necessary merely to affirm a belief in the brotherhood of man and the equality of all religions, but at the heart of the Society was the Esoteric Section to which membership was granted only after the applicant had proved his sincerity and usefulness to the Society.

The Esoteric Section took from the ancient wisdom of several religions

1

a hierarchy of great spiritual beings, the so-called Great White Brotherhood. Having accepted the theory that mankind evolves through a series of lives (reincarnation) to ultimate perfection (which everyone would attain in the end, however many lives it took), it was not difficult to believe that human beings were at all different stages of evolution, or in the so-called Masters. The Masters were perfected souls who, released from the wheel of karma, that inexorable law by which we reap what we sow, both of good and evil, through a series of lives, had elected to remain in touch with humanity in order to help it along the path of evolution. There were many Masters but the two who were said to have taken the Theosophical Society under their special protection were the Master Morya and the Master Kuthumi. In Madame Blavatsky's time these Masters were believed to live close to each other, in splendid human bodies in a ravine in Tibet from where they often emerged to travel in other parts of the world. They could also materialise themselves while remaining in Tibet and communicate in materialised letters to the leaders of the Society.* Madame Blavatsky claimed to have lived in Tibet with the Masters for many months, being given by her own adopted Master Morya the occult teaching she had always longed for and which she afterwards gave to the world through her mammoth books, *Isis Unveiled* and *The Secret Doctrine,*as well as through the Esoteric Section.[1]

Higher than the Masters in the hierarchy of spiritual beings was the Lord Maitreya, the Bodhisattva, who, it was believed by Theosophists at the time of Krishnamurti's 'discovery' in 1909, would before long take over a human vehicle especially prepared for him, just as two thousand years before he had taken over the body of Jesus to found a new religion. The Bodhisattva incarnated when the world had a special need of him. Above him in the hierarchy were even greater beings, including the Buddha.[2]

Madame Blavatsky died in 1891, and on the death in 1907 of the first President of the Theosophical Society, Colonel Olcott, Mrs Annie Besant was elected President and thereafter made her home at Adyar. She and her chief colleague, Charles Webster Leadbeater (a former Church of England clergyman and disciple of Madame Blavatsky), were both clairvoyant, though Mrs Besant later put aside her occult powers when she devoted most of her energies to the cause of Indian Home Rule. Both Mrs Besant and Leadbeater claimed to be in close touch with the Masters. It was Leadbeater, however, who became the

*Some of the Mahatma Letters, as they are called, are in the British Library.

2

spokesman for his own Master, Kuthumi (Mrs Besant's Master was Morya), carrying out his instructions and guiding his earthly pupils along the occult Path of Discipleship. The Masters were willing to consider pupils if they were sufficiently evolved. The steps on the Path were Probation, Acceptance and then four Initiations culminating in the fifth, Adepthood, which was the attainment of perfection, nirvana.

According to Leadbeater, the Masters still lived in the same ravine in Tibet, in the same bodies in which Madame Blavatsky had known them, miraculously preserved from ageing. They no longer left their valley, however, but could be visited on the astral plane in their homes.[3] Leadbeater would take candidates for discipleship in their astral bodies, while asleep, to the house of the Master Kuthumi and then announce to them in the morning whether they had been successful or not in reaching the step on the Path which they aspired to. It can be imagined what power Leadbeater came to exercise over his flock, who ardently believed in him and in the existence of the Masters and the other holy beings they were told about, and what snobbery and jealousy their faith gave rise to. Leadbeater maintained that he and Mrs Besant were both so highly evolved that they had already taken their fourth, or Arhat, initiation by the time Krishnamurti came to Adyar.

Jiddu Krishnamurti was born on 11 May 1895,* at Madanapalle, a small hill town between Madras and Bangalore. His father, Jiddu Narianiah, had married a cousin, Sanjeevamma, who bore him ten children, of whom Krishna was the eighth. This Telegu-speaking, strictly vegetarian Brahmin family were not badly off by Indian standards, Narianiah being an official in the Revenue Department of the British administration, rising before his retirement to the position of District Magistrate. Narianiah was a Theosophist and Sanjeevamma a worshipper of Sri Krishna, himself an eighth child after whom she called her own eighth child.

Sanjeevamma had a premonition that this eighth child was to be remarkable in some way and insisted, in spite of her husband's protests, that it should be born in the puja room. A Brahmin writer has pointed out that this prayer room could normally only be entered after a ritual bath and the putting-on of clean clothes: 'Birth, death and the

---

*This date is in accordance with Hindu astrological calculations which count the day as lasting from 4 am to 4 am. By Western reckoning, he would have been born at 12.30 am on 12 May.

menstrual cycle were the focus of ritual pollution ... that a child should be born in this room was unthinkable.'⁴ And yet it was so.

Unlike Sanjeevamma's other confinements, it was an easy birth. The next morning the baby's horoscope was cast by a well-known astrologer who assured Narianiah that his son was to be a very great man. For years it seemed unlikely that his prediction would be fulfilled. Whenever the astrologer saw Narianiah he would ask, 'What of the boy Krishna? ... Wait. I have told you the truth; he will be someone very wonderful and great.'

At the age of two Krishna almost died of malaria. Thereafter, for several years, he suffered from bouts of malaria and severe nose bleeds which kept him away from school and closer to his mother than any of her other children. He loved to go with her to the temple. He was such a vague and dreamy child, and so bad at school work, which he hated, that he appeared to his teachers to be mentally retarded. Nevertheless, he was extremely observant, as he was to be all his life. He would stand for long stretches at a time, watching trees and clouds, or squat to gaze at flowers and insects. He also had a most generous nature, another characteristic which he retained throughout his life. He would often return from school without pencil, slate or books, having given them to some poorer child, and when beggars came to the house in the mornings to receive the customary gift of unboiled rice and his mother sent him out to distribute the food, he would return for more, having poured all the rice into the first man's bag. When they came again in the evening for cooked food and the servants tried to drive them away, Krishna ran inside to bring food to them. If Sanjeevamma made the children special sweetmeats as a treat, Krishna would take only part of his share and give the rest to his brothers.

Krishna had another trait in his character which remained with him and which seems strangely at variance with his dreamy nature – a love of machinery. This first showed itself one day when he took his father's clock to pieces to find out how it worked and refused to go to school or even to eat until he had put it together again which, it seems, he succeeded in doing.

There was a special bond between Krishna and his brother Nitya-nanda (Nitya), who was three years younger. Nitya was as sharp and clever at school as Krishna was vague and unteachable, and as they grew older Krishna became more and more dependent on this little brother.

In 1904 Krishna's eldest sister died, a girl of twenty who was of a very spiritual nature. It was after her death that Krishna showed for the first time that he was clairvoyant: both he and his mother often saw the dead girl at a special place in the garden. The following year, however, when Krishna was ten and a half, a far worse tragedy befell the family: Sanjeevamma herself died. Krishna saw her after her death even more clearly than he had seen his sister, a fact which Narianiah confirmed.*

When Narianiah was compulsorily retired at the end of 1907, at the age of fifty-two on a pension of only half his former salary, he wrote to Mrs Besant offering his services in any capacity at Adyar. (Although an orthodox Brahmin, he had been a member of the Theosophical Society since 1882; Theosophy embraces all religions.) He told her that he was a widower with four sons ranging in age from fifteen to five, and that as his only daughter was married there was no one but himself to look after the boys. (Since Krishna was the eighth child, and had two younger brothers and a sister living, four other children must have died apart from the girl of twenty.) Mrs Besant declined his offer on the grounds that the nearest school was three miles away and that the boys would be a disturbing influence in the compound. Fortunately, Narianiah persisted and was eventually given a job at the end of 1908 as an assistant secretary. He moved to Adyar with his sons on 23 January 1909. As there was no house available inside the compound, the family were put in a dilapidated cottage just outside, with no indoor sanitation. The boys arrived in a shocking physical condition.

Narianiah's sister, who had quarrelled with her husband, came to look after the household for a time, but she seems to have been a slatternly woman and a very bad cook. The eldest boy, Sivaram, who wanted to be a doctor, joined the Presidency College in Madras while Krishna, not yet fourteen, and Nitya, who was also born in May, not yet eleven, walked six miles every day to and from the Pennathur Subramanian High School at Mylapore where Krishna was caned almost every day for stupidity. Little Sadanand, aged five, was neither physically nor mentally well enough to go to school and was to remain retarded all his life.

In 1906, when he was fifty-six, Charles Leadbeater had been involved in a sexual scandal which had split the Theosophical Society throughout the world. Between 1900 and 1905 he had been on long lecture tours

---

*The account of Krishna's birth and childhood was dictated by Narianiah in 1911 to an English Theosophist at Adyar and signed by Narianiah in the presence of two reliable witnesses.

in America, Canada and Australia, making converts for Theosophy and giving special instruction to adolescent boys (he had built up a great reputation as a tutor). Then two boys from Chicago confessed to their parents, without, apparently, any collusion, that he had been encouraging them in the habit of masturbation. This was at a time when homosexuality was not only abhorrent to the general public but masturbation was thought to lead to madness and blindness.* Mrs Besant wrote to Leadbeater in terrible distress when she heard this, for one of the essential requirements for initiation was absolute sexual purity. Leadbeater replied that he advocated masturbation in certain cases as a far lesser evil than guilty obsession with sexual thoughts; all the same he promised never again to advocate the practice within the Theosophical Society – for *her* sake, not because he did not believe in it.

Leadbeater was required to attend a Council meeting at the Grosvenor Hotel in London on 16 May 1906 to answer the charges against him. Before doing so, he handed in his resignation from the Society. In order to avoid publicity, Colonel Olcott, the President in India, accepted his resignation, to the intense indignation of many members who wanted him expelled, for he did not clear himself at the hearing. After that, Leadbeater lived quietly in the country, in England or in Jersey, for almost three years, with occasional trips to the Continent, teaching privately and being helped financially by the many friends he had retained in the Society. Most of his former pupils vouched for his purity. When Mrs Besant was elected President by a huge majority in June 1907, she succeeded, after an intense campaign, in having him readmitted into the Society at the end of 1908, though he was never again to hold any official position. She now sent for him to come to India where she wanted his help. On 10 February 1909 he arrived at Adyar, less than three weeks after Narianiah had settled there with Krishna and his brothers.

Leadbeater went to live at the small, so-called Octagon River Bungalow close to the Headquarters building. His chief work was dealing with the vast correspondence that came in from all over the world. He had brought with him as a secretary a young Dutchman, Johann van Manen, and was grateful for extra secretarial help from a young Englishman, Ernest Wood, who knew shorthand and had already been

---

* *The World Through Blunted Sight*, Patrick Trevor-Roper, p. 155 (Thames and Hudson, 1988).

at Adyar for three months working on the monthly magazine *The Theosophist*. In the room next to Wood's, in the cheap lodgings in which he lived, was a young Indian, Subrahmanyam Aiyar, who was a friend of Narianiah. These two men had met Krishna and Nitya and were helping them with their homework.

It became a habit for van Manen, Wood and Subrahmanyam to go down to the beach to bathe every evening where Krishna and Nitya, with some other children who lived outside the compound, were usually to be found paddling. Van Manen suggested to Leadbeater one day that he should go with them as he believed one of the boys might interest him. Leadbeater went and immediately picked out Krishna who, he said, had the most wonderful aura he had ever seen, without a particle of selfishness in it; he predicted to Wood that one day the boy would become a great spiritual teacher. Wood was amazed, for, having helped Krishna with his homework, he considered him particularly stupid.

Not long after seeing Krishna on the beach, Leadbeater asked Narianiah to bring the boy to his bungalow on a day when there was no school. This Narianiah did. Leadbeater seated Krishna beside him, put his hand on the boy's head and began to describe his former life. Thereafter, on Saturdays and Sundays, the visits and relation of past lives continued, written down by Narianiah who was, at first, always present, and later by Wood in shorthand. The name given to Krishna throughout the lives was Alcyone.* The date of Leadbeater's first meeting with Krishna in the Octagon Bungalow is uncertain but, since Mrs Besant left Adyar on 22 April for a lecture tour in America without apparently having heard anything about him, it was probably after that date.

Considering Leadbeater's homosexual tendencies, it must be emphasised that it could not have been Krishna's outward appearance that attracted him. Krishna, apart from his wonderful eyes, looked far from prepossessing at that time. He was scrawny, undernourished, covered in mosquito bites, with lice even in his eyebrows, crooked teeth and his hair shaved to the crown and falling in a pigtail at the back. Moreover, he had a vacant expression that gave him an almost moronic look. People who knew him then have said that there was little to choose between him and Sadanand. According to Wood, he was physically so weak that his father declared more than once that he was bound to die.

---

* *The Lives of Alcyone* was later published in monthly instalments in *The Theosophist*.

(Krishna himself was to say later in life that he would certainly have died had Leadbeater not 'discovered' him.)

We have Krishna's own account of his first meeting with Leadbeater, written some years later:

> When I first went over to his room I was much afraid, for most Indian boys are afraid of Europeans. I do not know why it is that such fear is created, but apart from the difference in colour, which is no doubt one of the causes, there was, when I was a boy, much political agitation and our imaginations were much stirred by the gossip about us. I must also confess that the Europeans in India are by no means generally kind to us and I used to see many acts of cruelty which made me still more bitter. It was a surprise to us, therefore, to find how different was the Englishman who was also a Theosophist.[5]

Shortly after these sessions began in the Octagon Bungalow, Leadbeater told Wood that the boy was to be the vehicle for the Lord Maitreya (or the World Teacher as he was more often called) and that he, Leadbeater, had been directed by the Master Kuthumi to help train him for that destiny.[6]

Leadbeater seemed to have forgotten or disregarded the fact that he had already chosen a vehicle – a good-looking fourteen-year-old boy, Hubert, son of Dr Weller van Hook of Chicago who had been a staunch supporter of his at the time of the scandal. At a public lecture in Chicago on 'The Coming Teacher', during her American tour, Mrs Besant announced: 'We look for Him to come in the Western world this time – not in the East as did Christ two thousand years ago.' Leadbeater had picked out Hubert in Chicago, when he was eleven; Mrs Besant had met him in Europe in 1907 and now, meeting him again in 1909, she persuaded his mother to take him to Adyar to be trained by Leadbeater. Mother and son were to arrive there in the middle of November, little suspecting that Hubert had been supplanted.*

Before long Leadbeater induced Narianiah to take Krishna and Nitya away from school and allow them to be educated under his supervision while still living with their father. (Krishna refused to do anything without Nitya.) Four tutors were provided for them, as well

---

*Hubert and his mother stayed at Adyar for five years. He afterwards went to Oxford, married and became an attorney in Chicago. He was very bitter about Leadbeater. *The Last Four Lives of Annie Besant*, A. H. Nethercote, p. 193n. (Hart-Davis, 1961).

as Leadbeater himself who taught them history – Ernest Wood, Subrahmanyam Aiyar, Don Fabrizio Ruspoli (who had resigned from the
Italian navy when he became a Theosophist) and Dick Clarke, a
newcomer to Adyar who had been an engineer. But the most important
subject taught was the English language so that the boys might be able
to talk to Mrs Besant when she arrived back in Adyar. They already
knew a certain amount of English and did not find this subject difficult.
They soon forgot their native Telegu and were not, unfortunately,
taught any other Indian language.

Dick Clarke was also given the task of grooming Krishna and Nitya.
They were deloused and provided with clean clothes every morning;
their hair was allowed to grow at the front and was cut to shoulder
length, and Krishna was fitted with a plate for his teeth which Clarke
had to tighten every day. In addition to their four tutors, John Cordes,
an Austrian living at Adyar, was responsible for building them up
physically. But it was Leadbeater who supervised their washing, making
sure that they washed between their legs. He deplored the ritualistic
Hindu way of bathing while wearing a loincloth. Exercise and nourish-
ing food were insisted on – long bicycle rides, swimming, tennis and
gymnastics. Krishna enjoyed these outdoor activities – he was a natural
athlete – but he was still hopeless at lessons. Instead of attending to the
tutor, he would stand by the open window, with his mouth open looking
at nothing in particular. Over and over again he was told by Leadbeater
to shut his mouth. He obeyed but it would immediately fall open again.
At last one day Leadbeater became so exasperated that he slapped him
on the chin. This, Krishna was to declare in later life, ended their
relationship. His mouth remained closed but he never felt the same
about Leadbeater again.

Leadbeater was even more concerned with the boys' occult training
than with their physical well being. On the night of 1 August he took
them in their astral bodies while asleep to the house of Master Kuthumi
who put them on probation, and thereafter, for the next five months
before Krishna was accepted, Leadbeater took him in his astral form
to the Master for fifteen minutes' instruction, at the end of which the
Master would summarize his talk in a few simple sentences. The next
morning in the Octagon Bungalow Krishna would write down what
he remembered of the Master's words. Dick Clarke and a lady living
at Adyar both vouched for the fact that these notes were written down
by Krishna himself with great laboriousness and that the only help he
received was with spelling and punctuation. It was these notes that
were afterwards made into a little book, *At the Feet of the Master* by

9

Alcyone, which has been translated into twenty-seven languages and is still in print. Alcyone wrote in the foreword: 'These are not my words; they are the words of the Master who taught me.'

On 17 November 1909 Mrs Besant arrived back in India and Krishna met her for the first time. It was the beginning of an undying love between them. Leadbeater had written to her in Europe on her return journey to tell her about the lives of Alcyone he was investigating, but it was not until she got to Adyar that she learnt of his expectations for the boy. During the three weeks which she stayed at Adyar before going up to Benares for the Theosophical Convention,* the boys were in her room at Headquarters every day, where she gave them reading lessons. She was able to soothe the growing friction between Narianiah and Leadbeater, who had no patience with the father's objection to his sons being removed further and further from his influence. She arranged, with Narianiah's consent, that while she was in Benares the boys should stay in her room in the Headquarters building.

On 31 December Leadbeater telegraphed to Mrs Besant to say that the Master Kuthumi had intimated that he was going to accept Krishna as his pupil that night and would she please be present.[7] Next day she sent Leadbeater her recollections of the ceremony and asked him to confirm whether it was true that the Lord Maitreya had given Krishna into her and Leadbeater's charge. Leadbeater replied: 'It is true that the Lord Maitreya solemnly gave him into our charge on behalf of the Brotherhood. Krishna was deeply impressed and has been different ever since.'

But soon a far more exciting event was to take place. On 8 January 1910, there was a dramatic exchange of telegrams. Leadbeater to Mrs Besant in Benares: 'Initiation ordered for eleventh. Surya [the Lord Maitreya's pseudonym in *The Lives of Alcyone*] in person will officiate. Ordered afterwards to visit Shamballa.† Involves thirty-six hour seclusion.' The reply was immediate: 'Close Shrine [room] and my verandah locking stairs door for time required. Use my room, my secretary's and Mrs Lubke's‡ as needed. You hold my authority for everything.'

* The annual conventions were held in alternate years at Adyar, the international headquarters of the Theosophical Society, and Benares, the headquarters of the Indian section. Mrs Besant had a house at Benares.

† An oasis in the Gobi Desert where lived the King of the occult hierarchy, the Sanat Kumara of Hindu scripture.

‡ An elderly lady who worked in the library. Her room was next to Mrs Besant's drawing room. Leadbeater found her 'a depleting influence', and this gave him an excellent opportunity to move her permanently and have her room whitewashed.

From the Monday evening of 10 January until the morning of the 12th, Krishna and Leadbeater were shut up in Mrs Besant's room with Nitya or Dick Clarke keeping a constant vigil outside the door. Clarke recorded that Leadbeater and Krishna remained 'away from their bodies during the best part of two nights and a day, coming back very occasionally and then only partially, though sufficiently to absorb nourishment (mostly warm milk) which we administered at their bedsides.' Krishna lay on Mrs Besant's bed and Leadbeater on the floor.[8]

According to Leadbeater, in a letter to Mrs Besant, Krishna woke on the morning of the 11th, crying out, 'I remember! I remember!' Leadbeater asked him to tell him all he remembered and these memories were written down on the 12th in a very long letter to Mrs Besant. Leadbeater assured her that these were in Krishna's own words, except for some help with his tenses and supplying a word here and there. As recorded by Krishna, the Master Morya was at the house of Master Kuthumi as well as Mrs Besant and Leadbeater; then they all went together to the house of the Lord Maitreya where several other Masters were present. Krishna was led in front of the Lord Maitreya with his sponsors, Mrs Besant and Leadbeater, and, having answered correctly the questions put to him by the Lord, he was welcomed into the Great White Brotherhood. The next night he was taken to see the King of the World, and that, as he wrote, 'was the most wonderful experience of all for He is a boy not much older than I am, but the handsomest I have ever seen, all shining and glorious, and when He smiles it is like sunlight. He is strong like the sea, so that nothing can stand against Him, and yet He is nothing but love, so that I could not be the least afraid of Him.'[9]

When Krishna emerged from Mrs Besant's room everyone waiting outside prostrated before him. It certainly looks from the photograph taken directly afterwards that he had undergone some very wonderful experience. He remembered nothing of all this in later years except what other people had told him.

In March, Narianiah agreed to transfer the legal guardianship of the two boys to Mrs Besant. She moved them to the room next to her own although they continued to have lessons in the Octagon Bungalow. In September she took them to Benares where they stayed with her at her house, Shanti-Kunja. Krishna picked out five men from Mrs Besant's special group of followers and asked if he might teach them the qualifications for discipleship as taught to him by the Master Kuthumi. Among these five were George Arundale, the thirty-two-year-old Principal of the Central Hindu College at Benares, and E. A. Wodehouse,

11

the English Professor there, elder brother of P. G. Wodehouse. Mrs Besant, delighted at the request, wrote to Leadbeater: 'It is so good to see him opening out, bless him... He is developing very rapidly, and shows no trace of shyness or timidity, but a pretty and gracious dignity...he fathers George [Arundale] quite quaintly.' Krishna himself asked Leadbeater to send him the notes he had made of the Master's teaching.*

Wodehouse wrote about Krishna at this time at Benares:

> What struck us particularly was his naturalness...of any kind of a side or affectation there was not a trace. He was still of a retiring nature, modest and deferential to his elders and courteous to all. To those whom he liked, moreover, he showed a kind of eager affection, which was singularly attractive. Of his 'occult' position he seemed to be entirely unconscious. He never alluded to it – never, for a moment, allowed the slightest hint of it to get into his speech or manner... Another quality was a serene unselfishness. He seemed to be not in the least preoccupied with himself... We were no blind devotees, prepared to see in him nothing but perfection. We were older people, educationalists, and with some experience of youth. Had there been a trace in him of conceit or affectation, or any posing as the 'holy child', or a priggish self-consciousness, we would undoubtedly have given an adverse verdict.[10]

Wodehouse's description could be truthfully applied to Krishna's nature for the rest of his life.

---

*Leadbeater typed out the notes before sending them (the notes themselves have disappeared) and it was this typed version that was used for *At the Feet of the Master*.

2

'A tremendous power'

Early in 1911 the International Order of the Star in the East was founded, with Krishna as its Head and Mrs Besant and Leadbeater its Protectors. The object of the Order was to draw together all those who believed in the near Coming of the World Teacher and to help prepare public opinion to receive him. George Arundale was made secretary to the Head. A quarterly magazine, the *Herald of the Star*, was founded and was printed at Adyar.

In February of that year Mrs Besant took the boys on a tour of Burma. Krishna, from seeing there so many beautiful statues of the Buddha, conceived a reverence for him that he never lost. On their return to Adyar, Leadbeater told Mrs Besant that it was the Master's wish that the boys should go to England. Mrs Besant, therefore, set off with them for Bombay on 22 March. In Benares, on the way, European clothes were bought for them and the large holes in their ears, which had been pierced when they were very young, were painfully sewn up by a doctor. (Krishna never lost the slight scars in his ears.) They were accompanied by Arundale who had taken a few months' leave from the Hindu College.

They sailed from Bombay on 22 April. Mrs Besant reported to Leadbeater, in the first of her weekly letters to him, that the boys were managing their European clothes very well, though they found their shoes 'restricting', and that Krishna was delighted because the Captain had allowed him 'to see something of the workings of the ship, particularly the "Marconi apparatus"'.

There was tremendous excitement among the English Theosophists who went to Charing Cross Station on 5 May to welcome Mrs Besant and her wards. The glorious destiny awaiting Krishna had not been kept secret. In the crowd was the thirty-six-year-old Lady Emily Lutyens whose life for the next twenty years was to revolve around Krishna. Mrs Besant, with the boys, went to stay with her closest friend in England, Miss Esther Bright, and her widowed mother at 82 Drayton Gardens. On 8 May a meeting was held at the Theosophical Headquarters in Bond Street at which Mrs Besant announced the formation of the Order of the Star in the East and said that all who wished to enrol as members should give their names to George Arundale. Lady Emily was one of the first to do so, and shortly afterwards Mrs Besant asked her to become National Representative of the Order for England. Two others to enrol, who had been converted to Theosophy by Lady Emily, were Miss Mary Dodge and Muriel, Countess De La Warr, the friend who lived with her in a huge house in St James's, Warwick House. Miss Dodge was an American who had lived in England for twenty years and was now so crippled with arthritis that she had to use a wheelchair. She had inherited from her grandfather, William Earle Dodge, a fortune derived from copper, real estate and railroads. She put a car at Mrs Besant's disposal while she was in England.

The boys were taken to see all the sights of London, but what they most enjoyed were the theatres. They hated walking because their European shoes were agony. Mrs Besant took them with her to the various places in England and Scotland where she held Theosophical meetings. Lady Emily accompanied them to Oxford and remembered them at a garden party there on a bitterly cold May day – two shivering little Indian boys looking so forlorn and cold that she longed to put her arms around them and mother them. She took them, along with the two eldest of her five children, to see the Coronation procession of George V on 22 June.

Later Mrs Besant gave three lectures at the Queen's Hall in London on 'The Coming of the World Teacher'. The interest was so great that, after filling the hall, hundreds of people were turned away. She was a magnificent, if flowery, orator. The writer, Enid Bagnold, who heard her speak on the same subject at the Queen's Hall in 1912, recounted in her autobiography: 'When she came on to the platform she was burning. Her authority reached everywhere.'

In August Mrs Besant and the boys stayed with the Brights at Esher in Surrey where they had a cottage. Lady Emily visited them there several times and recalled the terrible indigestion that Krishna suffered from as a result of the strict diet prescribed for him by Leadbeater, supposedly under orders from the Master Kuthumi: 'Innumerable glasses of milk had to be consumed during the day, and porridge and eggs for breakfast. I can see Krishna now, after a sleepless night of pain, struggling to eat his prescribed breakfast under Mrs Besant's stern eye. How I longed to snatch that plate from him and give his inside a rest. The digestive trouble, with acute pain, persisted until about 1916.'[11] Nitya, less docile than Krishna, complained to Miss Bright that there were no spices in the food.

According to Leadbeater, the Master wanted the boys to be educated in England and to go to Oxford; therefore, in August, their names were put down for New College, where Krishna was expected to take up residence in October 1914.

Back in India and rejoined by Leadbeater, what was said to be the first manifestation of the Lord Maitreya in Krishna took place at the Theosophical Convention at Benares on 28 December. Leadbeater described the occasion in a letter to Ruspoli at Adyar. Krishna was standing, giving out certificates to new members of the Order of the Star in the East when all at once Leadbeater felt 'a tremendous power flowing through him' [Krishna] and the next members, as they filed past, fell at his feet, some of them with tears pouring down their cheeks. Next day, at a meeting of the Esoteric Section, Mrs Besant said publicly, for the first time, that 'after what they had seen and felt, it was no longer possible to make even a pretence of concealing the fact that Krishna's body had been chosen by the Bodhisattva [The Lord Maitreya] and was even now being attuned to him.'

In January 1912 Mrs Besant received a letter from Narianiah threatening to bring a lawsuit against her to recover the custody of his sons. He was willing for her to take them to England to be educated only if she promised to sever them completely from Leadbeater, whom he detested. According to Narianiah, she gave him this promise. Leadbeater, however, was determined now to find a quiet place where he might prepare Krishna for his second initiation. Forbidden by Narianiah from taking the boy to the Nilgiri Hills as he had intended, Leadbeater left India secretly to find a suitable setting in Europe, while Mrs Besant, giving out that she was sailing with the boys from Bombay on 10 February, actually sailed on the 3rd. She wrote to Narianiah ordering him to leave Adyar immediately.

This time Dick Clarke accompanied them and also C. Jinarajadasa (Raja), a prominent leader of the Theosophical Society who had been abroad lecturing at the time when Krishna was 'discovered'. On 25 March, accompanied only by Clarke and Raja, the boys travelled to

Taormina in Sicily where Leadbeater had settled and where they were joined by Arundale. They remained there for nearly four months, occupying a whole floor of the Hotel Naumachia, Mrs Besant being with them from May to July. During their stay, Krishna and Raja were said by Leadbeater to have taken their second initiation and Nitya and Arundale their first.

Arundale went back to India in July while Mrs Besant, Raja and the boys returned to England, and Leadbeater, who never again visited England, went to Genoa for a short time. Mrs Besant wrote to tell him that she had received a letter from Narianiah calling on her to hand over the boys by the end of August. The letter was published in a Madras paper, *The Hindu*, which launched a vicious attack on Mrs Besant, Leadbeater and the Theosophical Society. The editor was a personal enemy of Mrs Besant and she and Leadbeater both believed that it was he who had got hold of Narianiah and was financing the suit he was soon to file against her. She was now afraid that this editor might try to kidnap the boys, so, before returning to India, leaving the boys in England, she ensured that they were hidden in the country. Lady De La Warr lent them her house, Old Lodge in Ashdown Forest, and there they remained for six months, with Raja and Dick Clarke as their tutors and two former pupils of Leadbeater's as bodyguards. Mrs and Miss Bright were in charge of the household. Lady Emily went down to see them many times. The mutual attachment between her and Krishna was deepening.

Narianiah's contention in the lawsuit he brought against Mrs Besant in the High Court of Madras was, briefly, that she had no right to delegate the guardianship of the boys that he had conferred on her to a person against whom he had the strongest aversion. He also alleged that there had been an 'unnatural association' between Leadbeater and the elder boy. Mrs Besant, conducting her own defence, lost the suit, though the most damaging accusation, of Leadbeater's unnatural association with Krishna, was dismissed. She was ordered to hand over the boys to their father. She immediately appealed but also lost the appeal. She then applied to the Privy Council in England; judgement was given in her favour and she was awarded costs. The appeal was allowed chiefly on the grounds that the boys' wishes had not been consulted and that they had not been represented in Court. The boys did not wish to return to India and the order of the Madras Court could not be carried out without their consent. But there had been so many delays that this judgement was not given until 25 May 1914, by which time Krishna was eighteen, the age at which boys attained their majority according to Indian law.[12]

Krishna wrote to Mrs Besant in India when he heard the verdict, thanking her for all her loving care since she first saw him on the platform at Madras: 'I know that the only thing you want is that I should help others as you have helped me, and I shall remember this always now that I am of age and free to follow my will without your guardianship.' Krishna never missed a mail in sending Mrs Besant loving little letters that told little of his real state of mind.

3

'Why did they pick on me?'

While the court hearings were continuing the two boys were moved around from place to place. In the summer of 1913 they were at Varengeville, on the coast of Normandy, where a house had been lent to them by M. Mallet.* Arundale had now resigned from the Central Hindu College to help tutor the boys. Instructions from the Master came through Leadbeater that Krishna was never to go out unless accompanied by two initiates – this meant Arundale and Raja. Raja was a much stricter disciplinarian than Arundale and the boys resented him as a tutor.

Lady Emily was also at Varengeville that summer, in another house with her five children, and in the afternoons there were games of tennis and rounders. The chief activity, however, was planning a new and enlarged *Herald of the Star*, to be published monthly in England with Lady Emily as its editor. During that summer Krishna became Lady Emily's 'entire life'. Her 'husband, home and children faded into the background'. She looked upon Krishna as both her 'son and her teacher',[13] and he, for the next few years, was almost equally devoted to her.

In the October of that year Miss Dodge settled £500 a year for life on Krishna and £300 on Nitya. This income seems to have given Krishna the courage to write to Leadbeater asserting his independence for the first time. He asked for Raja to be 'relieved of his duties' because he, Krishna, knew he could 'control and guide George [Arun-

---

*This was a second house which Edwin Lutyens had built for the Mallets, called Les Communes.

19

dale]'better without him. 'I think it is time now', he went on, 'that I took my affairs into my own hands... I have not been given any opportunity to feel my responsibilities and I have been dragged about like a baby.' Raja was recalled, but the request was not well received. Until then, Leadbeater had found Krishna entirely malleable.

Because of renewed fears of kidnapping, Arundale was told to take the boys again to Taormina in January 1914. This time Lady Emily went with them and was sharply reproved by Mrs Besant in a letter for leaving her children who were her responsibility to follow Krishna who was not. The boys' next move was to Shanklin on the Isle of Wight where Krishna learnt to play golf. E. A. Wodehouse had been sent from Benares as a tutor in place of Raja, and Arundale's aunt, Miss Francesca Arundale, was in charge of the household (Krishna received from Mrs Besant £125 a month for living expenses). Miss Arundale was a severe-looking woman who had been a disciple of Madame Blavatsky, with screwed-back grey hair and steel-rimmed spectacles. Lady Emily went frequently to visit them. Walking with her in the woods Krishna would see little fairy creatures and was surprised that she could not see them too. She recalled that he cared only for poetry in those days, especially Shelley and Keats, and parts of the Old Testament which she read aloud to him. He knew the 'Song of Solomon' almost by heart.

George Arundale had become very jealous of Lady Emily by this time and was sending reports to Mrs Besant of the harm she was doing Krishna. After Mrs Besant had won her Privy Council case in May, the boys, with their tutors, moved to Bude, a coastal town in Cornwall, where Lady Emily was banned by Arundale from visiting them. He told her that she was hindering 'the Master's work by emphasising Krishna's lower nature at the expense of the higher' and that she knew very little of him as he really was. He kept urging Krishna to 'bring through' what he remembered from the astral plane but Krishna never would 'bring through' anything that he felt was not genuine.

Krishna, as a compensation for not seeing Lady Emily, was allowed a motor bicycle at Bude. He enjoyed polishing it endlessly and tinkering with the engine. Dick Clarke said that he was a born mechanic. He also became very good at golf, practising with an excellent professional. (Five years later he was to win a championship at Muirfield which he said afterwards was the proudest moment of his life.)

In July, B. Shiva Rao was sent from India by Mrs Besant to Bude to teach Sanskrit to Krishna. Shiva Rao had known the boys at Adyar where he had helped Leadbeater to compile *The Lives of Alcyone*. A young man, he was an enlivening influence, but, when war broke out on 4 August 1914, he was recalled. The war made no difference to the dull life in the dreary lodgings at Bude. In the autumn, when Nitya went off to study with a tutor in Oxford, Krishna was even more isolated. Krishna longed for a normal life and wrote to Lady Emily: 'Why did they pick on me?' He had no young company, no one to laugh with, and he loved laughing, and, now that Lady Emily was banned, the severe Miss Arundale was the only female he saw.

It is doubtful whether Mrs Besant had any conception of Krishna's loneliness and unhappiness. She was now fully occupied with her work for Indian Home Rule, for which she campaigned so vigorously that in 1917 she was interned for three months at Ootacamund. Leadbeater, meanwhile, had been on a long lecture tour which ended in his settling in Australia, in 1915, where he set up a community. He seemed to have forgotten Krishna although he continued to write flowery articles in the Theosophical magazines about the Coming.

At the end of March 1915, Nitya, who was also very unhappy and lonely and had been overworking with his tutor at Oxford and had badly strained his eyes, escaped to France as a despatch rider for the French Red Cross. Krishna longed to go too and was thrilled when Mrs Besant cabled her consent. He rushed up to London to order a uniform but, to his intense disappointment, permission was suddenly withdrawn. It was thought more important that both boys should continue to study for Oxford, so back he went to Bude with only Wodehouse for companionship to even more dreary lodgings because Mrs Besant was finding it hard to keep up her monthly payments during the war. In contrast, Arundale, in a smart new uniform, went to work for the Anglo-French Red Cross in a London hospital. He and Krishna were never to be close again. Nitya was recalled from France and joined Krishna at Bude.

With Arundale out of the way the brothers grew much closer, and they were both happier, Krishna because he could see Lady Emily again and Nitya because he had won two gold medals for his work for the French Red Cross. Krishna, by hard work, hoped to pass Responsions (the entrance examination to Oxford) by October 1916, two years later than had been intended. This meant that Nitya would go up to Oxford before him.

At the end of April 1916 the boys left Bude for good when Wodehouse joined the Scots Guards. They spent two months in London, staying with Miss Dodge and Lady De La Warr at the large house they now shared, West Side House on Wimbledon Common, which had a

beautiful garden. Although the boys had often been to a meal at
Warwick House, West Side House provided them with their first experience of the luxurious conditions of a rich aristocratic home. They had
also come under the influence of a retired barrister, Harold Baillie-
Weaver, who, before his marriage and conversion to Theosophy, had
lived in great style. He was still impeccably dressed and full of *joie de
vivre*. He was the first 'man of the world' they had ever come in contact
with. He introduced them to his own tailor, formed their taste in clothes
and even taught them how to polish their shoes. Thereafter they wore
made-to-measure suits, shirts and shoes, grey spats and grey homburg
hats, and carried gold-headed canes (this style was made possible by
Miss Dodge's annuity). Krishna was never to lose his love of good
clothes and interest in them.

This period at West Side House was a comparatively happy one for
the boys. There were two tennis courts; they lounged about in dressing
gowns most of the morning and were free to go to cinemas whenever
they wanted, and to visit Lady Emily. They had always felt thoroughly
at home in the Lutyens' nursery, where the younger children treated
them as part of the family. The drawback to West Side House was that
they had to be on their best behaviour there, knowing that Lady De
La Warr would immediately report any undue frivolity to Mrs Besant.
She was a waspish little woman, very unlike Miss Dodge who had a
saintly nature.

But their studies soon had to be resumed. A coach was found for the
boys by Baillie-Weaver, the Rev. John Sanger, who lived with his wife
near Rochester in Kent and had only three other students. Krishna
found Mr Sanger an excellent teacher but was disappointed when he
was told that there was no hope of his passing Responsions before
March 1917. The examination was not the only problem, however.
New College had struck off the boys' names at the time of the lawsuit.
Now Baillie-Weaver was trying to get them into Christ Church or
Balliol.

After a visit to London, Krishna wrote to Lady Emily on his return
to Sanger's a letter which shows the quality of his love for her and the
unnecessary mischief Arundale had caused:

Mummy, dear, there will be so very many partings in this life that we must
get used to it if we want to be happy. Life is really one huge separation if
one loves anybody *very* much and *purely*. In this life we have got to live for
others and not for ourselves & not be selfish. My mother you don't know
how much you helped me lately, it is you who have created a desire in me

to work and to do what the Master wants me to do. It is also you who have made me live purely and think of pure things and cast away those thoughts which bother so many. You see, my *holy* mother, that you have helped me even though you very often think you have been a hindrance to me.

Although a very late developer, Krishna was a perfectly normal young man, but because of the need for absolute purity in an initiate which had been instilled into him, he was dreadfully worried by his 'bad dreams' which he found 'beastly'. He could not understand them because he knew that his thoughts were never anything but pure when awake. Lady Emily was able to help him by assuring him they were only a natural safety valve.

At the beginning of 1917 all hopes of getting the boys into Oxford had to be abandoned. No college would take them because of the lawsuit and Krishna's reputation as 'the Messiah'. Mr Sanger then tried unsuccessfully to get them into his old college at Cambridge. By June it was realised that there was no alternative but to try for London University, which meant an even stiffer examination than for Cambridge.

How bored Krishna must have been with the endless cramming in subjects for which he had no aptitude. One feels that he persevered to please Mrs Besant far more than for his own sake. He was, however, beginning to develop one of his own powers. He wrote to Raja on 11 November: 'You may be glad to know that I am doing Nitya's eyes. They have improved tremendously and he can see with his left eye [in which up to then he had been almost blind] ... Here [at Sanger's], when anybody has a headache or toothache he comes to me so you can imagine I am fairly popular.' And a few weeks later he was writing to Mrs Besant:

I have been thinking of you such a lot lately and I would do anything to see your dear face again. What a funny world it is! I am so very sorry you are feeling rather weak and I expect you are overworking as usual. Only I do wish I was there to look after you and I believe I would make you all right again. I am developing that power of curing people and I do Nitya's eyes every day and they are much better.

In January 1918 'the boys', as we still called them, although Krishna was twenty-three and Nitya twenty, came to London to sit for the four-day matriculation. Krishna felt he had done well, even in mathematics and Latin, his worst subjects, but in March they heard that, although Nitya had passed with honours, Krishna had failed. So back he had to go to Sanger's while Nitya remained in London to study for the Bar. Mr Sanger was intensely disappointed for Krishna. He gave the interesting opinion that, while Nitya had the sharper mind, Krishna's mind was the bigger of the two; he had a wider grasp of a subject but was handicapped by not being able to express his thoughts readily.[14]

Krishna left Mr Sanger's for good in May and spent most of the summer at West Side House. In September he sat again for matriculation, again with high hopes, only to fail in mathematics and Latin. That winter he travelled every day by bus from Wimbledon to London University to attend lectures in which he had no interest, until the beginning of 1919 when he moved with Nitya into a flat in London in Robert Street, Adelphi. He continued to go every day to London University while Nitya was still reading for the Bar. They spent a great deal of time at our house in London. It was a thrill to come home from school and see their grey hats and gold-headed canes on the hall table. Krishna, who had just discovered P. G. Wodehouse and Stephen Leacock, read *Piccadilly Jim* and *Nonsense Novels* aloud to us while standing against the bookcase in the drawing room (he hardly ever sat down except at meals), laughing so much that he could hardly get his words out. He had a most infectious laugh which he never lost. At weekends we would go to cinemas with them and they would join in games of hide-and-seek all over the house. They had a unique glamour for me; they created a charm round themselves wherever they went. They seemed more alike than English brothers because their foreignness set them equally apart. Their English accent had the same lilt, they had the same laugh, the same narrow feet which no ready-made shoes could fit, the same capacity to bend the first joint of their fingers without the second and they both smelt deliciously of some unguent they put on their glossy, straight black hair. And then they were so much cleaner and better dressed than anyone else I knew. They could not wear the same suits because Nitya was shorter than his brother, but they shared their shirts, ties, socks, underclothes and handkerchiefs, all marked with their joint initials JKN.

In June 1919 Mrs Besant came to England. It was four and a half years since she had seen the brothers, as they must now be called. While she was there Krishna presided over a Star meeting, the first work of the kind he had done since her last visit: he had never told her of his loss of interest in Theosophy and the Order of the Star in the East. Before she returned to India he asked her permission to go and live in France to learn French if he failed matriculation for the third time. Seeing the hopelessness of expecting him to study any longer for entry into London University, she agreed. In January 1920 Nitya passed his law examination, and in the same month Krishna sat for matriculation for the third time, but, feeling that he had no chance of passing, he left the papers blank. Four days later he was in Paris.

4

'I can never realise my dream'

At first Krishna lived in Paris with two Theosophists and Star members, Madame Blech and her sister, and, homesick for Lady Emily, reached the nadir of his unhappiness and disillusionment with his role. He wrote to Lady Emily on 1 February: 'I can *never* realise my dream, the more wonderful it is the more sadder and unalterable. You know my dream, mother, which is being with you ad infinitum. But I am a lusus naturae (a freak of nature) and nature enjoys its freak while the freak suffers.' And ten days later: 'Oh! mother, I am young, must I grow old with sorrow as my eternal companion? You have had your youth and your happiness and you have had that which can be given by man and God, a home!'

One of the first people that Krishna saw in Paris was Fabrizio Ruspoli. Ruspoli had rejoined the navy on the outbreak of war and was now in Paris as head of the Italian Naval Delegation to the Peace Conference. In a letter of 11 February, Krishna told Lady Emily:

Ruspoli and I lunched at a little restaurant. We two talked a long time. He is very upset like me. Poor old Ruspoli... He, at the age of 42 feels homeless, believes in none of the things C.W.L [Leadbeater] or Mrs Besant have said... He does not know what to do, has no ambition. In fact we are both in the same unfortunate boat... He thinks and feels all that I feel, but as he says What's to be done? We both felt miserable.

But soon Krishna's life was to be brightened by a family called de Manziarly who lived close to the Blechs. Madame de Manziarly, a Russian married to a Frenchman, was a beautiful, very intense little woman, who had three daughters and a son, all of whom she had made

27

Star members as children. Only the two younger girls, Marcelle and Yolande (known as Mar and Yo), aged nineteen and fifteen, were in Paris at this time. Mar, a fine pianist and a composer, became Krishna's special friend. Madame gave him French lessons, took him to exhibitions, to the Comédie-Française and to the Russian Ballet, but he far preferred going on picnics with the girls who treated him with a mixture of playfulness and reverence. He was embarrassed, though, to find that this family and their friends felt 'inspired' by him, that he was 'a living flame' to them. As he told Lady Emily, they wanted to see the Masters whereas 'I, as you know, don't care a damn'. Yet he did have one mystical experience which he related to Lady Emily:

> Suddenly while she [Madame de Manziarly] was talking, I became unconscious of her and the room and toute les choses. It was as though I fainted for a second and I forgot what I had been saying and asked her to repeat what I had been saying. It is absolutely indescribable, mother. I felt as though my mind and soul were taken away for a second and I felt most strange I assure you. Mme de M. was looking at me all the time and I said that I felt very strange and I said 'Oh! the room is *very* hot isn't it?' For I did not want her to think I was 'inspired' or anything of that kind but all the same I *felt* really inspired and very strange ... I had to get up and stand a bit and collect my ideas. I assure you mother it was most strange, most strange. Between ourselves *absolutely*, in the Theosophical language, there was someone there but I did *not* tell her.

Nitya visited Krishna in Paris in February 1920, and he and Madame de Manziarly became very fond of each other. Nitya felt that at last he had someone to care for him as himself and not just as Krishna's brother. Madame de Manziarly's husband died in February, after which she was able to devote herself entirely to Krishna who was now living alone in a little attic room. In July Krishna went for two months with the Manziarly family to Amphion on the Lake of Geneva, where they had taken a house. While he was there he read aloud to the girls *The Buddha's Way of Virtue* which awoke in him some of his former faith. The passage which struck him most was: 'All conquering and all knowing am I, detached, untainted, untrammelled, wholly freed by destruction of desire. Whom shall I call teacher? Myself found the way.'

This time at Amphion was probably the happiest normal holiday Krishna ever had. He was sad that Lady Emily could not be there. 'How you would enjoy all the childish and joyish side,' he wrote. He would have particularly liked her to be with him on an expedition to Chamonix. 'So calm and dignified those mountains looked ... I longed for you to see that which is to me the manifestation of God himself.' This was his first awareness of mountains, for which he never lost his love and reverence.

Krishna heard at this time that Raja was in England again, bringing with him, to go to Cambridge, a former pupil of Leadbeater's, Rajagopalacharyia (Rajagopal), a young man of twenty, said to have been St Bernard in a previous life and to have a wonderful future. Krishna supposed, as he told Lady Emily, that now Raja was there all the past lives and occult steps on the Path would start again. Raja, he had been told, wanted to start some kind of ceremonial in the Theosophical Society. 'I am going to write to Raja and tell him that as long as he does not use his blinking ceremony in the Star it is all the same to me... I suppose he believes what Lady D [De La Warr] says about us and our debts... If he had told me that they had spent so much on me in "educating"(?) me and that I must return it in "service" to the T.S. [Theosophical Society], I should then tell him that I never asked him to take me out of India etc. Anyway, it is all d—d rot and I am fed up with it.'

He was more disturbed when Raja sent him an advance copy of *The Disciple*, a new journal issued by the Esoteric Section of the Theosophical Society. He wrote to Lady Emily:

My hair stands on end... as you know I really do believe in the Masters etc and I don't want it to be made ridiculous... the *Disciple* is so dammed petty and unclean... I am in a most rebellious mood as you can imagine and personally I don't want to belong to anything of which I am ashamed... *if* [underlined four times] I am to occupy a leading position in the T.S. it will be because of [what] *I am* not what other people think of me or have created a position for me.

But he showed none of this rebelliousness to Mrs Besant – only the devotion he never ceased to feel for her. Writing to her for her seventy-third birthday in September, he expressed this with all his heart. He also told her that now he could read and understand French easily he intended to go to the Sorbonne to take up philosophy.

At the end of September, Krishna joined Nitya for a week in another flat in the Adelphi. He saw a good deal of Raja and met Rajagopal whom he found to be 'a very nice boy'. During those days in London before returning to Paris in September, his interest in the Order of the Star was reawakened, evidently due to Raja's influence, and he undertook to write the monthly editorial notes for *The Herald* which

Lady Emily was still editing. These notes were a great strain on him, which he came to dread more and more, but it made all the difference to the sale of the magazine which was in financial difficulties. Krishna himself wrote asking for donations and enough money came in to carry on. When Lady Emily's son Robert, now a professional journalist, became its editor, the magazine was making a profit.

Back in Paris Krishna attended the Sorbonne and also, on Lady Emily's advice, took elocution lessons, and at the end of the month spoke voluntarily at a Theosophical Society meeting. He reported that he was 'quaking with nerves' beforehand but once on the platform he was 'as cool as an experienced speaker... people clapped and grinned all over their faces... I am going to speak now as I like it and I am very glad as I have to do it some day'. This was an important step in his development.

Krishna wrote to Mrs Besant in January 1921 that his French was 'flourishing' and that he had taken up Sanskrit which 'will be useful in India', adding 'my one desire in life is to work for you and Theosophy. I shall succeed. I want to come out to India as Raja will have told you and take my part in the work.' He never did learn Sanskrit, however, and he stayed hardly any time at the Sorbonne. At the beginning of February he had bronchitis very badly and Madame de Manziarly moved him from the cheap little hotel where he was now staying to her own apartment in the Rue Marbeuf where she and the girls looked after him. At the same time, Nitya in London had a virulent form of chicken-pox. When the two brothers were better, they went to Antibes alone together for three months to recuperate. There Krishna had time to look seriously into himself as he told Lady Emily in March:

I have been thinking a great deal about the Order and the T.S. [Theosophical Society] Mais surtout de moi- même. I must find myself and then *only* can I help others. In fact, I must make the Old Gentleman [Ruspoli's expression for the ego or higher self] come down and take some responsibility. The body and mind is not spiritual enough and now I must waken them for 'his' habitation. If I am to help I must have sympathy and complete understanding and surtout infinite love. I am using well-worn phrases but to me they are *new*.

Since Krishna was still far from well when he returned to Paris, Madame de Manziarly took him to see a 'naturist' friend of hers, Dr Paul Carton, who put him on a very strict diet which he followed conscientiously. Although Krishna never ceased to be a vegetarian and never touched alcohol, tea or coffee, he continued to try new diets all his life without sticking to any of them for long. In old age he had almost a chemist's shopful of vitamins and other health foods and pills.

A great change now came over the lives of both brothers. In May it was discovered that Nitya had a patch on the lung. As soon as Krishna heard this, he summoned him to Paris to be treated by Dr Carton who maintained that the only way to cure him was to treat him as if he were in the last stages of tuberculosis; Madame de Manziarly therefore took him for a complete rest to Boissy-St-Leger near Paris, where a house was put at their disposal. It was the end of all thought of his becoming a barrister.

Mrs Besant was in Paris in July for a Theosophical International Convention, followed by the first Congress of the Order of the Star in the East, which Nitya was allowed to attend. The Order now had 30,000 members, of whom 2,000 attended the Congress. Mrs Besant and Krishna opened the Congress together in French, after which Krishna took everything into his own hands. Mrs Besant and Nitya were both surprised and delighted by the masterly way in which he conducted it. Mrs Besant wrote in the September issue of the *Theosophist* that 'he astonished all present by his grasp of the questions considered, his firmness in controlling the discussions ... but the Biggest thing about him was his intense conviction of the reality and omnipotence of the Hidden God in every man, and the, to him, inevitable results of the presence of that Divinity.'

The brothers spent August with Madame de Manziarly, Mar and Yo at Boissy-St-Leger, where Lady Emily, my sister Betty and I, now aged fifteen and thirteen, joined them in another house. Rajagopal was also of the party, staying with us, as well as John Cordes who had superintended Krishna's physical exercises at Adyar. Nitya, who was running a temperature, led an invalid life while the rest of us played rounders every afternoon and childish games in our garden in the evening, such as blind man's buff, 'statues' and Russian Whispering, amidst shrieks of laughter. Krishna put his whole heart into these games as if he cared for nothing else. Having been deprived of all such fun in his youth, it was as if he could not get enough of it now.

Before Mrs Besant returned to India, it had been decided that Krishna and Nitya should join her there that winter for Krishna to begin his mission. But by September Nitya was even worse, so, accompanied by Cordes, Krishna took him to Villars in the Swiss Alps. In the middle of the month, leaving Nitya with Cordes at Villars, Krishna went to stay with Baron van Pallandt who wanted to make over to Krishna his beautiful, early eighteenth-century ancestral home,

Castle Eerde, near Deventer in Holland, with 5,000 acres of woodland. On the way, Krishna stopped in Amsterdam where he met an attractive American girl of seventeen, Helen Knothe, who was staying with her Theosophical Dutch aunt and studying the violin. For the first time he fell in love.

Soon after Krishna returned to Villars it was settled that, Nitya's health permitting, the brothers should leave from Marseilles for Bombay on 19 November. Nitya's health had certainly improved, and towards the end of October Madame de Manziarly escorted him to Leysin to consult a well-known lung specialist, Dr Rollier, who, unfortunately, pronounced him well enough to travel to India. Krishna, meanwhile, after a fortnight in London saying his goodbyes, went to Holland for a week for a Theosophical and Star Convention. There he met Helen again and became even more deeply in love. In Paris, on the eve of his departure for Marseilles, he wrote to Lady Emily:

> I am very miserable as I am leaving you and Helen for a long time. I *am* awfully in love and it is a great sacrifice on my part but *nothing* else can be done. I feel as if I have an awful wound inside me ... I think, I know, she has felt it too, but what else is there to be done ... You don't know how I am feeling. I have never realised it all before and what it means ... 'Enough of idle wishing. How it steals the time.' How one is miserable!! God bless you.

The brothers received a royal welcome when they arrived at Bombay and Adyar. At Adyar, Mrs Besant had built for them their own room with a verandah, on top of a house connected to the Headquarters building where she herself lived, and with the best view in Adyar over the river to where it joins the sea. They both thought Adyar the most beautiful place they had ever seen. Krishna particularly enjoyed the beauty of walking to the sea at sunset through the palm groves. They had changed into Indian dress as soon as they had arrived in Bombay. (Krishna was always to wear Indian clothes in India and western in the West, wanting to look as inconspicuous as possible. But sometimes, in the evenings, in Europe he would change into Indian dress.)

Soon after the brothers arrived at Adyar they went to see their father who lived in Madras, prostrating themselves and touching his feet with their foreheads like good Indian sons. The old man was so pleased to see them that he could not speak for tears.*

---

*Narianiah died in February 1924. His eldest son, Sivaram, had become a doctor and died in 1952, leaving four sons and four daughters. Krishna's youngest brother,

The brothers stayed only three and a half months in India, during which time they travelled with Mrs Besant to various parts of the country, and Krishna gave one of the Convention lectures at Benares. (Neither then, nor at any other time in his life, did he use notes for his talks.) In Benares he met George Arundale again, who had recently married a beautiful Brahmin girl of sixteen, Rukmini Devi – a marriage which caused a great stir. Krishna also gave a talk at Adyar on the 'Coming Teacher' which accurately forecast the future: 'He is not going to preach what we want, nor give us the sop to our feelings which we all like, but on the contrary He is going to wake us all up whether we like it or not.'[15]

Krishna did not see much of Mrs Besant at Adyar, for she spent every day at the office of *New India*, the daily paper she had edited since 1915, in Madras. Unhappy and homesick for Helen, he was distressed to find so many jealous factions at Adyar. He gave tea parties every day in his room in an attempt to bring people into harmony and to 'smash their cliques'. 'Everybody is very anxious to see me and talk to me and take my advice,' he told Lady Emily. 'Lord only knows why. I don't. No, mother, don't be afraid, I won't have a swollen head.'

Almost as soon as the brothers arrived in India it had been settled that they should go on to Sydney, where Leadbeater was still living as head of a community, to attend a Theosophical Convention in April 1922. The damp heat of Colombo, from where they sailed with Raja in March, brought on Nitya's cough once more, and he was not at all well during the voyage. At Freemantle, Krishna received a telegram from Perth saying: 'The Brothers of the Star welcome you.' He wrote to Lady Emily: 'I have a cold shiver down my back, here are people waiting to welcome me, have you ever heard of such a thing – welcome me – and I am wishing I was anywhere but here ... it will be like this all my life. Oh Lord, what have I done ... oh! how I dislike it all.' Yet in his editorial notes for the July *Herald* he gave such a lyrical description of the beauty of the drive from Adelaide to Perth, and the excitement of being in a new country, that no one could have had an inkling of his true feelings.

At Perth, Krishna had to undergo the 'torture' of speaking twice. 'I never wanted to speak and all the people were so pleased and thanked

Sadanand, lived with Sivaram until his death in 1948. With the mental age of a child, he was very playful, enjoyed games, and was much loved by his nephews and nieces. (Information from Sivaram's eldest son, Giddu Narayan.)

me for what I said. You don't know how I abhor the whole thing, all the people coming to meet us, the meetings and the devotional stuff. It all goes against my nature and I am not fit for the job.' 'T.S. people' did not appeal to him, he wrote; he did not feel he belonged to their circle, yet outside it he was a 'crank of the superlative degree'.

Leadbeater met them at the docks at Sydney and seemed as pleased to see them as they were pleased to see him after nearly ten years. 'He is really a marvellous old man,' Nitya wrote to Ruspoli. 'He is absolutely unchanged, except that he has grown milder...just as at Adyar he takes everything for granted, never a question of doubt, never a question that anyone else can doubt.' A great difference, though, was that he was now a bishop in the Liberal Catholic Church, an offshoot of the Old Catholic, or Jansenist, Church which claimed apostolic succession. He wore a long red cassock, a pectoral cross and a bishop's ring, and spent most of his time conducting religious services which Krishna deplored. Krishna attended one out of politeness and almost fainted from boredom.

Nitya went to a doctor in Sydney who found, by X-ray, that not only was his left lung diseased but his right lung was now also affected; he was advised to return to Switzerland immediately for treatment. To go by way of India would be too hot, so the brothers decided to travel via San Francisco and break the journey in the Ojai (pronounced O-high) Valley. Mr A. P. Warrington, General Secretary of the Theosophical Society in America, who was in Sydney for the Convention, would travel with them. He had a Theosophical friend, Mrs Mary Gray, who was willing to lend them a cottage for three or four months. The valley, near Santa Barbara, 1,500 feet up, was said to have an excellent climate for consumptives. Before leaving Sydney, Krishna received a message through Leadbeater from the Master Kuthumi which he copied and sent to Lady Emily:

Of you, too, we have the highest hopes. Steady and widen yourself, and try more and more to bring the mind and brain into subservience to the true Self within. Be tolerant of divergencies of view and of method, for each has usually a fragment of truth concealed somewhere within it, even though oftentimes it is distorted almost beyond recognition. Seek for that tiniest gleam of light amid the Stygian darkness of each ignorant mind, for by recognizing and fostering it you may help a baby brother.

Krishna commented; 'It was just what I wanted as I am inclined to be intolerant and not look for the brother!'

Krishna and Nitya were both enchanted by California. After being shown over Berkeley University, Krishna wrote to Lady Emily:

> That arrogance of class and of colour was not to be found there ... I was so thrilled that I wanted to carry the physical beauty of the place with me to India for the Indians who alone know how to create the proper scholastic atmosphere. Here this atmosphere was lacking, they are not dignified as we Indians are ... oh, for such a university to be transplanted to India, with our professors for whom religion is as important, if not greater, as [sic] education.

The brothers were alone at Ojai in a small pine cottage, where they arrived on 6 July. It was at the further, eastern, end of the valley, surrounded by orange and avocado groves. A woman came in to cook their breakfast and lunch but they became proficient at getting their own supper of scrambled eggs and chipped potatoes, though Heinz 'came in very useful'. Mr Warrington was in another cottage close by. All went well for the first few weeks – they rode in the mountains and bathed in the stream that ran down the canyon, thoroughly enjoying the freedom from all restraint which they had never had before. Then Nitya started running a temperature and began to cough badly. Krishna was nervous at being alone with him, especially as Nitya became very irritable if he tried to make him rest. It seemed providential when a friend staying with their hostess, Mrs Gray, came into their lives. This was Rosalind Williams, a pretty, fair-haired girl of nineteen, seemingly a born nurse. They both took to her at once. 'She is very cheerful, gay and keeps Nitya in a good humour which is essential,' Krishna told Lady Emily. 'Her sister is a T.S. [Theosophical] person and so she knows all about it and in spite of all that she is very nice.' She obtained her mother's consent to stay on with Mrs Gray in order to look after Nitya. It was understood from the first that she was Nitya's rather than Krishna's friend. Krishna was still writing love letters to Helen Knothe.

Many people had urged Nitya to have treatment from an electric machine invented by a Dr Albert Abrams which, Abrams claimed, was able to diagnose and cure, from a few drops of blood, many diseases, including tuberculosis. The brothers decided to try this method, and drops of Nitya's blood were sent on a piece of blotting paper to a pupil of Dr Abrams in Los Angeles without any information beyond the name. Two days later the report was received: TB in the left lung, kidneys and spleen. Mr Warrington managed to hire one of the rare machines (a black box called an Oscilloclast) and Nitya sat for several hours a day with plates attached by electric wires to the affected parts while Krishna read O. Henry and the Old Testament to him. The contents of the box were a well-kept secret. The machine ticked like a loud clock but gave no sensation at all.

5

'God-intoxicated'

The Master's message to Krishna in Sydney had greatly influenced him. He wrote to Lady Emily on 12 August that for the past fortnight he had been meditating on it for half an hour every morning and again before sleeping. '*I am going to get back* my old touch with the Masters and after all that's the only thing that matters in life.' Five days after writing this, on the 17th, he underwent a three-day experience that entirely revolutionised his life. It was not for a fortnight, however, that an account of it, written by Nitya, was sent to Mrs Besant and Leadbeater:

> Our cottage is on the upper end of the valley and no one else lives near except Mr Warrington who has a cottage all to himself a few hundred yards away; and Krishna, Mr Warrington and I have been here for nearly eight weeks, taking a rest and getting well. We have an occasional visitor in Mr Walton, the Vicar-General of the Liberal Catholic Church of America, who has a house in the valley, and Rosalind, a young American girl stays a week or two nearby, spending her time with us. About two weeks ago happened this incident which I want to describe to you when all five of us chanced to be together.
>
> Of the true meaning of what happened, of the exact importance of it, you of course will be able to tell us if you will, but here we seem to have been transported into a world where Gods again walked among men for a short space of time, leaving us all so changed that now our compass has found its lodestar. I think I do not exaggerate when I say that all our lives are profoundly affected by what happened.
>
> Krishna himself, properly speaking, should relate the sequence of events, for all of us were mere spectators, willing to help when necessary; but he

does not remember all the details, as he was out of his body a great part of the time, and everything remains clear in our memory, for we watched him with great care the whole time with a feeling that his body was entrusted partly to us. Mr Warrington is not in perfect health, and I am not yet allowed to move about much, so it was Rosalind's good fortune to look after Krishna and I think she has already received her reward [by being put on probation].

On the evening of Thursday the seventeenth Krishna felt a little tired and restless and we noticed in the middle of the nape of his neck a painful lump of what seemed to be a contracted muscle about the size of a large marble. The next morning he seemed all right, until after breakfast, when he lay down to rest. Rosalind and I were sitting outside, and Mr Warrington and Krishna were inside. Rosalind went in at Mr Warrington's call and found Krishna apparently very ill, as he was lying on the bed, tossing about and moaning as if he were in great pain. She went and sat with him and tried to find out what was the matter with him, but Krishna could give no clear answer. He started again moaning and a fit of trembling and shivering came upon him, and he would clench his teeth and grip his hands tight to ward off the shivering. It was exactly the behaviour of a malarial patient, except that Krishna complained of frightful heat. Rosalind would hold him quiet for a bit, and again would come the trembling and shivering, as of ague. Then he would push her away, complaining of terrible heat and his eyes full of a strange unconsciouness. And Rosalind would sit by him until he was quiet again, when she would hold his hand and soothe him like a mother does her young. Mr Warrington sat at the other end of the room, and realized, so he told me later, that some process was going on in Krishna's body, as a result of influences directed from planes other than physical. Poor Rosalind, who at first was very anxious, raised questioning eyes and Mr Warrington assured her that all would be well. But during the morning things got worse, and when I came and sat beside him he complained again of the awful heat, and said that all of us were full of nerves and made him tired; and every few minutes he would start up in bed and push us away; and again he would commence trembling. All this while he was only half conscious, for he would talk of Adyar and the people there as if they were present; then again he would lie quiet for a little while until the rustle of a curtain or the rattling of a window, or a sound of a far-off plough in the field would rouse him again and he would moan for silence and quiet. Persistently every few minutes he would push Rosalind away from him when he began to get hot, and again he would want her close to him.

I sat near, but not too near. We tried our best to keep the house quiet and dark, but slight sounds which one scarcely notices are inevitable, yet Krishna had become so sensitive that the faintest tinkling would set his nerves on edge.

Later as lunch came he quieted down and became apparently all right and fully conscious. Rosalind took him his lunch which he ate, and while we all finished our meal he lay quiet. Then a few minutes afterwards he was groaning again, and presently, poor fellow, he could not keep down the food he had eaten. And so it went on all the afternoon; shivering, groaning, restless, only half conscious, and all the time as if he were in pain. Curiously enough, when the time came for our meals, even though he ate nothing himself, he became tranquil and Rosalind could leave him long enough to have her food, and at bedtime he was quiet enough to sleep through the night.

The next day, Saturday, it recommenced after his bath, and he seemed less conscious than the day before. All through the day it lasted, with regular intervals to give him a rest and allow Rosalind to have her food.

But Sunday was the worst day and Sunday we saw the glorious climax. All through the three days all of us had tried to keep our minds and emotions unperturbed and peaceful, and Rosalind spent the three days by Krishna's side, ready when he wanted her and leaving him alone when he wished it. It was really beautiful to see her with him, to watch the way she could pour out her love unselfishly and absolutely impersonally. Even before all this happened we had noticed this great characteristic in her, and though we wondered then if a woman should be nearby at that moment yet the eventual happening showed that probably she was specially brought here at that moment to help Krishna and all of us. Though she is only nineteen and knows little of Theosophy she played the part of a great mother through these three days.

On Sunday, as I have said, Krishna seemed much worse, he seemed to be suffering a great deal, the trembling and the heat seemed intensified and his consciousness became more and more intermittent. When he seemed to be in control of his body he talked all the time of Adyar, A.B. [Annie Besant], and the members of the Purple Order in Adyar [an inner group formed by Mrs Besant who wore purple silk shawls], and he imagined himself constantly in Adyar. Then he would say, 'I want to go to India! Why have they brought me here? I don't know where I am,' and again and again and again he would say, 'I don't know where I am.' If anyone moved in the house he nearly jumped off the bed and every time we entered his room we had to give him warning. Yet towards six o'clock when we had our evening meal he quieted down until we had finished. Then suddenly the whole house seemed full of a terrific force and Krishna was as if possessed. He would have none of us near him and began to complain bitterly of the dirt, the dirt of the bed, the intolerable dirt of the house, the dirt of everyone around, and in a voice full of pain said that he longed to go to the woods. Now he was sobbing aloud, we dared not touch him and knew not what to do; he had left his bed and sat in a dark corner of the room on the floor, sobbing aloud that he wanted to go into the woods in India. Suddenly he announced his intention of going for a walk alone, but from this we managed to dissuade him, for we did not think he was in any fit condition for nocturnal ambulations. Then as he expressed a desire for solitude, we left him and gathered outside on the verandah where in a few minutes he joined us, carrying a cushion in his hand and sitting as far away as possible from us. Enough strength and consciousness were vouchsafed him to come outside but once there again he vanished from us, and his body, murmuring incoherences, was left sitting there on the porch.

We were a strange group on that verandah; Rosalind and I on chairs, Mr Warrington and Mr Walton opposite, facing us sitting on a bench, and Krishna to our right a few yards away. The sun had set an hour ago and we sat facing the far-off hills, purple against the pale sky and the darkening twilight, speaking little, and the feeling came upon us of an impending climax; all our thoughts and emotions were tense with a strangely peaceful expectation of some great event.

Then Mr Warrington had a heaven-sent inspiration. In front of the house a few yards away stands a young pepper tree, with delicate leaves of a tender green, now heavy with scented blossom, and all day it is the 'murmurous haunt of bees', little canaries, and bright humming birds. He gently urged Krishna to go out under the tree, and at first Krishna would not, then went of his own accord.

Now we were in a starlit darkness and Krishna sat under a roof of delicate leaves black against the sky. He was still murmuring unconsciously but presently there came a sigh of relief and he called out to us, 'Oh, why didn't you send me out here before?' Then came a brief silence.

And now he began to chant. Nothing had passed his lips for nearly three days and his body was utterly exhausted with the intense strain, and it was a quiet weary voice we heard chanting the mantram sung every night at Adyar in the Shrine Room. Then silence.

Long ago in Taormina, as Krishna had looked with meditative eyes upon a beautiful painting of our lord Gautama [the Buddha] in mendicant garb, we had felt for a blissful moment the divine presence of the Great One, who had deigned to send a thought. And again this night, as Krishna, under the young pepper tree, finished his song of adoration I thought of the Tathagata [the Buddha] under the Bo tree, and again I felt pervading the peaceful valley a wave of that spendour, as if again He had sent a blessing upon Krishna.

We sat with eyes fixed upon the tree, wondering if all was well, for now there was a perfect silence, and as we looked I saw suddenly for a moment a great Star shining above the tree, and I knew that Krishna's body was being prepared for the Great One. I leaned across and told Mr Warrington of the Star.

The place seemed to be filled with a Great Presence and a great longing came upon me to go on my knees and adore, for I knew that the Great Lord of all our hearts had come Himself; and though we saw Him not, yet all felt the splendour of His presence. Then the eyes of Rosalind were opened and she saw. Her face changed as I have seen no face change, for she was blessed enough to see with physical eyes the glories of that night. Her face was transfigured, as she said to us, 'Do you see Him, do you see Him?' For she saw the divine Bodhisattva [The Lord Maitreya] and millions wait for incarnations to catch such a glimpse of our Lord, but she had eyes of innocence and had served our Lord faithfully and we who could not see saw the Splendours of the night mirrored in her face pale with rapture in the starlight. Never shall I forget the look on her face, for presently I who could not see but who gloried in the presence of our Lord felt that He turned towards us and spoke some words to Rosalind; her face shone with divine ecstasy as she answered, 'I will, I will,' and she spoke the words as if they were a promise given with splendid joy. Never shall I forget her face when I looked at her; even I was almost blessed with her vision. Her face showed the rapture of her heart, for the innermost part of her being was ablaze with His presence but her eyes saw and silently I prayed that He might accept me as His servant and all our hearts were full of that prayer. In the distance we heard divine music softly played, all of us heard though hidden from us were the Gandharvas [cosmic angels who make the music of the spheres]. The radiance and the glory of the many Beings present lasted nearly an half hour and Rosalind, trembling and almost sobbing with joy, saw it all, 'Look, do you see?' she would often repeat, or 'Do you hear the music?' Then presently we heard Krishna's footsteps and saw his white figure coming up in the darkness and all was over. And Rosalind cried out, 'Oh, he is coming; go get him, go get him' and fell back in her chair almost in a swoon. When she recovered, alas, she remembered nothing, nothing, all was gone from her memory except the sound of music still in her ears.

The next day again there was a recurrence of the shuddering and half-waking consciousness in Krishna though now it lasted but a few minutes and at long intervals. All day long he lay under the tree in samadhi* and in the evening, as he sat in meditation as on the night before, Rosalind again saw three figures around him who quickly went away, taking Krishna with them, leaving his body under the tree. Since then and every evening he sits in meditation under the tree.

I have described what I saw and heard but of the effect of the incident upon all of us I have not spoken, for I think it will take time, at least for me to realize fully the glory that we were privileged to witness, though I feel now that life can only be spent in one way, in the service of the Lord.

*A Sanskrit word, here used probably as a state of trance. A simple definition is: 'The excellent process of Samadhi destroys death, leads to eternal happiness and confers the supreme Bliss of Brahman [Reality]'.

Krishna himself also wrote an account of this experience to Mrs Besant and Leadbeater but, since he had been unconscious, or semi-conscious, he remembered very little of it. He ended his account:

> I was supremely happy, for I had seen. Nothing could ever be the same. I have drunk of the clear and pure waters at the source of the fountain of life and my thirst was appeased. Nevermore could I be thirsty. Never more could I be in utter darkness; I have seen the Light. I have touched compassion which heals all sorrow and suffering; it is not for myself, but for the world. I have stood on the mountain top and gazed at the mighty Beings. I have seen the glorious and healing Light. The fountain of Truth has been revealed to me and the darkness has been dispersed. Love in all its glory has intoxicated my heart; my heart can never be closed. I have drunk at the fountain of Joy and eternal Beauty. I am God-intoxicated.

Earlier on in his account he had written:

> On the first day while I was in that state and more conscious of the things around me, I had the first most extraordinary experience. There was a man mending the road; that man was myself; the pickaxe he held was myself; the very stone which he was breaking up was a part of me; the tender blade of grass was my very being, and the tree beside the man was myself. I also could feel and think like the roadmender and I could feel the wind passing through the tree, and the little ant on the blade of grass I could feel. The birds, the dust, and the very noise were a part of me. Just then there was a car passing by at some distance; I was the driver, the engine, and the tyres; as the car went further away from me, I was going away from myself. I was in everything, or rather everything was in me, inanimate and animate, the mountain, the worm and all breathing things. All day long I remained in this happy condition.

Mr Warrington also wrote an account of the experience, vouching for the truth of the other two. Copies of the three accounts were sent to Miss Dodge and Lady Emily with a request to the latter to have a few copies made by some very reliable person since they were strictly private. She chose Rajagopal, who had learnt to type, for this task.[16]

After a quiet fortnight, during which Krishna continued to meditate every evening under the pepper tree, the strange, semi-conscious states began again on 3 September, but this time they occurred regularly from 6.30 to 8.30 or nine o'clock in the evening after his meditation, and were accompanied by pain in the spine which built up after a few days into agony. Nitya made daily notes of Krishna's condition which he later put together to form a long narrative to send to Mrs Besant and Leadbeater.[17] Krishna's 'ego', as Nitya called it, would withdraw, leaving his body in charge of the 'physical elemental'* who bore the pain so that Krishna had no recollection of it when he 'came back'. The descriptions of the physical torture suffered by the body night after night for the next three months are harrowing. Nitya and Mr Warrington, who was there the whole time, did not believe that such pain was possible. The 'physical elemental' mistook Rosalind, who came to the cottage every evening while what was eventually known as 'the process' took place, for his dead mother.

At times Krishna had the sensation of being burnt so that he wanted to rush out and immerse himself in the stream and had to be forcibly restrained, for he was apt to fall on his face in a faint with 'a fearful crash' wherever he happened to be. He usually lay in the semi-dark on a mattress on the floor so that he could not fall off the bed. He could not bear too much light. Nitya said it was like watching a man being burnt to death. The pain, which affected different parts of the body, would come in long spasms. When there was a slight lull Krishna would converse with certain invisible beings or one being who seemed to come every night 'to conduct the operations'. Krishna would refer to them only as 'they' or 'them'. Apparently he was given indications as to what was going to happen, for he was heard to say such things as, 'Oh, it is going to be bad tonight? All right, I don't mind.' As the pain intensified he would sob and writhe about and give terrible shrieks and sometimes cry aloud for a respite. The 'physical elemental' would sob, 'O, please, please I cannot', and then it would break off and Krishna's voice would say, 'It's all right. I didn't mean that, please go on', or, 'I'm ready now, let's go on.'

At nine o'clock, after the night's work on his body, he would sit with the others drinking his milk (he never had any supper on those evenings) and they would tell him what had happened. He listened as if they were talking of a stranger and his interest in what was happening was as great as theirs; it was all new to him since his memory retained none of it.

On one very bad evening he groaned, 'O, mother, why did you bear me for this?' He begged for a few minutes' rest and the others would hear him talking to his mother or to 'them' to whom he would say,

---

*The part of the body that controls its instinctive and purely physical actions when the higher consciousness is withdrawn. It is at a low stage of evolution and needs guidance.

with a great deal of assurance, 'Yes, rather! I can stand a lot more; don't mind the body, I can't stop it from weeping', and sometimes 'They' would say something to him and they would 'laugh whole-heartedly'. Once they heard the 'physical elemental' calling out, 'Please come back, Krishna.' If Krishna came back 'the process' would stop. It seemed that a certain amount of work on the body had to be accomplished every evening and if there was an interruption in the middle it was made up at the end.

Krishna's body was becoming more and more tired and emaciated, and having to watch his suffering was a tremendous strain on the others. At the beginning of October 'They' began work on his eyes, a more appalling torture than ever. 'They told Krishna that night,' Nitya wrote, 'that his eyes were being cleansed so that he might be allowed to see "Him". But that cleansing was a ghastly process to listen to. We heard him say, "It's like being tied down in the desert, one's face in the blazing sun with one's eyelids cut off".'

One early evening, when Krishna came from his bath to meditate under the pepper tree before the evening business began, he told the others that there was to be a 'Great Visitor' that night (they understood that this was not the Lord Maitreya who was said to have been there once or twice). Krishna asked Nitya to put the picture of the Buddha in his room where he would return after his meditation, so Nitya had no doubt as to who the 'Great One' would be. That night's work seemed to be the most agonising that Krishna's body had yet been through but also the most glorious since that first Sunday night in August under the pepper tree, for they all felt that the 'Great Presence' came for a moment. Later, when Nitya and Rosalind were with Krishna in his room, Krishna began talking to people they could not see. Apparently 'the work' had been assured of success and they were congratulating him. They heard him say, 'There is nothing to con-gratulate me about, you'd have done the same yourself.' When the congratulators had left, Krishna, still unconscious, said, 'Mother, every-thing will be different now, life will never be the same for any of us after this. I've seen Him, mother, and nothing matters now.'

But this was not the end of Krishna's physical suffering. 'They' now started opening up something in his head which caused such 'indescribable torture' that he kept on screaming out, 'Please close it, please close it.' When the pain became unbearable, 'They' did close it and then a little later opened it again and the body would start screaming until it fainted. This went on for some forty minutes. When it eventually stopped, the body, to the amazement of the others, started chattering away in the voice of a child of about four, recalling incidents from his childhood.

'The process' continued unabated every night, except for a few days when Krishna and Nitya were in Hollywood, until the beginning of December, and when it was over each evening the little boy prattled away for an hour or more to his mother, for whom he still mistook Rosalind, about events in his childhood. He told her about a talkative fairy playmate he had had and how he had hated going to school. He described his mother's death, 'He thought she was ill and when he saw the doctor giving her medicine he begged her, "Don't take it, mother, don't take it, it is some beastly stuff and it won't do you any good, please don't take it, the doctor does not know anything, he is a dirty man." A little later, in a tone of horror he said,"Why are you so still, mother, what's happened, and why does father cover his face with his dhoti, mother, answer me, mother."'

While 'the process' was going on every evening, Krishna was writing in the mornings, as he told Lady Emily in a letter of 17 September, 'an article of rather a curious nature. I have written so far 23 pages, absolutely unaided.'[18]

Both Mrs Besant and Leadbeater attributed Krishna's experience of 17–20 August to the passing of the third initiation but they could find no explanation for 'the process'. Krishna himself was convinced that it was something he had to go through for the preparation of his body for the reception of the Lord Maitreya and that no attempt must be made to prevent or alleviate it. Only one medical practitioner ever saw him in this state, Dr Mary Rocke, an English Theosophist and Star member whom he knew well and trusted. She was unable to throw any light on its cause and she could not have examined him without his regaining consciousness. If any strange doctor or psychologist had entered the house, let alone the room, Krishna would have been aware of it immediately and 'the process' would undoubtedly have stopped.

So what was 'the process'? The explanation given by Nitya at the time and adopted by others was that it was the awakening of Krishna's *kundalini*, sometimes called the 'Serpent Fire', which was centred at the base of the spine and when awakened by the practice of true yoga brought a release of tremendous energy and clairvoyant powers. Leadbeater disputed this, writing to Mrs Besant that he had suffered no more than discomfort when *his kundalini* had been awakened. Krishna developed no greater clairvoyant powers after 'the process' than he had shown as a boy. Anyway, 'the process' went on too long for the *kundalini* explanation to be valid. From time to time doctors, psychologists and others have made suggestions as to what it might have been. Migraine, hysteria, epilepsy and schizophrenia have all been suggested. None of these fits the case. Many mystics, of course, have seen visions and heard voices, but have these ever been accompanied by such physical agony? Is there any physical explanation? Is one forced to the conclusion that there can only be a mystical one? What seems certain is that whatever happened to Krishna's body for the next few years made it possible for him to become a channel for some super force or energy that was the source of his later teaching.

6

'There is a loneliness'

The opportunity arose in the following February of buying Pine Cottage and six acres of land surrounding it, including another, larger house. When Krishna expressed a wish to acquire this, pointing out how sacred the place had become after all that had happened there, the money was provided by Miss Dodge. Krishna called the larger house Arya Vihara (Noble Monastery), and soon afterwards another seven acres were bought and the Brothers' Trust set up to hold the property. All through Krishna's life money, in the form of donations and legacies, came in when needed, and later on he made money from his books; he never, though, kept anything for himself except Miss Dodge's annual allowance of £500.

From the beginning of 1923 Krishna began to work hard from Ojai, dealing with dozens of official letters, writing his monthly notes for the *Herald*, reorganising the Star in California, giving talks in the neighbourhood and raising money for a school in India. In May he and Nitya who, as a result of further Abrams treatment, was said once again to be cured, toured the United States, ending up in Chicago for the Theosophical Convention. In June the brothers went to England. It had been arranged for them to attend the Theosophical and Star Congress in Vienna in July. Lady Emily met them at Plymouth and reported to Mrs Besant that Krishna seemed outwardly little changed, though perhaps more beautiful, but 'one was conscious at every moment of a controlled but immense concentrated power flowing through him'. After the Congress, where Krishna was to meet Helen Knothe again (she had remained in Amsterdam), he asked if he might have a 'family' holiday in some quiet place where he was not known. A friend of John

47

Cordes put a chalet, the Villa Sonnblick, at his disposal outside the village of Ehrwald in the Austrian Tyrol, and there he and Nitya spent seven weeks with a party of friends consisting of Lady Emily, my sister Betty and me, Helen, Mar de Manziarly, Rajagopal (who was now at Cambridge), Cordes, and Ruth Roberts, an English girl with whom Krishna had had a flirtation in Sydney. Krishna, Nitya, Lady Emily, Helen and Rajagopal stayed in Sonnblick, where we all had our meals, while the rest of us slept in another chalet. The first fortnight was a really happy holiday; it was an ideal place for mountain walks and there was a flat field on which we could play rounders. At picnics in the mountains, Krishna, Nitya and Rajagopal would chant Indian Mantrams, which sounded particularly beautiful in the woods.

Then, in mid August, 'the process' started again in earnest, every evening, and continued until 20 September. Krishna, or rather the 'physical elemental', now mistook Helen for his mother when he 'went off'. Lady Emily sent diary letters to Mrs Besant recounting all that happened. 'To see him [Krishna] leaping down the hills, so full of grace and beauty and vitality,' she wrote, 'it is almost impossible to believe what his poor body has endured each night.' After one evening of torture he cried out, 'It has never been as bad as this.' Nitya was to write afterwards, 'During the last days at Ehrwald they tried the experiment of leaving Krishna conscious while the pain was still fairly strong, but this consciousness was only for 10 or 20 seconds at a time, and as soon as the pain became too intense, Krishna would leave the body.'

On the evening of 20 September Krishna 'brought through' a message for Nitya, supposedly from the Master Kuthumi, which Nitya wrote down:

Nitya Listen. This is finished here, this is the last night, but it will be continued in Ojai. But this depends upon you. You both should have more energy. On what you do in the next month will depend the success. Let nothing stand in the way. It has been a success here. But Ojai depends entirely on you, there it will be continued with much greater vigour if you are ready.

When you leave this place you have to be exceedingly careful. It is like a fresh vase just out of the mould, and any bad vibrations may crack it, and this will mean repairing and remodelling and this would take a long time; if you fail it will mean beginning everything from the beginning.

This message is particularly interesting in that the style is totally unlike either Krishna's or Nitya's

On leaving Ehrwald, most of the party went to stay at Castle Eerde in Holland with Baron van Pallandt who had offered the property to Krishna. This was the last time that it was used as a private house. A Trust was formed, with Krishna as President, to which the estate was made over and Eerde became the international headquarters of the Order of the Star in the East.

Believing that 'the process' was to continue at Ojai, Nitya felt it was necessary to have another initiate there, so Rajagopal (who had become an initiate before coming to England) took a year off from Cambridge to go with them. They now lived at Arya Vihara while Rosalind lived at Pine Cottage with her mother. (Helen had had to go home to New York.)

Soon after their arrival, 'the process' did start again and was so bad that for the first time Nitya became worried and wrote anxiously to Leadbeater to ask if everything was 'all right'. Krishna was now being made to bear the pain himself which was growing more and more intense. 'Nowadays,' Nitya told Leadbeater, 'there is no Helen with him and though Rosalind is next door to us he does not seem to want her; after the pain is over Krishna leaves the body and the body weeps heart-brokenly with exhaustion. He calls for his mother, and I've discovered he wants Helen, not Rosalind. As far as I can make out from what Krishna's body occasionally says, there is still a great deal of work to be done on the body, perhaps it means many months.'

On 26 November Krishna's body 'brought through' a message which Nitya included in this letter to Leadbeater: 'The work being done now is of gravest importance and exceedingly delicate. It is the first time this experiment is being carried out in the world. Everything in the household must give way to this work, and no one's convenience must be considered, not even Krishna's.'

It is strange that Leadbeater did not want to go to Ojai to witness this strange phenomenon for himself. He merely wrote to Mrs Besant saying that he was 'much troubled about the whole affair . . . so utterly opposed to what I myself have been taught. I hope you can assure me that all is well.' Mrs Besant, although she had now laid aside her occult powers, was apparently able to reassure him, and from then on Leadbeater left all responsibility for Krishna to her. To Nitya he wrote: 'I do not understand the terrible drama that is taking place in our beloved Krishna.'

To Lady Emily Krishna was to write at the beginning of 1924 after 'the process' had been going on for two months:

I am getting more and more irritable and I am getting more and more tired, I wish you and the others were here. I feel like crying so often nowadays and that used not to be my way. It's awful for the others and myself... I wish Helen were here but that is an impossibility and also probably They don't want anybody to help me along. So I have to do it all myself... However hard one may try, there is a loneliness, that of a solitary pine in the wilderness... Last ten days, it has been really strenuous, my spine and neck have been going very strong and day before yesterday, I had an extraordinary evening. Whatever it is, the source or whatever one calls the bally thing, came up my spine, up to the nape of my neck, then it separated into two, one going to the right and the other to the left of my head till they met between the two eyes, just above my nose. And I saw the Lord and Master. It was a tremendous night. Of course the whole thing was painful in the extreme... I'm sure we are going to have a holiday soon.

Krishna described this experience to Mrs Besant also, and Nitya, too, gave her an account of it. Nitya presumed it meant the 'opening of the third eye'. In treatises on yoga the 'third eye' is often referred to as the Eye of Shiva. It is in the middle of the forehead and, like *kundalini*, is associated with clairvoyance. 'Krishna's clairvoyance has not yet begun,' Nitya added, 'but I imagine it is only a question now of time. So far we've had 110 nights of the process since we've been here.'

It was at the end of March that Dr Rocke arrived at Ojai, having been sent by Leadbeater from Sydney, where she now lived, to report on Krishna. She stayed a fortnight, watching 'the process' every evening. Krishna wrote to Lady Emily that 'she was tremendously struck by the whole thing and we are not entirely mad'. Dr Rocke was still there on 11 April – 'a marvellous night for us all', as Nitya told Mrs Besant, when Krishna 'brought through' a message, the first part of which Nitya believed was from the Lord Maitreya himself:

My Sons, I am pleased with your endurance and bravery. It has been a long struggle and as far as We have gone it has been a good success. Though there were many difficulties We have surmounted them with comparative ease... You have come out of it well, though the entire preparation is not over... We are sorry for the pain, long drawn out, which must have seemed to you apparently endless, but there is a great glory awaiting each one of you... My Blessing is with you.
Though We *shall* begin at a later date I do not want you to leave this place for Europe until after Wesak [the great occult festival of the full moon

of May, which fell that year on 18 May], when you shall see Me. Though
We have guarded the three places in your body there is sure to be pain. It
is like an operation; though it may be over you are bound to feel the effects
afterwards.

Unfortunately, we have no account from Dr Rocke herself of what she
thought of 'the process'.

The brothers, with Rajagopal and Helen, whom they met in New York,
arrived in England on 15 June. Mrs Besant was also in England and
the brothers were caught up in her ceaseless activities, culminating in
a Theosophical and Star Congress at Arnhem in Holland, followed by
the first camp at Ommen, a mile from Castle Eerde on part of the land
given by Baron van Pallandt. This camp was to be an annual event
right up to the war.

After this Krishna was at last free to enjoy the 'family' holiday he
longed for. The chosen place that year was an eleventh-century castle-
hotel at the top of a steep hill above the village of Pergine in the
Dolomites, where Krishna arrived with his friends on 18 August. The
party was the same as in the previous year, with the exception of Mar
de Manziarly and the addition of an Italian lady and a few Indian
friends. We occupied two towers at corners of the battlements as well
as some rooms in the hotel and had meals at one end of a vast dining
room, screened off from the other guests and with our own vegetarian
Austrian cook. Just below the castle was a flat field, for rounders, as
there had been at Ehrwald. But Krishna was given less than a week
before 'the process' started again. It was more agonising than ever,
which seemed hardly possible after Ojai. Now, however, Helen was
there and was able to help him.

Nitya, Lady Emily, Helen and Rajagopal were living under the same
roof as Krishna in the round tower. When 'the process' started, the
occupants of that tower did not come to supper with us in the hotel.
The rest of us knew that *something* was going on every evening –
something to prepare Krishna's body for the occupation of the Lord
Maitreya – but it was not until the following year that I was told about
'the process' and Krishna's and Nitya's accounts of the Ojai experience
were read aloud to me.

There was a definite purpose in that year's holiday. It had been
settled that the four girls – Helen, Ruth, Betty and I – should, at
Krishna's urging, go to Sydney to be 'brought on' along the Path of
Discipleship by Leadbeater. (Rosalind had gone there when the

51

brothers left Ojai in June.) All Krishna's public talks in the various places he had been to with Mrs Besant that summer had stressed that, for discipleship, it was necessary to take leaps in the dark, to live dangerously, to feel strongly enough to be able to jump out of the window, to change oneself radically. Now, at Pergine, at Lady Emily's suggestion, he began to talk on those lines to the party assembled there. After the morning game of rounders he would sit under an apple tree in the field and try to drum into us the qualities to aim for. He told the girls that although it was only human nature for them to want marriage and a home of their own they could not have those things *and* serve the Lord when he came; if they tried to play at both lives they would become bourgeois and nothing was worse than mediocrity. But they must not become hard; to grow by love and radiant happiness was the only way to develop. Complete mental and physical purity were also essential.

Four passionate young girls of whom I, at just sixteen, was the youngest, were being told to live celibate lives outside a nunnery. Krishna's attitude to sex and marriage was to change after a few years. When he had heard in 1922 that Mar de Manziarly was engaged to be married he had said that she might as well commit suicide. (The engagement was broken off before she went to Ehrwald.) He was very hard on us all at Pergine, often making us cry by the home truths he told us. He found us all dreadfully unresponsive; he told Lady Emily that it was like talking to a lot of sponges who just sucked it all up. He wished he could 'bruise' us more. 'You are like people in a dark room waiting for someone to turn on the light for you instead of groping in the dark and turning it on for yourselves.'[19]

Yet in spite of his harshness one felt his great love for us and his longing that we should grow into beautiful human beings – his terror that we should become 'mediocre'.

'The process' stopped on 24 September when Krishna 'brought through' a message which he believed to be from the Lord Maitreya:

> Learn to serve Me, for along the Path alone you will find Me.
> Forget yourself, for only then am I to be found.
> Do not look for the Great Ones when they may be very near you.
> You are like the blind man who seeks sunshine,
> You are like the hungry man who is offered food and will not eat.
> The happiness you seek is not far off; it lives in every common stone.
> I am there if you will only see. I am the helper if you will let Me help.

These lines, very different from the other messages, are more in the style of the poems which Krishna was soon to be writing.

7

'An old dream is dead'

Lady Emily's husband was strongly opposed to the Sydney plan
when he heard of it, but when Miss Dodge offered to pay both her
return fare and those of the four girls, there was nothing he could do
to prevent it without the risk of breaking up his marriage. It was
doubtful whether Krishna was aware of his opposition for, although he
was against marriage for would-be disciples, he was not a home breaker.

Krishna and Nitya, with Lady Emily and the four girls, set off for
Bombay from Venice on 2 November. (Rajagopal had returned to
Cambridge for his final year.) On the last day of the voyage Nitya
suddenly expectorated blood. The next twelve months were to be ones
of grave anxiety for Krishna over this much-loved brother.

We were to stay in India, first at Adyar, then Delhi, before going on
to Sydney the following year. Soon after arriving at Adyar, where we
found Madame de Manziarly, Mar and Yo, Krishna's 'process' started
again without help from Helen who, with Ruth, had travelled straight
to Sydney. Nor did he have any help from Nitya who was now very ill
again and had gone up to Ootacamund with Madame de Manziarly.
'I suppose it will all stop some day,' Krishna wrote from Adyar in
January to Mrs Besant, who was in Delhi, 'but at present it is rather
awful. I can't do any work etc. It goes on all day and all night now.'
But it was not nearly so intense as it had been. Shortly before writing
this, Krishna had been to Madanapalle, his birthplace, to look for a
site for a university he was longing to build. He discovered a lovely
place in the Tettu valley about ten miles from the town and 2,500 feet
above sea level. The following year he was able to form a Trust to buy
300 acres there. He re-named it Rishi Valley from the Rishi Conda

mountain that dominated it, and there a school, not a university, was founded. It was the first of eight schools that Krishna was to found altogether.

The brothers had been invited to attend the Theosophical Convention in Sydney in April so they travelled out there with the Lutyens family. Raja went with them to help look after Nitya who was still very ill. A specialist in Sydney pronounced that he would need all his strength to pull through and must leave the city immediately, so he went up to Leura in the Blue Mountains where a superior log cabin was taken for him. Rosalind, who was still in Sydney, went with him as his nurse, as well as a married chaperone. Krishna divided his time between Leura and Sydney. Although he had done all he could to get the girls to Sydney, it was evident that he hated the church atmosphere there and was not welcomed by Leadbeater who found him a disruptive influence. He would grin and wink at us through the window as we sat in a stuffy room, trying to meditate with other members of the large community at The Manor, in the suburb of Mosman.[20] He was dreadfully impatient of everyone's feverish concern with taking steps on the Path as doled out by Leadbeater and which led to jealousy and snobbery. Compared to Krishna, everyone at The Manor seemed coarse and mediocre. He tried to talk to Leadbeater about 'the process' but the latter had nothing helpful to say; it was quite outside his range of experience and certainly not a necessary preparation for initiations.

Parcels of land had been given to Krishna for his work in many parts of Australia, and a great white stone amphitheatre had just been built on a glorious site on the edge of the harbour at Balmoral, close to The Manor, where it was expected the Lord would speak when he came. This and the land were held by different trusts at Krishna's request.

By June the specialist considered Nitya well enough to travel. When the brothers sailed for San Francisco on 24 June, with Rosalind and a Theosophical Swedish doctor, I felt that the light had gone out of my life for ever. My mother, who had supposedly passed her first initiation in Sydney, had already returned to England, leaving Helen, Ruth, Betty and me at The Manor.

It was a fearful voyage as Nitya grew weaker and weaker. Towards the end of it Krishna wrote to Mrs Besant: 'We will pull through and Nitya will be well once again. It has been and is a most anxious time, my own beloved mother, but you and the Masters are there.' After only a fortnight at Ojai of daily Abrams' treatment, Nitya's condition had improved. The remission was short lived, however, and for the next three months all Krishna's energies were taken up in nursing him as he became too ill to get out of bed at all. Krishna would have despaired if he had not been assured by both Mrs Besant and Leadbeater that the Masters would not allow Nitya to die; his life was too valuable.

In the meantime Mrs Besant had gone to England with Shiva Rao to give lectures at the Queen's Hall. George Arundale, who had been on a world lecture tour with his wife, Rukmini, was staying at a Theosophical community at Huizen in Holland, not far from Castle Eerde, run by a Theosophical bishop of the Liberal Catholic Church, James Ingall Wedgwood. A young Norwegian called Oscar Kollerstrom, a former pupil of Leadbeater in Sydney and a priest in the Liberal Catholic Church, was also at Huizen. Arundale telegraphed to Mrs Besant in London to say that amazing things were taking place: Oscar had just taken his third initiation, Wedgwood his second and Rukmini her first; *kundalini* had just been awoken in Wedgwood and Rukmini. (Arundale was already a second initiate and he and Oscar both claimed clairvoyance.) After another exciting telegram, Mrs Besant cancelled her Queen's Hall lectures and went to Huizen, accompanied by Esther Bright, Lady Emily, Shiva Rao and Rajagopal.

Two days after Mrs Besant arrived, on 26 July, Arundale was ordained a priest, Miss Bright, Lady Emily and Rajagopal were said to have taken their second initiation, and on the night of 1 August Arundale and Wedgwood took their third initiation and Rukmini her second. On the 4th Arundale was consecrated a bishop. Leadbeater's consent for this step had been requested by cable; when no reply came, Arundale asserted that he had received Leadbeater's 'cordial consent' on the astral plane. When they returned from the ceremony Mrs Besant found a cable from Leadbeater strongly disapproving of the step. None of the Huizen happenings was ever confirmed by Leadbeater.

Arundale kept on 'bringing through' instructions from the Masters: no initiate was to share a room with a non-initiate; silk underwear must be worn by all the Liberal Catholic priests (this was very hard on the poor ones, Lady Emily noted); copes were to be carefully chosen but no hats worn (for the first time Miss Dodge struck when she was asked to buy gorgeous vestments for the bishops); Mrs Besant, Wedgwood and the Arundales were to give up eating eggs in any form. (According to Lady Emily, Mrs Besant was the only one who adhered to this instruction, with the consequence that she was half starved from then onwards.)

On the night of 7 August Krishna (at Ojai), Raja (in India), Arundale and Wedgwood were said by Arundale to have taken their fourth or Arhat initiation, and two nights later Arundale 'brought through' the names of ten of what he said were to be the Lord's twelve apostles. These were Mrs Besant, Leadbeater, Raja, Arundale, Wedgwood, Rukmini, Nitya, Lady Emily, Rajagopal and Oscar Kollerstrom. Krishna had not been consulted but it was taken for granted that he would know all about it on the astral plane.

In the June issue of the *Herald* Arundale had announced that Krishna would not be able to attend the Ommen camp that year because of Nitya's health but that Mrs Besant and he would be there and he hoped that everyone would consider it a special duty to attend. There were few cancellations, therefore, and on 10 August the Huizen party moved to Ommen where the camp and Congress were opened that afternoon (Mrs Besant stayed in the Castle). At a talk next day Mrs Besant announced publicly that the Lord had already chosen his apostles but that she was only allowed to give out the names of seven of them, those who had already become Arhats – herself and Leadbeater, Raja, Arundale, Krishna, Oscar Kollerstrom and Rukmini who, she was assured, was to become an Arhat in a few days' time.[21] It was not until it was pointed out to her afterwards that she realised she had left out Wedgwood and named Krishna as one of his own apostles. She rectified these mistakes in another public talk on the 14th. The camp broke up that day and the Huizen party returned there. Arundale kept saying excitedly, 'I know something else has happened but it seems impossible.' The next morning Mrs Besant called Esther Bright, Lady Emily, Rukmini and Shiva Rao into her room and shyly told them that she, Leadbeater, Krishna, Raja, Arundale, Wedgwood and Oscar had all taken their fifth and final initiation on the night of the 13th, but it was to make no difference to the way they were to be treated.

Lady Emily had been caught up in the hysteria of that time at Huizen and had written enthusiastically to Krishna about it. He cabled back, asking her whether Leadbeater had confirmed all these happenings. She cabled in reply that Mrs Besant herself was making the announcements, adding 'Put your faith in her.' When Lady Emily returned to London she found a very unhappy letter from Krishna full of scepticism. She destroyed, at his request, all his letters to her during this crazy period; he feared they might fall into other hands and hurt Mrs Besant who was writing to him begging him to confirm all that Arundale had 'brought through'. Not wanting to wound her, he merely replied that he had been far too busy looking after Nitya to be conscious of any of it. Earlier on he had asked if Rajagopal might be sent to Ojai to help with nursing Nitya. This request had been granted and Rajagopal had left for America before the camp opened.

Mrs Besant very much wanted Krishna to go with her to India that winter for the Convention at Adyar to celebrate the fiftieth anniversary of the founding of the Theosophical Society. He did not at all want to leave Nitya but when, at the end of October, Nitya seemed better and Madame de Manziarly offered to go to Ojai to look after him, Krishna very reluctantly came to England, with Rosalind and Rajagopal, to please Mrs Besant. Lady Emily had a long talk with him as soon as he arrived and found him terribly unhappy about all the recent happenings at Huizen and Ommen. Something which to him was beautiful, private and sacred had been made publicly ugly, vulgar and ridiculous. Lady Emily asked him why he did not tell Mrs Besant what he felt. He said, what was the good? They would only say that the Black Powers had got hold of him. All the same, he did try several times to talk to her but she did not seem to take it in. Lady Emily felt that Mrs Besant had been hypnotised by Arundale and that she herself had been ludicrously gullible.

The party that set out from Naples for Colombo on 8 November consisted of Mrs Besant, Krishna, Lady Emily, Rosalind, Rajagopal, Shiva Rao, Wedgwood, Arundale and Rukmini. The two bishops, walking around Naples in long red cassocks, told Krishna that Nitya's life would be spared if he would acknowledge them as Adepts and his chosen apostles. Krishna would do no such thing and tried to avoid speaking to them. Shiva Rao believed that Krishna never for a moment doubted the Masters' power to save Nitya. Just as they were entering the Suez Canal, on the night of the 13th, a telegram was delivered to Mrs Besant announcing Nitya's death. According to Shiva Rao, who was sharing a cabin with Krishna, the next ten days were agonising. At night Krishna would sob and moan and cry out for Nitya, sometimes in his native Telegu which, in his waking consciousness, he could not speak. However, by the time they reached Colombo he had transformed his grief into what was almost a blessing and had written a piece about Nitya which was published in his editorial notes for the *Herald* of January 1926:

The pleasant dreams my brother and I had of the physical are over . . . We had great fun in life though we were of different temperaments. We somehow understood each other without effort . . . It was a happy life and I shall miss him physically all through this life.

An old dream is dead and a new one is being born, as a flower that pushes through the solid earth . . . A new strength born of suffering is pulsating in the veins and a new sympathy and understanding is being born out of the past suffering. A greater desire to see others suffer less and, if they must suffer, to see that they bear it nobly and come out of it without too many scars. I have wept but I do not want others to weep but if they do I now know what it means... On the physical plane we could be separated and now we are inseparable... As Krishnamurti I now have greater zeal, greater faith, greater sympathy and greater love for there is also in me the body, the Being, of Nityananda... I know now, with greater certainty than ever before, that there is real beauty in life, real happiness that cannot be shattered by any physical happening, a great strength which cannot be weakened by any passing event, and a great love which is permanent, imperishable and unconquerable.

Nitya's death was a terrible shock to Mrs Besant, though it did not undermine her faith, whereas from that time onwards Krishna seems to have lost all faith in the Masters as presented by Leadbeater, though not in the Lord Maitreya and his own role as the vehicle. Arundale and Wedgwood made it quite clear that Nitya had died because Krishna had refused to acknowledge them.

Leadbeater, with a party of seventy, including Helen, Ruth, Betty and me, arrived at Colombo a few days later. We had heard of Nitya's death at Melbourne. Mrs Besant, Krishna and others, who had gone to Adyar, returned to Colombo to meet us. Leadbeater's greeting to Krishna was: 'At least *you* are an Arhat.'

After the crossing to India there was a special train to Madras for the whole party, with crowds, garlands and prostrations at every station. Krishna, who knew that I had passionately loved Nitya, sat beside me in the train. 'Krishna was perfectly delicious,' I wrote in my diary, 'and talked to me about Nitya. They are together all the time now. K himself is so much more wonderful, and much softer.'

The situation at Adyar was very painful. Ruth revealed that Leadbeater did not believe in any of the initiations given out at Huizen. There were, therefore, two factions – the Arundale–Wedgwood party and the Leadbeater party, with Krishna and his own adherents standing aloof from both, and Mrs Besant, who had lost none of her love and reverence for Krishna, trying to reconcile them all. She went up to Krishna's room one morning, took him by the hand and led him down to her own drawing room where Leadbeater, Raja, Arundale and Wedgwood were assembled and, placing him on the sofa between herself and Leadbeater, asked him if he would accept them as his disciples. He replied that he would accept none of them except perhaps Mrs Besant herself. (The memory of this incident is one of the very few that Krishna retained for the rest of his life, for it would not be long before he was to lose practically all recollections of the past.)

The Star Congress followed the Theosophical Convention on 28 December. At the first Star meeting, under the banyan tree at eight o'clock in the morning, with over 3,000 people present, when Krishna was coming to the end of a talk about the World Teacher, he was suddenly transformed. He had been saying: 'He comes only to those who want, who desire, who long', when his face changed and his voice rang out with an extraordinary authority: 'And I come for those who want sympathy, who want happiness, who are longing to be released. I come to reform, not to tear down, I come not to destroy but to build.'[22]

It was an electrifying moment for those of us who noticed the change. (Wedgwood and Arundale said they thought that he was merely quoting scripture.) Mrs Besant certainly noticed it. At the last meeting of the Star Congress she was to say: '... that event [of 28 December] marked the definite consecration of the chosen vehicle... the final acceptance of the body chosen long before... the Coming has begun.' And in the January 1926 issue of the *Theosophist*, she wrote: 'There was no excitement, no flurry, even on the 28th December when, as our Brother Krishnaji was concluding his "speech" his sentence was broken into by our Lord the World Teacher, who took possession of his body and spoke a couple of sentences.' Leadbeater was no less certain. After he returned to Sydney he stated that there was not 'a shadow of doubt' that 'He' had used 'the Vehicle more than once' at the Jubilee Convention.[23]

Krishna himself had no doubts either. At a talk to the National Representatives of the Order of the Star at Adyar, he said: 'The memory of the 28th should be for you as if you were guarding some precious jewel and every time you look at it you must feel a thrill. Then when He comes again, and I am sure that He will come again very soon, it will be for you a nobler and far more beautiful occasion than even last time.'[24] And at a pupils' meeting he said: 'I personally feel quite different from that day... like a crystal vase, a jar that has been cleansed and now anybody in the world can put a beautiful flower in it and the flower shall live in the vase and never die.'[25]

Lady Emily noted in her diary that Krishna told her that he now felt like a shell – so absolutely impersonal. When she described to him how his face had changed as well as his voice, he said wistfully, 'I wish I could have seen it.' Did he believe that it was the face of the Lord Maitreya? To almost the end of his life he was stressing the importance that Mrs Besant and Leadbeater had always given to 'the face', but this seems to have referred to the beauty of his own face which he always regarded quite impersonally as he did his whole body. The body, apparently, had been given into his charge to look after. This sense of complete dissociation from his body was a phenomenon that lasted throughout his life.

8

'Constant turmoil within'

K rishna remained in India until May when he travelled to England with Rosalind and Rajagopal. (My mother, Betty and I had left at the end of January when Helen and Ruth returned to Sydney.) It seemed natural for Rajagopal to step into Nitya's shoes as Organising Secretary of the Star. He also became International Treasurer of the Order, a new appointment. He was a born organiser and Krishna was only too pleased to leave all financial concerns in his efficient hands.

At Krishna's request, Rajagopal arranged a three-week gathering at Castle Eerde from 3 July before the Ommen camp that year; an invitation to attend was sent from West Side House at Wimbledon to special friends who were asked to pay £2 a week for board and lodging. Thirty-five people of many different nationalities accepted; Mar de Manziarly, John Cordes, Rosalind, Rajagopal and the three Lutyenses were among them. The Castle now had electricity and proper plumbing installed by the Trust (formerly there had been oil lamps and oubliettes going straight into the moat where enormous carp devoured what descended on them), and the bedrooms had been turned into dormitories. Only Krishna had a room to himself. For the first three days he was in bed with bronchitis; thereafter he spoke to us every morning for an hour in the large drawing room, sitting cross-legged on the sofa under a Gobelin tapestry. Lady Emily, Mar and I all made notes in our diaries, confirming independently the belief that the Lord spoke through him several times.

The weather was perfect and there were enough of us for exciting games of volleyball. 'There is nothing so nice in the world,' I wrote in my diary, 'as to feel as one feels here, really alive physically, mentally and emotionally. To have, as K said, that sense of well-being through-out.' I became very close to Krishna during this gathering. Lady Emily recorded in her diary that at the talk on the last day, Krishna 'spoke as never before and one feels that his consciousness and that of the Lord are so completely blended that there is no distinction any more. He said, "Follow me and I will show you the way into the Kingdom of Happiness. I will give each of you the key with which you can unlock the gate into the garden", and the face of the Lord shone through the face of Krishna.'

Most of Krishna's friends and followers now called him Krishnaji – the suffix 'ji' indicating affectionate respect; to go on calling him Krishna in this book seems too familiar, Krishnaji too Indian, and Krishnamurti too laboured; therefore for the rest of the book he will be referred to as K, which was how he referred to himself.

When the camp opened on 24 July, the Eerde party, with the exception of K who remained at the Castle, moved into tents among the pinewoods a mile away. About 2,000 people* attended the camp which was beautifully organised. Mrs Besant, when she came to Europe at the beginning of July, went straight to Huizen. Nevertheless, she and Wedgwood attended the camp talks while staying at the Castle. In the heart of the camp was an amphitheatre made of rough-hewn logs where meetings were held when it was fine, and every evening there was a camp fire at sunset. K would change into Indian dress for the camp fires and light the fifteen-foot high pyramid of logs while chanting a hymn to Agni, god of fire. He would then give a talk as the fire blazed.

On the evening of the 27th Lady Emily, according to her diary, knew 'that directly Krishna appeared He [the Lord] was there. He looked so stern and full of power.' And Mrs Kirby, an Italian married to an English banker in Genoa, who had known K since 1909 at Adyar and had been with us at Pergine, wrote that there was an unusual dignity in his appearance that evening and that the power in his voice went on increasing, sounding deeper and fuller until 'the Lord was there and He was speaking . . . When it was over I discovered that I was trembling from head to foot.' When she saw him next morning, 'He was as dear and affectionate as ever and as I was telling him how his whole appearance had changed he said, "I wish I could see it

---

*The annual report of the Order of the Star in the East for 1926 gave the total number of members as 43,000 in forty countries. Two thirds of these were also members of the Theosophical Society.

too"... Krishnaji looked as if he badly needed a rest... What a life, poor Krishnaji. There is no doubt about his being the *Sacrifice*.'[26]
Part of his talk that evening is given below:

> I would ask you to come and look through my window, which will show you my heaven, which will show you my garden and my abode. Then you will see that what matters is not what you do, what you read, what any person says you are or are not, but that you should have the intense desire to enter into that abode where dwells Truth... I would have you come and see it; I would have you come and feel it... and not say to me: 'Oh, you are different, you are on the mountain top, you are a mystic.' You give me phrases and cover my Truth with your words. I do not want you to break with all you believe. I do not want you to deny your temperament. I do not want you to do things that you do not feel to be right. But, are any of you happy? Have you, any of you, tasted eternity?... I belong to all people, to all who really love, to all who are suffering. And if you would walk, you must walk with me. If you would understand you must look through my mind. If you would feel, you must look through my heart. And because I really love, I want you to love. Because I really feel, I want you to feel. Because I hold everything dear, I want you to hold all things dear. Because I want to protect, you should protect. And this is the only life worth living, and the only Happiness worth possessing.[27]

At the end of the talk Wedgwood was seen to lean towards Mrs Besant and whisper something to her. As soon as she and K got back to the Castle, she told him that it was a powerful black magician, whom she knew well, who had been speaking through him. K, utterly astounded, said that if she really thought that he would never speak in public again. The black magician was never afterwards mentioned. I happened to be sleeping at the Castle that night and K himself told me of this incident and said, 'Poor Amma'. He realised that her mind was going and that she believed anything Wedgwood told her.

Mrs Besant made a sudden decision to go with K to America where she had not been since 1909. A lecture tour was quickly arranged for her, and she set off with K, Rajagopal and Rosalind on 26 August. Twenty reporters came on board in New York who were disappointed to find K dressed in a well-cut grey suit. One journalist described him as 'a shy, badly-frightened nice-looking Hindu boy.' K was deeply embarrassed by the headlines: 'Cult of star awaits glory of Coming Lord'; 'New Messiah in Tennis Flannels'; 'New Deity Comes in Plus Fours', etc.

Forty reporters interviewed K alone at the Waldorf-Astoria Hotel next day. He was far less shy without Mrs Besant. *The New York Times* reported that many interviewers 'tried to trip him up with shrewdly worded questions; he skilfully avoided all the pitfalls and earned their admiration by coming out triumphant'. K often mentioned in later life that at this time he was offered $5,000 a week by a film company to play the title role in a life of Buddha. This pleased him because it made him feel that he could have earned his living had he wanted to.

It was not until 3 October, after Mrs Besant had given thirty lectures, that K met her in San Francisco and had the joy of taking her to Ojai. He had been having a rest at Warm Springs, Virginia, with Rajagopal. He had been away from Ojai for about a year. Two days after arriving there he wrote to Lady Emily: 'Here I am without Nitya... When I went into the room in which he was ill and from which he went away, I am afraid my body cried. It is a strange thing, the body. I wasn't really upset but my body was in an extraordinary state... I am getting used to his physical absence – which is rather a difficult thing to do, as we lived here more than anywhere, where we both suffered and where we were both happy.'

Because of a painful swelling in the breast (which eventually subsided), two doctors in Hollywood forbade K to go to India that winter as he had planned to do. Mrs Besant decided to remain with him at Ojai and he wrote to Lady Emily begging her to join him there with Betty and me. Betty had just joined the Royal College of Music and did not want to go, but my mother and I set off joyfully at the end of November and spent nearly five heavenly months at Ojai with K and Mrs Besant, Rajagopal and Rosalind. K and Mrs Besant had never had such a long, peaceful, happy time together. He was writing poetry then. Every evening we would walk to see the sunset which inspired him so much that he would return to write a poem.* He was his most human self while we were there, getting very irritable with me when he taught me to drive his Packard, and then being frantic with worry when I took the car out on my own in revenge.

In January what he called 'the old business' of intense pain in his neck and the base of his spine started again, though he now seemed able to bear it without 'going off'. It was only after it was over that he needed to relax and would leave his body for an hour or so to become a child. In this, I was able to help him. When I first went to him the

---

*His first poem, 'Hymn of the Initiate Triumphant', had been published in the *Herald* in January 1923. About 60 other poems of his were published, both in the *Herald* and in book form, until 1931, when he stopped writing poetry.

'physical elemental' asked me who I was and then said: 'Well, if you are a friend of Krishna's and Nitya's I suppose you are all right.' It was like a child of about four speaking, who called me 'Amma'. The child seemed very much in awe of K and would say things like, 'Take care, Krishna's coming back.' When K did come back he had absolutely no recollection of what the child had been saying.

When Lady Emily asked him one day what he meant by possessive love, he replied: 'Everybody is the same – they all think they have some special claim, some special road to me.' This went on all his life – people thinking they possessed him in some way, that they understood him better than anyone else. In fact, did anyone ever fully understand him? Certainly no one possessed him.

On 9 February he was to write to Leadbeater: 'I know with certainty that I am blending into the consciousness of the one Teacher and that He will completely fill me. I feel and know also my cup is nearly full to the brim and that it will overflow soon. I long to make, and will make, everybody happy.'

Soon after Mrs Besant arrived at Ojai she bought 450 acres of land in the upper Ojai valley for K to build the school which he so wanted. She then tried to raise money for a further 240 acres at the lower end for an annual camp as at Ommen. Yet another trust was formed, the Happy Valley Foundation, and an appeal launched for $200,000.* All the money was eventually subscribed, and the land bought, but the Happy Valley School was not started for twenty years.

Before leaving Ojai with K in April, Mrs Besant issued a statement to the Associated Press of America, beginning: 'The Divine Spirit has descended once more on a man, Krishnamurti, one who in his life is literally perfect, as those who know him can testify,' and ending: 'The World Teacher is here.'

There was a month's gathering at Castle Eerde before the Ommen camp that year. One of the large barns flanking the entrance to the Castle had been converted into small rooms on two floors so now there was room for sixty people. For the first week K had bad bronchitis again. While he was ill Lady Emily would read his poems aloud to us

---

*Mrs Besant wrote in the April *Theosophist* when making this appeal: 'I am risking on this new venture a reputation based on fifty-three years of public work and all my financial future.'

in the mornings while he lay in bed reading Edgar Wallace. On 30 June he was well enough to come down and give talks.

There were many discussions at the gathering between Lady Emily and Rajagopal about the reorganisation of the Order. Since so many people now believed that the Teacher had come, the objectives of the Order were no longer valid. On 28 June new objectives were drawn up: '1. To draw together all those who believe in the presence in the world of the World Teacher. 2. To work for Him in all ways for His realisation of His ideal for humanity. The Order has no dogmas, creeds or systems of belief. Its inspiration is the Teacher, its purpose to embody His universal life.' The name of the Order was changed from the Order of the Star in the East to the Order of the Star, and the magazine from the *Herald of the Star* to the *Star Review*. Henceforth, every country was to publish its own version of the magazine but there was to be, in addition, an *International Star Bulletin*, published by the Star Publishing Trust which had been set up in Holland in 1926 and which was for many years to publish K's talks.

K's theme this year at Eerde was Liberation whereas the year before it had been the Kingdom of Happiness. Lady Emily made some notes of what he said:

You must become liberated not because of me but in spite of me ... all this life and especially during the last few months I have struggled to be free – free of my friends, my books, my associations. You must struggle for the same freedom. There must be constant turmoil within. Hold a mirror constantly before you and, if there is anything you see there which is unworthy of the ideal you have created for yourself, change it ... You must not make me an authority. If I become a necessity to you what will you do when I go away? ... Some of you think I can give you a drink that will set you free, that I can give you a formula that will liberate you – that is not so. I can be the door but you must pass through the door and find the liberation that is beyond it ... Truth comes like a burglar – when you least expect it. I wish I could invent a new language but as I cannot I would like to destroy your old phraseology and conceptions. No one can give you liberation, you have to find it within, but because I have found it I would show you the way ... He who has attained liberation has become the Teacher – like myself. It lies in the power of each one to enter into the flame, to become the flame ... Because I am here, if you will hold me in your heart I will give you strength to attain ... Liberation is not for the few, the chosen, the select.

K's own philosophy was at last beginning to emerge, to the consternation of most of those at the gathering, especially the members of the Esoteric Section of the Theosophical Society who were accustomed to being told what to do and what steps they had taken on the Path. He was saying, in effect, that the Masters and all other gurus were unnecessary, that everyone had to find truth for himself. He spoke a great deal to Lady Emily at the gathering about his longing to become a *sanyasi*. He said himself that this was the last great temptation he had to resist.

Arundale, Wedgwood and even Raja, who was personally devoted to K, were all declaring at this time from Huizen, where they were staying, that they did not believe that K's consciousness was as yet blended with that of the Lord but a united front must be maintained. K himself had now changed his terminology: the blending of consciousness had become for him 'union with the Beloved', which was liberation.

The old Theosophical leaders were clinging desperately to their power; their influence was being undermined. What would happen to their authority if they could no longer train pupils for discipleship and dole out steps on the Path? How could they continue to lecture on the 'Coming of the World Teacher' if the Teacher was making revolutionary statements which struck at the very heart of the Esoteric Section?

Mrs Besant was at the camp again that year but she had evidently wanted to be at the Eerde gathering too. K must have dissuaded her from coming, for she wrote a pathetic letter to him from London on 28 July, three days before the camp opened:

> My beloved one . . . I have felt for a considerable time that the climax would come at Eerde this year and I wanted so much to be there for this beautiful time, and be nothing but just one of your own people, so that I have been feeling rather sad at not being there with all the fortunate people who have had that great blessing. Silly of me, perhaps, but I did so want to be there. I don't think you know how much I love you, dear, because I don't hang round you and fuss. So I have done my little weep all by myself over my bad karma. You didn't know I was such a goose, did you, or that I wanted so badly to be there instead of only coming in with the crowd.[28]

The day before the camp opened, before Mrs Besant arrived, K gave his first public answer to the question troubling so many: did he or did he not believe in the Masters and the occult hierarchy? It was perhaps the most important statement of his own position that he ever made:

When I was a small boy I used to see Sri Krishna, with the flute, as he was pictured by the Hindus, because my mother was a devotee of Sri Krishna ... When I grew older and met with Bishop Leadbeater and the Theosophical Society, I began to see the Master K.H. – again in the form that was put before me, the reality from their point of view – and hence the Master K.H. was to me the end. Later on, as I grew, I began to see the Lord Maitreya. That was two years ago and I saw him constantly in the form put before me ... Now lately, it has been the Buddha whom I have been seeing and it has been my delight and my glory to be with Him. I have been asked what I mean by the Beloved. I will give a meaning, an estimation, which you will interpret as you please. To me it is all – it is Sri Krishna, it is the Master K.H., it is the Lord Maitreya, it is the Buddha, and yet it is beyond all these forms. What does it matter what name you give? ... What you are troubling about is whether there is such a person as the World Teacher who has manifested-Himself in the body of a certain person, Krishnamurti; but in the world nobody will trouble about this question. It is an unfortunate thing that I have to explain, but I must. I wanted to be as vague as possible, and I have made it so. My Beloved is the open skies, the flower, every human being ... Till I was able to say with certainty, without any undue excitement, or exaggeration in order to convince others, that I was one with my Beloved I never spoke. I talked of vague generalities which everybody wanted. I never said: I am the World Teacher; but now that I feel that I am one with my Beloved, I say it, not in order to impress my authority on you, not to convince you of my greatness, nor of the greatness of the World Teacher, nor even of the beauty of life, but merely to awaken the desire in your hearts and in your own minds to seek out the Truth. If I say, and I will say, that I am one with the Beloved, it is because I feel and know it. I have found what I longed for, I have become united, so that henceforth there will be no separation, because my thoughts, my desires, my longings – those of the individual self, have been destroyed ... I am as the flower that gives scent to the morning air. It does not concern itself with who is passing by ... Until now you have been depending on the two Protectors of the Order [Mrs Besant and Leadbeater] for authority, on someone else to tell you the Truth, whereas the Truth lies within you ... It is no good asking me who is the Beloved. Of what use is explanation? For you will not understand the Beloved until you are able to see him in every animal, every blade of grass, in every person that is suffering, in every individual.[29]

Mrs Besant went to the camp from Huizen with Raja and Wedgwood. Although her main speech during the meetings was 'The World Teacher is Here', she could not reconcile what K was actually saying with her preconceived idea of what the Lord would say. She returned to Huizen on 15 August, thus missing a talk which K gave two days later to the voluntary workers who had run the camp. The talks were usually taken down in shorthand and published but there is no official record of this talk (it was probably suppressed for Mrs Besant's sake). We have only one sentence from it, recorded in Lady Emily's diary: 'You cannot help until you yourself are beyond the need of help.' Reports of this talk reached Mrs Besant and greatly upset her and also, as she said, upset many others. K, who was resting at Villars with Rajagopal, wrote to her saying that he could not remember what he had said. 'I am afraid they all object to think for themselves,' he added, 'It's so much easier to sit in comfort in the thoughts of others . . . Mother, we two must stick together and nothing else matters.'

But, according to Peter Freeman, MP, the General Secretary of the Theosophical Society for Wales: 'He [K] told us that he had never been able to read a Theosophical book in his life – could not understand our Theosophical "jargon" and although he had heard many Theosophical lectures, none of them had convinced him of their knowledge of truth.'[30]

After Villars K went to Paris where he had promised to sit for the sculptor, Antoine Bourdelle. Bourdelle, then sixty-six, was immediately captivated by K. 'When one hears Krishnamurti speak one is astonished,' he is quoted as saying – 'so much wisdom and so young a man . . . Krishnamurti is a great sage and were I fifteen years of age I would follow him.'[31]*

K was not present when Rajagopal and Rosalind were married at a registry office in London on 3 October, with a religious ceremony afterwards at St Mary's Liberal Catholic Church. Mrs Besant gave Rosalind away. It was Mrs Besant who had urged the marriage, so that Rosalind might travel with K with propriety, although Rajagopal was certainly deeply in love with her. Arya Vihara at Ojai was to become their home. K had no recollection of what he thought about the marriage. His feelings about marriage in general had now changed, however; he no longer regarded it as a disaster.

---

*Bourdelle's bust of K, considered to be among his finest works, is now in the Bourdelle Museum in Paris.

9

'I refuse to be your crutch'

K went to India with Mrs Besant in October 1927. Landing at
Bombay on the 27th, Mrs Besant made a statement about him to
the reporters who met them: 'I bear witness that he has been accounted
worthy... to blend his consciousness with that of a fragment, an *amsa*,
of the omnipresent consciousness of the World Teacher... and now he
has come back to you, to his own people, to his own race, yet trans-
cending both, for he belongs to the whole world.'

The effect of this pronouncement on Indians, whose natural tendency
is to prostrate themselves in worship, can be imagined. Arundale,
however, wrote an article in *Theosophy in India* which illustrates the
impossible situation which K faced that winter, and the bewilderment
of Theosophists: 'Our President has been declaring that the Lord is
here... Now it is impossible for me to reconcile this statement... with
my own knowledge of the Lord as He is in His glorious body.'

Leadbeater was at Adyar for the Theosophical Convention in
December. On the 8th K wrote to Lady Emily: 'I had a long talk to
him... he agrees with me to an astonishing extent. He asked me what
I felt like and I told him there was no Krishna – the river and the sea.*
He said, yes, like the books of old, it's all true. He was very nice and
extraordinarily reverential.'

In January K was writing to Lady Emily again to tell her that his
head had been terribly bad and that he must have fainted several times.
It hardly ever left him now, though it did not prevent him from touring

---

*The tradition in Eastern philosophy that, at the end of evolution, the ego, after its
long windings of successive lives, leaves the river of life to lose itelf in the sea of Nirvana.

India giving talks. He was disappointed that Leadbeater could give no explanation for the continuance of the pain. K had accepted all he had suffered physically as preparation of the body for the occupancy of the Lord, yet now that he had obtained 'union with the Beloved' he was puzzled as to why the pain should continue.

The companion who travelled with him, now that Rajagopal was at Ojai with Rosalind, was an old friend, Judunandan Prasad (Jadu). Jadu had been at Pergine and at the Eerde gathering the previous summer. He was an attractive young man, far more like Nitya in temperament than Rajagopal, and K felt a more natural affinity with him. He travelled back to Europe with K at the end of February. For the first time on a voyage, K held discussions with his fellow passengers after repeated requests from them to do so.

On 31 March K gave his first public talk in England at the Friends' Meeting House. There was so much interest that hundreds had to be turned away. Jadu sailed with him to America four days later. The first Star camp was to be held at Ojai in May, on the land bought by Mrs Besant at the lower end of the valley, which included a grove of holm oaks, the beautiful evergreen oaks of California. But, before the camp, K gave his first public talk in America, on the evening of 5 May, at the Hollywood Bowl, to an audience of 16,000 who, according to the *Los Angeles Times*, listened in 'apparently rapt attention' to his talk on 'Happiness through Liberation'.

Only about 1,000 people attended the first Ojai camp. Nevertheless, it was a great success. K's morning talks were held in the Oak Grove. On 30 May, two days after the camp closed, K, Rajagopal and Jadu left for England while Rosalind remained at Ojai. Mrs Besant came to England at the same time and K went with her to Paris where, on 27 June, he broadcast in French on 'The Secret of Happiness' for the Eiffel Tower Radio Station to an estimated two million listeners.

There was a larger gathering than ever at Castle Eerde that summer before the Ommen camp. The other barn had now been converted so there was room for more than Star members. Leopold Stokowsky and his wife came for a few days and Sir Roderick Jones, the Chairman of Reuters, with his wife, the author, Enid Bagnold. K had innumerable friends now, of many different nationalities, but a couple with whom he became particularly close for many years were Egyptians who lived in Paris, Carlo and Nadine Suàres.

*

74

Mrs Besant had intended to be at the Ommen camp at K's special request, conveyed in a very loving letter, but illness prevented it. Although he was greatly concerned for her health, her absence enabled him to say what he wanted at the camp fire talks without fear of hurting her. He told the organisers of the camp, before it opened, that he would abolish the Order of the Star at once if it 'claimed to be a vessel that holds the Truth and the only Truth'. During the meetings he was asked questions such as: 'Is it true that you do not want disciples?'; 'What do you think of rituals and ceremonials?'; 'Why do you tell us that there are no stages along the Path?'; 'As you tell us there is no God, no moral code and neither good nor evil, how does your teaching differ from ordinary materialism?'; 'Are you the Christ come back?' Extracts given below from K's answers show how little those who asked the questions had understood him.

I say again that I have no disciples. Every one of you is a disciple of the Truth if you understand the Truth and do not follow individuals... Truth does not give hope; it gives understanding... There is no understanding in the worship of personality... I still maintain that all ceremonies are unnecessary for spiritual growth... If you would seek the Truth you must go out, far away from the limitations of the human mind and heart and there discover it – and that Truth is within yourself. Is it not much simpler to make Life itself the goal than to have mediators, gurus, who must inevitably step down the Truth and hence betray it?... I say that Liberation can be attained at any stage of evolution by a man who understands, and that to worship stages, as you do, is not essential... Do not quote me afterwards as an authority. I refuse to be your crutch. I am not going to be brought into a cage for your worship. When you bring the fresh air of the mountain and hold it in a small room, the freshness of that air disappears and there is stagnation... I have never said there is no God. I have said that there is only God as manifested in you... but I am not going to use the word God... I prefer to call this Life... Of course there is neither good nor evil. Good is that of which you are not afraid; evil is that of which you are afraid. So, if you destroy fear, you are spiritually fulfilled... When you are in love with life, and you place that love before all things, and judge by that love, and not by your fear, then this stagnation which you call morality will disappear... Friends, do not concern yourself with who I am; you will never know... Do you think Truth has anything to do with what you think I am? You are not concerned with the Truth but you are concerned with the vessel that contains the Truth... Drink the water if the water is clean: I say to you that I have that clean water; I have that balm which shall purify, that shall heal greatly; and you ask me: who are you? I am all things because I am Life.[32]

He closed the Convention with the words: 'There have been many thousand people at these camps and what they could not do in the world if they all understood! They could change the face of the world tomorrow.'

Poor Mrs Besant, now eighty years old, was having a very unhappy old age trying to reconcile irreconcilables. In order to fall in with all K was saying, she closed the Esoteric Section throughout the world before he arrived in India in October 1928. (She was to reopen it in less than a year.) K recognised this as a very wonderful thing for her to have done. She was unable to be there to greet him when he arrived at Adyar, but wrote, 'Beloved...I am suspending the E.S. altogether indefinitely, leaving all teaching to you'; and the next day, 'Welcome home, Beloved. I have done my best to make a clear field for you, you the only authority.'[33] As K told Lady Emily, Mrs Besant wanted to resign the Presidency of the Theosophical Society in order to follow him everywhere but her Master would not allow it. At all the meetings in India that winter she insisted on sitting on the ground with the rest of the audience instead of with him on the platform as she had always done before. At the same time she was upholding Arundale who was saying to K, as K reported to Lady Emily: 'You go your way and we will go ours. I have also something to teach.' Mrs Besant also supported Leadbeater who had written to her: 'Of course our Krishnaji has not the Omniscience of the Lord', by writing herself in the December *Theosophist*: 'Krishnamurti's physical consciousness does not share the omniscience of the Lord Maitreya', and quoting Sri Krishna's dictum: 'Mankind comes to Me along many roads.' K wrote to Lady Emily that presently there would be 'a clear-cut division' between him and the Theosophical Society, which would be 'much better than this pretence'. His head and spine were very bad and no one could help, 'not as before'.

While K was at Benares that year, the Rishi Valley Trust acquired from the military authorities 300 acres of land which K wanted for another school. This was at Rajghat, a lovely place on the banks of the Ganges just north of Benares. The pilgrims' path runs through the estate, linking Kashi with Saranath where the Buddha preached his first sermon after enlightenment. All the capital in the Trust would be spent on this land but it 'could not be helped'.

*

1 K, Nitya and Leadbeater, Adyar, 1910

2 Nitya, Mrs Besant, K and Arundale arriving at Charing Cross Station, London, May 1911

3 K in London in 1911

Opposite:

5 (*above*) In Baron van Palland motor car, Eerde, 1923. *Left to rig* Helen, Mary, Nitya, Betty, K, La Emily

6 (*below*) Playing ball below the Cast Hotel, Pergine, 1924

4 Lady Emily in 1912

8 (*left*) K in doorway of the Round Tower, Castle-Hotel, Pergine, 1924
9 (*below*) Rajagopal at Ehrwald, 1923

Opposite:
7 Nitya in India, 1924

11 (*left*) Mrs Besant and K at Ojai, 1927

12 (*below*) K at Ommen, *c.* 1928

pposite:
) Leadbeater in Sydney with two
his young pupils, 1925

13 K at Eerde, *c.* 1929

14 K and the author at Scheveningen, Holland, 1953.
A rare picture of K, aged 48

K and Jadu sailed for Europe in February 1929. After brief visits to Paris, Eerde and London, they went on to New York. In London I had told K that I was engaged to be married. From boardship he wrote to Lady Emily: 'At first I was frankly upset about it all – you know what I mean – and I carefully thought about it while I was with you and it's alright now. My ideas and my outlook must not interfere with Mary's growth. There will be very few who will go with me the whole way. I hope she will come out of it a full-blossomed flower.' On the same day, 5 March, he was writing to Mar de Manziarly: 'I will never give up anyone but everyone will give me up.' Of the old friends it was only Mar who followed him continuously until his death. Madame de Manziarly found an outlet for her energy in the ecumenical Christian movement; Ruth was already married to a bishop in the Liberal Catholic Church; K and Helen drifted apart (in the early 1930s she married Scott Nearing); my sister Betty reacted violently against him; Rajagopal became separated from him, as will be seen. Of course, many of the older ones were faithful until *their* deaths, and many whom he met later were faithful until *his* death and beyond, but there were others who turned against him, usually out of jealousy and hurt feelings. In the early days, when he said something to people which they liked, they would maintain that it was the Lord speaking through him; when he told them something they did not want to hear, it was K speaking. In the same way in the future, when he said something unpalatable, he would be accused of having been 'influenced' by someone or other.

In spite of K's certainty of his union with 'the Beloved', he had not lost, and was never to lose, his human side. At Ojai that year he, Rajagopal and Jadu 'talked and talked, quarrelled and got excited', as he told Lady Emily. They also laughed a great deal and played the fool and ragged each other. Rajagopal had a memorable laugh – more of a giggle – whereas K's laugh was louder and deeper. He remained all his life shy and self-effacing with strangers, with no social small talk. At our house in London, and with Mrs Besant, he had met Bernard Shaw, who declared him to be 'the most beautiful human being he ever saw',[34] but K was too shy to speak a dozen words to him.

K was physically a perfectly normal man who had been brought up to believe that sex must be sublimated in all those who aimed to become pupils of the Masters, and even more so in the vehicle of the Lord. He was to lose completely this intolerance of sex, yet he never considered it anything to make a problem over. Because of his looks, if nothing else, it was inevitable that many women should fall in love with him. There was to be more than one crazy woman who would write claiming to be his wife, and if he was seen publicly in the company of some girl, the press would immediately report an engagement.*

During the six weeks that K was at Ojai this year, before the camp, the pain in his head and spine was very bad and he felt so tired that a new doctor warned him that the frequent attacks of bronchitis he was having might lead to tuberculosis if he did not rest more; therefore he cancelled all his talks for the summer, including three lectures at the Queen's Hall in London, and decided to confine himself to the Ojai and Ommen camps and the Eerde gathering.

The Ojai camp, beginning on 27 May, had doubled its attendance. He pronounced in one of his talks in the Oak Grove: 'I say now, I say without conceit, with proper understanding, with fullness of mind and heart, that I am that full flame which is the glory of life, to which all human beings, individuals as well as the whole world, must come.'[35] It was rumoured during the camp that he was soon to dissolve the Order of the Star. This he did some weeks later. At the first meeting of the Ommen camp, on 3 August, in the presence of Mrs Besant and over 3,000 Star members, with thousands of Dutch people listening on the radio, he ended an epoch in his own history. Part of what he said is given below:

> I maintain that Truth is a pathless land, and you cannot approach it by any path whatsoever, by any religion, by any sect. That is my point of view and I adhere to that absolutely and unconditionally... If you first understand that, then you will see how impossible it is to organize a belief. A belief is purely an individual matter, and you cannot and must not organize it. If you do, it becomes dead, crystallized; it becomes a creed, a sect, a religion, to be imposed on others.
>
> This is what everyone throughout the world is attempting to do. Truth is narrowed down and made a plaything for those who are weak, for those who are only momentarily discontented. Truth cannot be brought down, rather the individual must make the effort to ascend to it. You cannot bring the mountain top to the valley... So that is the first reason, from my point of view, why the Order of the Star should be dissolved. In spite of this, you will probably form other Orders, you will continue to belong to other organizations searching for Truth. I do not want to belong to any organization of a spiritual kind; please understand this...
>
> If an organization be created for this purpose, it becomes a crutch, a weakness, a bondage, and must cripple the individual, and prevent him

---

*There was a report of his engagement to Helen Knothe in the New York papers, and my father managed to stop an announcement of my engagement to him in 1927.

from growing, from establishing his uniqueness, which lies in the discovery for himself of that absolute, unconditioned Truth. So that is another reason why I have decided, as I happen to be the Head of the Order, to dissolve it.

This is no magnificent deed, because I do not want followers, and I mean this. The moment you follow someone you cease to follow Truth. I am not concerned whether you pay attention to what I say or not. I want to do a certain thing in the world and I'm going to do it with unwavering concentration. I am concerning myself with only one essential thing: to set man free. I desire to free him from all cages, from all fears, and not to found religions, new sects, nor to establish new theories and new philosophies. Then you will naturally ask me why I go the world over, continually speaking. I will tell you for what reason I do this; not because I desire a following, nor because I desire a special group of special disciples. I have no disciples, no apostles, either on earth or in the realm of spirituality.

Nor is it the lure of money, nor the desire to live a comfortable life which attracts me. If I wanted to lead a comfortable life I would not come to a Camp or live in a damp country! I am speaking frankly because I want this settled once and for all. I do not want these childish discussions year after year.

A newspaper reporter who interviewed me considered it a magnificent act to dissolve an organization in which there were thousands and thousands of members. To him it was a great act because he said: 'What will you do afterwards, how will you live? You will have no following, people will no longer listen to you.' If there are only five people who will listen, who will live, who have their faces turned towards eternity, it will be sufficient. Of what use is it to have thousands who do not understand, who are fully embalmed in prejudice, who do not want the new, but would rather translate the new to suit their own sterile, stagnant selves! . . .

For eighteen years you have been preparing for this event, for the Coming of the World Teacher. For eighteen years you have organized, you have looked for someone who would give a new delight to your hearts and minds, who would transform your whole life, who would give you a new understanding; for someone who would raise you to a new plane of life, who would give you a new encouragement, who would set you free – and now look what is happening! Consider, reason with yourselves, and discover in what way that belief has made you different – not with the superficial difference of the wearing of a badge, which is trivial, absurd. In what manner has such a belief swept away all unessential things of life? That is the only way to judge: in what way are you freer, greater, more dangerous to every society which is based on the false and the unessential? In what way have the members of this organization of the Star become different? . . .

You are depending for your spirituality on someone else, for your happiness on someone else, for your enlightenment on someone else . . . when I

say look within yourselves for enlightenment, for the glory, for the purification, and for the incorruptibility of the self, not one of you is willing to do
it. There may be a few, but very, very few. So why have an organization?...
You use a typewriter to write letters, but you do not put it on an altar
and worship it. But that is what you are doing when organizations become
your chief concern. 'How many members are there in it?' That is the first
question I am asked by all newspaper reporters. I do not know how many
there are. I am not concerned with that... You have been accustomed to
being told how far you have advanced, what is your spiritual status. How
childish! Who but you yourself can tell if you are incorruptible?
...But those who really desire to understand, who are looking to find that
which is eternal, without a beginning and without an end, will walk together
with greater intensity, will be a danger to everything that is unessential, to
unrealities, to shadows... Such a body we must create, and that is my
purpose. Because of that true friendship – which you do not seem to know –
there will be real co-operation on the part of each one. And this not because
of authority, not because of salvation, but because you really understand,
and hence are capable of living in the eternal. This is a greater thing than
all pleasure, than all sacrifice.
So those are some of the reasons why, after careful consideration for two
years, I have made this decision. It is not from a momentary impulse. I have
not been persuaded to it by anyone – I am not persuaded in such things.
For two years I have been thinking about this, slowly, carefully, patiently,
and I have now decided to disband the Order. You can form other organizations and expect someone else. With that I am not concerned, nor with
creating new cages, new decorations for those cages. My only concern is to
set men absolutely, unconditionally free.[36]

10

'*I am going on my way*'

After the dissolution of the Order, Castle Eerde and all its land, apart from the 400 acres on which the camp was built, was returned to Baron van Pallandt, while all those parcels of land in Australia, and the amphitheatre on the edge of Sydney harbour, were given back to their donors. Although K went to Adyar with Mrs Besant that winter, and for her sake kept up a pretence of harmony with the Theosophical Society, he resigned from the Society when Mrs Besant reopened the Esoteric Section throughout the world before the end of the year. Nevertheless, their personal love for each other never wavered. Writing to her on leaving India in February 1930 as 'My own beloved Mother', he said: 'I know, and it doesn't matter to me, that C.W.L. [Leadbeater] is against me and what I am saying but please don't worry over it. All this is inevitable and in a way necessary. I can't change and I suppose they won't change and hence the conflict. It doesn't matter what a million people say or don't say, I'm certain what I am and I am going on my way.'

Leadbeater in Sydney was now saying that 'The Coming has gone wrong'; Arundale that he would allow K 'a niche in the Theosophical Pantheon but no more'; Raja that K's teaching was 'one more colour in the spectrum'; and Wedgwood that Mrs Besant was 'non compos' so that when she said that K's consciousness was blended with that of the Lord Maitreya she could not be relied upon.[37]

Hundreds of people were distressed by the dissolution of the Order. One of them was Lady De La Warr, who was to die in 1930. Miss Dodge remained loyal to K until her death five years later. The person

81

to suffer most was probably Lady Emily, not so much because of the dissolution but because of K's declaration that he did not want followers. For eighteen years she had been waiting for him to say: 'Follow me', and she would joyously have given up home, husband and family; now her existence had become utterly purposeless. She wrote in her autobiography, *Candles in the Sun*: 'Krishna had managed to transcend personal love but I could not. It was not that he did not love, but no one person was necessary to him any longer. He had attained to universal love. As he said himself: "Pure love is like the perfume of the rose, given to all. The sun does not care on whom it shines... The quality of true love, of pure love, knows no such distinction as wife and husband, son, father, mother".' Lady Emily felt that this was too abstract to be of any help to those who had to live in the world with family responsibilities – that K was, in fact, escaping from life. He tried most patiently to carry her with him, writing to her from Ojai:

> I am sorry you feel that way about what I say. The ecstasy that I feel is the outcome of this world. I wanted to understand, I wanted to conquer sorrow, this pain of detachment and attachment, death, continuity of life, everything that man goes through every day. I wanted to understand and conquer it. I have. So, my ecstasy is real and infinite, not an escape. I know the way out of this incessant misery and I want to help people out of the bog of this sorrow. No, this is not an escape.

She now told him how miserable she was to feel that she had disappointed him, to which he replied: 'Mummy darling, I am not "disappointed" in you – what a thing to say and what a thing for you to write to me. I know what you are going through, but don't worry about it... only you have to transfer your emphasis. Look, one must have no beliefs or even ideas for they belong to all kinds of reactions and responses... if you are alert, free from ideas, beliefs etc. in the present, then you can see infinitely and this perception is joy.' But she was more mystified than ever when told that she must have no beliefs or ideas.

The annual camps at Ommen and Ojai were now open to the public and no less well attended, for they were attracting a different kind of audience – those who were interested in what K had to say rather than in what he was. This was how he wanted it. He stayed now at Ommen, in a hut that had been built for him. (Several people had built huts among the pine trees.) Donations for his work continued to come in.

Rajagopal looked after all his financial affairs, arranged his tours and saw to the printing of his talks by the Star Publishing Trust; Rajagopal also edited the *International Star Bulletin*.

After the Ommen camp of 1930, K travelled with Rajagopal to Athens, Constantinople and Bucharest, where he had been invited to give public talks. From Athens he wrote to Lady Emily: 'I have never seen anything more beautiful, simple, forceful than the Parthenon. The whole of the Acropolis is amazing, breath taking and *everything* else in nature of the expression of man is vulgar, mediocre and confused. What people those wonderful few Greeks were.' The only other works of art that had so far thrilled him were the Winged Victory at the Louvre and a stone head of Buddha in the Boston Museum. (He had written an article about this head of Buddha in the *Herald* of March 1924.)

In Bucharest he had two private interviews with Queen Marie of Roumania, a granddaughter of Queen Victoria, who asked to see him at the palace. He also had to have a police escort there, night and day, since some nationalistic Catholic students had threatened to kill him. He treated the police precautions as a great joke. In January and February 1931, he was speaking in Yugoslavia and Budapest; wherever he travelled, he gave private interviews as well as public talks.

At a public talk given in London in March, a subtle development in K's teaching can be noticed and a change in his style:

> In everything, in all men, there is the totality, the completeness of life ... By completeness I mean freedom of consciousness, freedom from individuality. That completeness which exists in everything cannot progress: it is absolute. The effort to acquire is futile, but if you can realise that Truth, happiness, exists in all things and that the realisation of that Truth lies only through elimination, then there is a timeless understanding. This is not a negative. Most people are afraid to be nothing. They call it being positive when they are making an effort, and call that effort virtue. Where there is effort it is not virtue. Virtue is effortless. When you are as nothing, you are all things, not by aggrandisement, not by laying emphasis on the 'I', on the personality, but by the continual dissipation of that consciousness which creates power, greed, envy, possessive care, vanity, fear and passion. By continually being self-recollected you become fully conscious, and then you liberate the mind and heart and know harmony, which is completeness.[38]

When, as he wrote to Raja, a reporter asked him if he was the Christ, he answered: 'Yes, in the pure sense but not in the traditional, accepted sense of the word.' Later he told Lady Emily: 'You know, mum, I have *never* denied it [being the World Teacher], I have only said it does not matter who or what I am but that they should examine what I say which does not mean that I have denied being the W.T.' He was never to deny it.

In August the news came that Jadu, who had remained in America that year, had died of a stroke. His death was a great blow to K who had felt very close to him. After more travelling, and the Ommen camp, K returned, exhausted, to Ojai in October, determined to have a complete rest instead of going to India. The Rajagopals now had a baby daughter, Radha, to whom K became devoted. When the family went to Hollywood, where Rajagopal was to have his tonsils out, K was left quite alone for the first time in his life. He wrote to Lady Emily on 11 December from Pine Cottage, where he was living while the Rajagopals were away: 'My being alone like this has given me something tremendous, and it's just what I need. Everything has come, so far in my life, just at the right time. My mind is so serene but concentrated and I am watching it like a cat a mouse. I am really enjoying this solitude and I can't put into words what I am feeling. But I'm not deceiving myself either. For the next three months, or as long as I want to, I am going to do this. I can never be finished but I want to finish with all the superficialities I have.' He added that when the Rajagopals returned he would have his meals in the cottage on a tray. It seems to have been from this time of living alone that K lost his memory of the past almost entirely. This was consistent with his later teaching that memory, except for practical purposes, is a weight that should not be carried over from one day to the next.

It is only from K's letters to Lady Emily that we know something of his state of mind in the early 1930s. In March the following year he was writing to her: 'I am trying to build a bridge for others to come over, not away from life but to have more abundance of life... The more I think of what I have "realised" the clearer I can put it and help to build a bridge but that takes time and continual change of phrases, so as to give true meaning. You have no idea how difficult it is to express the inexpressible and what is expressed is not truth.' All his life he continued trying to express the inexpressible in different words and phrases.

Far from being carried along with K, Lady Emily was highly critical of him, telling him what many people no doubt thought and said behind his back without the courage to say it to him outright. In September this year, for instance, she was writing:

You seem surprised that people do not understand you but I should be far more surprised if they did!! After all, you are upsetting everything in which they have ever believed – knocking out their foundations and putting in its place a nebulous abstraction. You speak of what you yourself say is indescribable – and not to be understood till discovered for oneself. How then do you expect them to understand? You are speaking from another dimension and have quite forgotten what it is like to live in a world of three dimensions... You are advocating a complete destruction of the ego in order to achieve something about which you can know nothing until you achieve it! Naturally people prefer their egos of which they do know something... No human problem means anything to you because you are ego-less and your abstraction of bliss means nothing to people who are still desirous to live in the world as they know it.[39]

On the same day as she was writing this, he was writing to her, during a tour of America: 'I am full of something tremendous. I can't tell you in words what it is like, a bubbling joy, a living silence, an intense awareness like a living flame... I have been trying my hand at healing, two or three cases, and asked them not to say anything about it and it has been pretty good. One lady who was going blind will I think be all right.'

K did undoubtedly have some power of healing but he was always very reticent about it since he did not want people to come to him as a physical healer. In answer to a question at a meeting, he had replied:

Which would you rather have: a Teacher who will show you the way to keep permanently whole or one who will momentarily heal your wounds? Miracles are fascinating child's play. Miracles are happening every day. Doctors are performing miracles. Many friends of mine are spiritual healers. But although they may heal the body, unless they make the mind and heart also whole, the disease will return. I am concerned with the healing of the heart and the mind, not with the body. I hold that no great Teacher would perform a miracle, because that would be a betrayal of the Truth.[40]

In his youth K had certainly had clairvoyant powers which he might have developed; instead, he deliberately suppressed them. When people came to him for help he did not want to know more about them than they were willing to reveal to him. Most people came to him wearing a mask, he said; he hoped they would remove it; if not, he would no more try to look behind it than to read their private letters.[41]

Up till the war, K's life was travel, travel, travel, giving talks and private interviews wherever he went, with rests in between at Ojai. He asked Lady Emily to send him the names of any books on current affairs that she thought he ought to read and also *The New Statesman and Nation.* This she did but he really had no time for reading anything but detective stories, what with a huge correspondence and correcting his own talks for publication which he was doing at this time. Everywhere he went he made new contacts, new friends, spoke to a great variety of people, gaining a far more valuable knowledge of what was going on in the world than from any book.

In November 1932 he went with Rajagopal to India. Mrs Besant was ill and rapidly losing her mind, but she managed to be present at the Theosophical Convention at Adyar, which Leadbeater as well as K attended. K had a long talk with Raja as he told Lady Emily: 'They all have one phrase by heart – you go your way and we by our way but we shall meet... I believe they didn't want me to come here. There's distinct antagonism... Adyar is lovely but the people are *dead.*'

After the Convention he toured India, returning to Adyar in May 1933, where he saw Mrs Besant for the last time on his way back to Europe. She just recognised him and was very affectionate. (She died on 20 September.)* K was not to return to the Theosophical Head-quarters for forty-seven years.

The next time K and Rajagopal were at Adyar, three months after Mrs Besant's death, they stayed for the first time at Vasanta Vihar, 64 Greenways Road, a house which had just been built as K's Indian headquarters, with six acres of land. It was on the north side of the Adyar river, whereas the Theosophical Society's estate (of 260 acres) was on the south side, stretching to the sea. Vasanta Vihar was a far larger house than K had wanted, and Lady Emily scolded him for building it so close to the Theosophical compound. He replied that he and Rajagopal had considered Madras the best place 'for printing, people, workers, etc.', and this was the only land they could find. 'We have nothing against the T.S. and its tenets,' he added. 'I am not fighting *them* but the world's ideas, ideals.' He begged Lady Emily, in this same letter, to criticise him as much as possible: 'the more one is critical the more we can understand each other.' She took advantage

---

*George Arundale became the next President of the Theosophical Society, and, on his death in 1945, he was succeeded by Raja, who held the position until a few months before his death in 1953.

of this and hardly ever stopped criticising him, though her letters were always full of love for him as well.

During this visit to India, K drove to Rishi Valley, 170 miles west of Madras, where, it may be remembered, land had been bought for his work in 1928. J. V. Subba Rao was the first Principal of the co-educational school that had opened there, and was to remain so for thirty years while the school grew and flourished. During K's visit, he talked to the teachers for five hours every day.

Education was one of K's most passionate concerns throughout his life. He always loved children and felt that if they could be brought up to flower fully without prejudices, religions, traditional ideologies, nationalism and competitiveness, there might be peace in the world. But where to find the teachers? For an adult to uncondition himself was obviously much harder than for a child to remain unconditioned. It would mean a complete self-transformation. To give up one's preju-dices was virtually to give up one's personality, bearing in mind that to K ideals such as patriotism, heroism and religious faith were all prejudices. In this field of education there was an anomaly in K. He expected the schools he founded to achieve 'academic excellence' without competition. This might have been possible if parents had not insisted on their children taking university degrees; in India, particu-larly, a degree was essential for getting a good job.

Talks in Australia and New Zealand followed at the beginning of 1934. The Australian press was very friendly; not so the Theosophical members. Leadbeater had just died in Perth, on his way back from Adyar where he had attended Mrs Besant's funeral. K happened to be in Sydney when his body was sent there for cremation and he reported to Lady Emily that he went to the funeral service but stayed outside the chapel. 'The Manor people are bewildered by his death, and were asking who was going to tell them when they had taken steps [on the Path] now he is gone.' In New Zealand the newspapers were even more friendly. He was not, however, allowed to broadcast because he was 'anti-religious'. 'Bernard Shaw, who is on a visit, told the people that it was scandalous as I am a great religious teacher. He wrote to me about it. Unfortunately I didn't meet him. I had tremendous meetings and a good deal of interest. I think friends there will keep it up.'

Back in Ojai that year K began to learn Spanish from a Linguaphone course in preparation for a tour in South America which had been arranged for him. He had lost none of his ecstatic enthusiasm; he was writing to Lady Emily in November: 'I am bursting with the immensity of love, anything one likes to call it. I am intoxicated intelligently, wisely. It's amazing and it's so absurd to put it into words; it becomes so banal. Imagine the state of mind of the man who wrote the Song of Songs, that of Buddha and Jesus, and you will understand what mine is. It sounds rather bombastic but it's not – so simple and consuming.'

In writing this he had evidently not taken exception to a letter that Lady Emily had sent him in August:

How do you know that you have not merely found an escape? You cannot face life as it is – in all its ugliness – you have always been wrapped in cotton wool – figuratively speaking – you have always escaped ugliness by flying to the most beautiful places. You are always 'retreating'. You have found an escape that gives you ecstasy – but so have all religious mystics... How can I as an outsider know that you are any more right than someone else who says they have attained ecstasy – God – Truth etc.? [There is no reply to this letter.]

After speaking three times in New York early in 1935, and staying for a while with some old friends, Robert Logan and his wife Sarah, who had a house and a large estate, Sarobia, near Philadelphia, K set off with Rajagopal on 3 March for Rio de Janeiro. This was the beginning of an eight-month tour, in which he gave talks in Brazil, Uruguay, Argentina, Chile and, on the way back, Mexico City.[42]

Hundreds of people who attended these talks could not understand him for he spoke only in English, yet apparently they sat 'spell-bound'. He began each talk by declaring that he belonged to no religious sect or political party: 'Organized belief is a great impediment,' he said, 'dividing man against man... What I want to do is to help you, the individual, to cross the stream of suffering, confusion and conflict through deep and complete fulfilment.'

There was so much publicity in Montevideo (where he had been asked to speak by the Minister of Education) and Buenos Aires, with photographs of him and broadcasts, that he could not go out without attracting a crowd. At the same time, many antagonistic articles were published in the Catholic papers and efforts made by Catholics to get him deported. K was surprised that there was so much interest and enthusiasm. But the highspot of the tour for him was the hour and twenty minutes' flight across the Andes in a Douglas twin-engine aircraft (his first flight) which he had thoroughly enjoyed, although he had been told that it was 'the most dangerous flight in the world'.

In one of his talks he made his first public pronouncement about sex in answer to the question: 'What is your attitude to the problem of sex, which plays such a part in our daily life?' He answered:

It has become a problem because there is no love. When we really love there is no problem, there is an adjustment, an understanding. It is only when we have lost the sense of true affection, that profound love in which there is no sense of possessiveness, that there arises the problem of sex. It is only when we have completely yielded ourselves to mere sensation, that there are many problems concerning sex. As the majority of people have lost the joy of creative thinking, naturally they turn to the sensation of sex which becomes a problem, eating their minds and hearts away.

It took K a long time to pick up his strength, resting at Ojai and at Villars in Switzerland, after the exhaustion of this tour (he weighed less than 112 lbs at the end of it). He was, however, revived enough to go to India with Rajagopal in the winter of 1936 where he gave talks in the garden of Vasanta Vihar. Raja, who was to remain friendly with K until his death in 1953, in spite of their differences, went several times to see him. 'This smashing of the old,' K wrote to Lady Emily at the beginning of 1937, 'the crystallized, is not a day's process. There needs to be a constant, choiceless awareness. I am intoxicated and thrilled with it all.'

'Choiceless awareness' were words which K was to use frequently thereafter. Lady Emily did not understand them and they do need some clarification. Choice implies direction, an action of the will. K, as he explained it, was talking about awareness from moment to moment of all that was taking place inside oneself without any effort to change or direct it. It was a matter of pure observation, of looking, which would lead to self-transformation without effort.

K was appalled by conditions in India at this time – the terrible poverty, misery and hatred which existed and which Indians believed could be solved by nationalism. 'We have to find new people [for his work] and it's difficult. We must begin here as if nothing had happened here for the last ten years.' K maintained that no social reform would ever end human misery; people would always transform any new system into what they themselves were; throughout history every utopian revolutionary movement had reverted to the old order of things because the people in them had not changed at all; society of any kind was the result of the individual and the individual was the result of society; the individual was you and me; society could not be transformed from the outside; it could be transformed only by transforming totally the human being, by each one of us, within himself.

11

'A deep ecstasy'

K and Rajagopal were in Rome in the spring of 1937. Mussolini had banned all public talks in Italy so a gathering had been arranged for K in the house of a Contessa Rafoni. Here he was to meet Vanda Passigli who was later to play a prominent part in his life. She was the daughter of Alberto Passigli, an aristocratic landowner, prominent in Florentine society and founder of two important musical societies in Florence and friends with all the great musicians of the time. Vanda herself was a pianist of professional standing. In 1940 she was to marry Marchese Luigi Scaravelli, also a fine musician, who became Professor of Philosophy at the University of Rome. After the gathering, the Passiglis asked K to visit them at their house above Fiesole, Il Leccio. K was often to stay there in the future, after Vanda and her brother inherited it from their parents.

That summer at Ommen K suffered for the first time from the hay fever which was to plague him on and off for the rest of his life. And, as usual, he had a bout of bronchitis. He was thankful to get back to Ojai where, for the winter of 1937–8, he rested and saw no one but the Rajagopals. 'I am deeply thrilled with the discovery inside oneself,' he wrote to Lady Emily, 'there are many ideas and I am slowly trying to find suitable words and expressions for them. There is a deep ecstasy. There is a maturity that is not to be forced, not to be artificially stimulated. It alone can bring about abundant fullness and reality to life. I am really glad for this quietness and apparently purposeless meditation.'

This is probably K's first mention of what was to him 'real' meditation – 'making unexpected and amazing discoveries within oneself' without any direction or purpose. At such times his mind was at its keenest, most probing and alive. The popularly understood idea of meditation, tranquillising the mind by fixing it on one word or object, or practising some other form of technique, was, to him, deadening and useless.

In the spring of 1938 a most enlivening new friendship began for K when he met Aldous Huxley. In February that year Huxley's friend, Gerald Heard, who was living in California, had asked to come and see K. Huxley was then in hospital so it was not until April that Heard brought Huxley and his Belgian wife, Maria, to Ojai. (The Huxleys and their son had arrived in California in 1937.) There was an immediate rapport between K and Huxley. In November Huxley started treatment for his eyes by a method of eye exercises introduced by an American, Dr W. H. Bates. K was later to practise this method daily himself, not because there was anything wrong with his eyes but as a preventative. Whether or not it was the result of these exercises, he never had to wear glasses for the whole of his long life.

At first K was rather overawed by Huxley's intellectual brilliance but, once he discovered that Huxley would have given all his knowledge for one mystical experience not induced by drugs, he found that he could talk to him about what he called 'the points' he was making. K, referring to himself in the third person, described taking a walk with Huxley:

> He [Huxley] was an extraordinary man. He could talk about music, the modern and the classical, he could explain in great detail science and its effect on modern civilization and of course he was quite familiar with the philosophies, Zen, Vedanta and naturally Buddhism. To go for a walk with him was a delight. He would discourse on the wayside flowers and, though he couldn't see properly, whenever we passed in the hills in California an animal close by, he would name it, and develop the destructive nature of modern civilization and its violence. Krishnamurti would help him to cross a stream or a pothole. Those two had a strange relationship with each other, affectionate, considerate and, it seems, non-verbal communication. They would often be sitting together without saying a word.[43]

The last camp ever to be held at Ommen, the fifteenth, took place in August that year. (After the German invasion of Holland in 1940, the camp became a concentration camp.) 1938 was the year of the Munich crisis. K was, of course, a pacifist. Rajagopal did not go with him that year to India. Instead K travelled with an old friend who had been at Pergine, V. Patwardhan (known as Pat). In Bombay, where they arrived on 6 October, K found his Indian friends immersed in the 'petty jealousies' of politics. Several of them, followers of Gandhi, had been in prison. K met Gandhi several times but did not admire him; K never got caught up in politics. He saw no difference between German aggression and British Imperialism. 'Having grabbed half the earth,' he wrote to Lady Emily, 'the British can afford to be less aggressive', though at heart they were as 'brutal and greedy' as any other nation. And in November, still in India, he wrote again:

I quite agree with you that the poor Jews are having a horrible and degrading time. It's so utterly mad the whole thing. That human beings should behave in that bestial manner is revolting; the Kaffirs are treated most brutally and inhumanely; the Brahmins in the south in certain parts have lost all sense of humanity with regard to the untouchables; the white and brown bureaucratic rulers of the land are mostly machines carrying out a system that's brutal and stupid; the negroes in the south of U.S.A. have a bad time; one dominant race exploits another, as is shown all over the world. There's no reason, sanity, behind all this greed for power, wealth and position. It's difficult for the individual not to be sucked into the storm of hate and confusion. One must be an individual, sane and balanced, not belonging to any race, country or to any particular ideology. Then perhaps sanity and peace will come back to the world.

And later on he wrote: 'It's so easy to curse Hitler and Mussolini and Co. but this attitude of domination and craving for power is in the heart of almost everyone; so we have wars and class antagonism. Until the source is cleared there will always be confusion and hate.'

In addition to travelling to many parts of India, giving talks, at the end of the year K visited the second school he had founded, Rajghat, near Benares, which had been officially opened in 1934, and from there he went to Rishi Valley at the beginning of 1939 – one school by the river and one in the hills, each extremely beautiful in its own way and the two places in India he came to love best. On 1 April he sailed with Pat from Colombo for Australia and New Zealand. When he at last returned to Ojai, Pat went back to India where he died suddenly of a brain haemorrhage. Another friend gone. Nitya, Jadu, Pat: the old lot were thinning out.

K did not leave America in 1939 because of the threat of war, and he was to spend the next nine years in California with the Rajagopals, nearly all the time at Ojai. After Hitler had overrun Holland and

Belgium in May 1940, K had no news of his many Dutch friends, and there was scarcely any news from India. France capitulated on 22 June. The de Manziarlys managed to escape to the United States and the Suarès' to Egypt. K had started giving group discussions twice a week at both Ojai and in Hollywood. He also saw a good deal of the Huxleys. (K's pacificism assuaged Huxley's guilt at remaining in California throughout the war.) In the spring of 1940 K gave eight talks in the Oak Grove but when he preached pacifism, saying, 'The war within you is the war you should be concerned with, not the war outside,' many of the audience left in disgust. At the end of August he went to Sarobia to the Logans who had arranged a gathering for him; this was the last time that he spoke in public until 1944.

K made two trips with the Rajagopals in 1941–42 to the Sequoia National Park, 250 miles north of Ojai at a height of 6,000 feet, where some of the sequoias were said to be 3,000 years old. Halfway through the second of these trips, in September 1942, the Rajagopals had to return to Ojai for the beginning of Radha's school term, leaving K alone there in a log cabin for another three weeks, doing his own cooking, walking about ten miles a day, meditating two or three hours a day and seeing many wild animals. This time alone, which he hugely enjoyed, as he always did enjoy being quite alone, made such an impression on him that he described it in several of his books, dwelling on his friendship with a squirrel and a dangerous encounter with a mother bear and her cubs. It was one of his very few indelible memories.

When America entered the war (the Japanese having bombed Pearl Harbour on 7 December 1941), K had difficulty in renewing his American visa. Considering his anti-war propaganda it is something of a miracle that it was renewed. There were food shortages in America, the cost of living had gone up and petrol was soon to be rationed. K and the Rajagopals were growing their own vegetables and keeping bees, chickens and a cow. K took long solitary walks every day at Ojai. He told Lady Emily that he was leading 'an extraordinary life inwardly, very creative and joyous'. But Lady Emily, who had been through the Blitz and had already lost two grandsons in the war, wrote to him bitterly, accusing him of escaping all the horror. He replied on 14 April 1942:

I don't think any evil can be overcome by brutality, torture or enslavement; evil can be overcome by something that's not the outcome of evil. War is the result of our so-called peace which is a series of everyday brutalities, exploitations, narrowness and so on. Without changing our daily life we can't have peace, and war is a spectacular expression of our daily conduct. I do not think I have escaped from all the horror, but only there's no answer, no final answer, in violence, whoever wields it. I have found the answer to all this, not in the world but away from it. In being detached, the true detachment which comes from being, or attempting to be, more [word left out] to love and understand. This is very strenuous and not easily to be cultivated. Aldous Huxley and his wife are here for the week-end. We have long talks about all this and meditation which I have been doing a good deal lately.

Those quiet years of lying fallow during the war were invaluable to K as a teacher. Huxley, too, helped him by encouraging him to write. K was a much better writer than speaker. In spite of his years of practice, he never became a good speaker, though his personal magnetism came through his talks to enthral his audiences. K recorded Huxley saying to him one day: '"Why don't you write something?" So I did and showed it to him. He said, "It's marvellous. Keep going." So I kept going.' After that, K continued to write every day in a notebook. It seems that what he showed to Huxley must have been the beginning of *Commentaries on Living*, although this book was not published until 1956, after two other books had been brought out by well-known English and American publishers.

Commentaries on Living is a collection of short pieces derived from K's private interviews given in various parts of the world. Each piece starts with a description of the person or group of people who came to see him, or of a place. In order to make the interviews anonymous, he 'scrambled' them. Thus, we have *sanyasis* in Switzerland and obvious Westerners sitting cross-legged in India. The book begins splendidly with the line: 'The other day three pious egotists came to see me.' In one piece he writes on the subject of love: 'Thought invariably denies love. Thought is founded on memory and memory is not love... Thought inevitably breeds the feeling of ownership, that possessiveness which consciously or unconsciously cultivates jealousy. Where jealousy is, obviously love is not; and yet with most people, jealousy is taken as an indication of love... Thought is the greatest hindrance to love.'

In another piece he had more to say about love and thought in a relationship:

We fill our hearts with the things of the mind and therefore keep our hearts ever empty and expectant. It is the mind that clings, that is envious, that holds and destroys... We do not love and let it alone, but crave to be loved; we give in order to receive, which is the generosity of the mind and not of the heart. The mind is ever seeking certainty, security; and can Love be made certain by the mind? Can the mind, whose very essence is of time, catch love, which is its own eternity?[44]

It is uncertain when K wrote his first book, *Education and the Significance of Life*, published in 1953. On page 17 of this he says: 'The ignorant man is not the unlearned but he who does not know himself, and the learned man is stupid when he relies on books and knowledge and on authority to give him understanding. Understanding comes only through self knowledge, which is awareness of one's total psychological process. Thus education, in the true sense, is the understanding of oneself, for it is in each one of us that the whole of existence is gathered.'

The second book, *The First and Last Freedom*, published in 1954, with a long foreword by Aldous Huxley, has probably attracted more people to K's teaching than any of his other publications. It covers the whole spectrum of his teaching up to the uncertain date when it was written. His uncompromising refusal to offer comfort is one of the things that distinguishes him so uniquely from other religious teachers. He refuses to be our guru; he will not tell us what to do; he merely holds up a mirror to us and points out the causes of violence, loneliness, jealousy and all the other miseries that afflict mankind, and says: 'Take it or leave it. And most of you will leave it, for the obvious reason that you do not find gratification in it.' Our problems can be solved by no one but ourselves.

K began to give talks again in the Oak Grove at Ojai on ten successive Sundays in the summer of 1944. In spite of petrol rationing, people came from all over the United States to attend them and to seek private interviews with K. To a questioner who asked: 'What should be done with those who have perpetrated the horrors of the concentration camps?', K replied: 'Who is to punish them? Is not the judge often as guilty as the accused? Each one of us has built up this civilization, each one of us has contributed towards its misery . . . By shouting loudly the cruelties of another country you think you can overlook those of your own.'

One can sympathise with another member of the audience who said: 'You are very depressing. I seek inspiration to carry on. You do not cheer us with courage and hope. Is it wrong to seek inspiration?' K's stern reply could not have cheered him: 'Why do you want to be inspired? Is it not because in yourself you are empty, uncertain, lonely? You want to fill this loneliness, this aching void; you must have tried different ways of filling it and you hope to escape from it again by coming here. This process of covering up the arid loneliness is called inspiration. Inspiration then becomes a mere stimulation and with all stimulation it soon brings its own boredom and insensitivity.'

An authentic report of these 1944 talks, printed in India, was published the following year by Krishnamurti Writings Inc (KWINC), as the Star Publishing Trust had now become. After this, K stopped revising his own talks. KWINC was a charitable trust, as the SPT had been, set up for the sole purpose of disseminating K's teaching throughout the world. K and Rajagopal, with three others, were the trustees. Later on, K unfortunately resigned his trusteeship because he could not be bothered with financial meetings, and Rajagopal became President of KWINC. All donations in support of Krishnamurti's work were sent to this international organisation.

At last, after twenty years, in September 1946, a school was opened on the land at the upper end of the Ojai valley, bought for the purpose by Mrs Besant in 1926–27. A small, co-educational, secondary school, called the Happy Valley School, it was financed by the Happy Valley Association of which K, Aldous Huxley and Rosalind Rajagopal were three of the original trustees, and it was run by Rosalind. K had planned to leave Ojai directly after the opening for a tour of New Zealand, Australia and India, but a few days before he was due to set out he fell seriously ill with a kidney infection. He was in bed for two months. For the first month he was in great pain, and it took him more than six months after that to recover. K retained only a faint and inaccurate memory of this illness. 'I was ill for a year and a half,' he was to say in 1979, 'tremendously ill. There was a doctor but they did not give me anything.' As he did not want to go to hospital, Rosalind nursed him: it is probable that he refused to take any medicaments, fearing what they might do to his sensitive body, even though he did not feel the bearing of this pain was necessary as the pain of 'the process' had been.

K's plans now depended on whether he could get a further extension of his visa. After India was granted independence on 15 August 1947, he, like all Hindus and Muslims, was given the option of keeping his British passport or of taking out a national one. Although he considered nationality one of the greatest of evils, he had, of course, to have a passport in order to travel, and he chose an Indian one. He could hardly have done otherwise when so many of his Indian friends had suffered in the fight for freedom. A further extension of his visa was granted which enabled him to stay on at Ojai recuperating until

September 1947. He then left for India via England, having abandoned the plan of going to New Zealand and Australia.

K stayed for three weeks with Lady Emily in London (her husband had died of lung cancer in 1944). They had not seen each other for nine years and all her indignation evaporated at the sight of him. He was now fifty-two and she seventy-three, and although they were to write less and less often to each other, she continued to love him with all her heart until her death in 1964. He came with her to spend a weekend with me and my second husband in our house in Sussex. I also invited Mar de Manziarly who had come to England to see him since he was not going to Paris. He looked older, of course; there was some grey in his hair, but he was just as beautiful and his personality was quite unchanged. He was as affectionate as ever and as full of passionate enthusiasm for life, with the same exquisite manners and natural courtesy. We sat in our dressing gowns over breakfast, talking and laughing, and he said it was just like old times when we had been on holiday together with Nitya. He could not remember Ehrwald or Pergine or his 'process' there, but he did have some recollection of the happiness and fun we had had. He asked me what Nitya looked like and was surprised when I told him that he had had a very slight squint.

K had been cooped up so long at Ojai with the Rajagopals, who were inclined to bully him, that he seemed full of relief at being free again and able to travel. He flew alone to Bombay in October – his first flight to India, where he was to remain for eighteen months. This visit was crucial since he met there a new group of followers who, for the rest of his life, were not only to be his chosen companions but invaluable for his work in India.

Prominent among this group, meeting him for the first time, were two sisters, both married – Pupul Jayakar and Nandini Mehta, daughters of V. N. Mehta (no relation to Nandini's husband), a Gujarati Brahmin who had been a distinguished member of the Indian Civil Service and a Sanskrit and Persian scholar. He had died in 1940. His widow, who had a long record of social service, lived in Bombay where her daughters also lived. The younger, Nandini, was unhappily married, with three children, to Bhagwan Mehta, a son of Sir Chuninal Mehta, a devotee of K's from before the war. Sir Chuninal took Nandini to meet K when he arrived at Bombay; she fell under his spell and later went with her father-in-law to listen to his talks. A few months afterwards she told her husband that she wanted to lead a celibate life. After K left India she was to file a petition against her husband in the High Court of Bombay asking for a separation and custody of her children, aged nine, seven and three, on the grounds of cruelty. Her husband defended the suit, claiming that she had been unduly influenced by Krishnamurti's teaching. His lawyer read out in Court long extracts from K's talks in which he had spoken of the inferior position of Indian women and their bondage to their husbands. But nothing at all improper was suggested throughout the hearing. Nandini lost the case and her children were taken from her. She had already left her husband and sought refuge in her mother's house. A telegram was sent to K giving him the result, to which he replied, 'Whatever will be is right'.[45] A false rumour was circulated in England that K had been cited as co-respondent in a divorce case. For the rest of his life, K felt a very special tenderness for Nandini. In 1954 a small Krishnamurti day school for deprived children, Bal Anand, was founded in Bombay, of which Nandini became the Director.

K did not meet the elder sister, Pupul Jayakar, until the beginning of 1948. She had been a social worker since the early 1940s and was largely responsible for the development and export of hand-woven Indian textiles and crafts; she was later to become Chairman of the Festival of India Committee. An old friend of Indira Gandhi, she attained a good deal of influence in India after Mrs Gandhi became Prime Minister in 1966. She had a more forceful character than Nandini, though Nandini must have had great inner strength to leave her husband.

Among others belonging to the group which K gathered round him at this time were Sunanda Patwardhan and her husband Pama, a partner in the publishing firm of Orient Longman (no relation to Pat), and his elder brother, Achuyt, an old friend of K's who had been a great freedom fighter and was for the next two years to remain involved in politics. Sunanda had a Ph.D. from Madras University and was now studying law. She was in future to act as K's secretary when he was in India, travelling round with him, taking shorthand notes of the group discussions he held. Later on, she and her husband went to live at Vasanta Vihar. Two other members of the group were Dr V. Balasundaram, a young teacher at the Institute of Science at Bangalore, who was to become Principal of the Rishi Valley school, and R. Madhavachari, the secretary of KWINC in India who lived at Vasanta Vihar. Madhavachari held Rajagopal's power of attorney and made all the arrangements for K's talks and travels in India, edited his Indian talks and saw them through the press.

K had arrived in Bombay only two months after Partition, and Hindus and Muslims were butchering each other in the north. Nevertheless, he went up to Karachi and Delhi but had left Delhi before Gandhi's assassination on 30 January 1948. (It has been written that 'When the light had gone out with Gandhi's assassination, it was to Krishnamurti that Jawaharlal Nehru brought, in secret, his solitary anguish.'[46] K confirmed that this was more or less true; he had had great affection for Nehru.)

K spoke several times in the north, then gave twelve public talks in Bombay, between 1 January and 28 March 1948, which were attended by more than 3,000 people, followed by private discussions at Vasanta Vihar in Madras throughout most of April. (He told Lady Emily that he had never worked so hard in his life.) In each talk he tried to approach the various problems of existence from a different point of view but, since he was speaking to new audiences, there was inevitably a great deal of repetition. Fundamentally, there was no difference in his talks in India from those anywhere else. Anything new that had come out of those quiet war years at Ojai had flowered in his writings, particularly in *The First and Last Freedom* and *Commentaries on Living*. His Indian audiences were far more reverential, though; he was treated as a sublime guru.

In May K went up to Ootacamund, the hill station for Madras, for a complete rest. He stayed with some friends at a house called Sedgemoor, and, at his request, Pupul Jayakar and Nandini Mehta joined him there, staying at a nearby hotel. Mrs Jayakar has recorded some occurrences at Sedgemoor which show that 'the process' had started again much as it had been at Ojai, Ehrwald and Pergine. It must have been a frightening experience for these sisters who did not as yet know him well and, presumably, knew nothing of the former happenings.

K had been out for a walk with the sisters when he suddenly said he felt ill and must return to the house. He asked them to stay with him, not to be frightened by whatever happened, and not to call a doctor. He said he had a pain in his head. After a time he told them he was 'going off'. His face was 'weary and full of pain'. He asked them who they were and whether they knew Nitya. He then spoke of Nitya, told them that he was dead, that he had loved him and wept for him.* He asked them whether they were nervous but did not appear at all interested in their reply. He stopped himself from calling for Krishna

---

*It was at Ooty, at the beginning of 1925, where he had gone with Madame de Manziarly, that Nitya had become ill again. When K went back there, after Nitya's death, he had written to Lady Emily: 'I am staying in the same room as Nitya. I feel him, see him and talk to him but I miss him grievously.' Staying there again, although in a different house, may well have brought something of this back to K.

to come back: 'He has told me not to call him.' He then spoke of death. He said it was so close – 'Just a thread-line' – how easy it would be for him to die, but he would not like to because he had work to do. Towards the end he said: 'He is coming back. Do you not see them all with him – spotless, untouched, pure – now that they are here he will come. I am so tired but he is like a bird – always fresh.' Then suddenly it was Krishna again.

The record of this episode is undated. The next is dated 30 May 1948:

Krishna was getting ready to go for a walk, when suddenly he said he was feeling too weak and not all there. He said, 'What a pain I have' and caught the back of his head and lay down. Within a few minutes the K we knew was not there. For two hours we saw him go through intense pain. He suffered as I have never seen suffering. He said he had pain at the back of his neck. His tooth was troubling him, his stomach was swollen and hard and he groaned and pressed down. At times he would shout. He fainted a number of times. When he came to the first time he said: 'Close my mouth when I faint.' He kept on saying: 'Amma, oh, God give me peace. I know what they are up to. Call him back, I know when the limit of pain is reached – then they will return. They know how much the body can stand. If I become a lunatic look after me. Not that I'll become a lunatic. They are very careful with this body – I feel so old – only a bit of me is functioning. I am like an india rubber toy, which a child plays with. It is the child that gives it life.' His face throughout was worn and racked with pain. He kept clenching his fists and tears streamed from his eyes. 'I feel like an engine going uphill.' After two hours he fainted again. When he came to he said: 'The pain has disappeared. Deep inside me I know what has happened. I have been stocked with gasoline. The tank is full.'

He then started to talk and describe some of the things he had seen on his travels; he spoke of love: 'Do you know what it is to love? You cannot hold a cloud in a gilded cage. That pain makes my body like steel and oh so flexible, so pliant, without a thought. It is like a polishing, an examining.' Pupul Jayakar asked if he could stop having the pain, to which he replied, 'You have had a child. Can you stop it coming once it starts?' He now sat up cross-legged, his body erect. The pain had gone from his face, Mrs Jayakar noted: 'It was timeless. His eyes were closed. His lips moved. He seemed to grow. We felt something tremendous pour into him. There was a throbbing in the atmosphere. It filled the room. Then he opened his eyes and said, "Something happened – did you see anything?" We told him what we had felt. He said, "My face will be different tomorrow." He lay down and his hand went out in a gesture of fullness. He said, "I will be like a raindrop – spotless." After a few minutes he told us that he was all right and that we could go home.'

Two other occurrences of the same nature took place in June. On 17 June, K had been for a walk alone and had asked Pupul and Nandini to wait for him in his room. When he returned he was a stranger.'K had gone. He started saying he was hurt inside; that he had been burnt; that there was a pain right through his head. He said: "Do you know, you would not have seen him tomorrow. He nearly did not return." He kept on feeling his body to see if it was all there. He said: "I must go back and find out what happened on the walk. Something happened and they rushed back but I do not know whether I returned. There may be bits of me lying on the road."'

The next evening Pupul and Nandini again waited for him in his room while he went for a solitary walk. When he returned at about seven he was 'a stranger' once more. He went to lie down. 'He said he felt burnt, completely burnt. He was crying. He said: "Do you know I found out what happened on that walk. He came fully and took complete charge. That is why I did not know if I had returned. I knew nothing. They have burnt me so that there can be more emptiness. They want to see how much of him can come."' Again Pupul and Nandini felt the same throbbing filling the room as on the evening of 30 May.[47]

The fact that these sisters knew nothing of what had happened in the past gives this account a particular value in that there are so many similarities between it and those other accounts of what happened at Ojai, Ehrwald and Pergine – the frequent fainting with the pain, the body's awe of Krishna and fear of calling him back, his realisation that the pain would stop if Krishna did come back but so would 'the process'. Then the allusion to the closeness of death. (At Ehrwald, when the church bells suddenly rang out while Krishna was 'off', they caused the body such a shock of agony that Krishna had to come back. He said afterwards, according to Lady Emily, 'That was a very narrow shave. Those bells nearly tolled for my funeral.') Pupul Jayakar's notes tell us that, apart from K, there were other presences, just as there had been on those other recorded occasions – the 'they' who were very careful of the body, presumably the same 'they' who had returned with K on the first occasion mentioned by Pupul – 'spotless, untouched, pure'. Then there was the 'he' who had come 'fully' during the walk on 17 June and 'taken complete charge'. The being lying in agony on

102

the bed had been 'burnt' to create more emptiness so that more of this 'he' could enter into K or the body.

So now there appeared to be three entities apart from the unnamed number referred to as 'they': – the being left behind to bear the body's pain; K, who goes away and comes back again; and the mysterious 'he'. Were all these entities different aspects of K's consciousness or were they separate beings? Alas, the one person who might have been able to enlighten us, K himself, remembered nothing of these happenings at Ooty any more than he remembered anything about 'the process' at earlier times. Since he was out of his body it is not surprising. He had always been conscious of being 'protected' by something or someone outside himself, and he believed that whoever was travelling with him shared this same protection. But from where that protection emanated he could not say. More importantly, what we learn from this account is that there was still preparation being done on K's body.

After this time at Ooty, K continued his talks in many places in India and visited his schools at Rajghat and Rishi Valley. He did not return to Ojai until April 1949, having been away from there for nineteen months.

12

'To enter the house of death'

The Rajagopals noticed a new independence in K on his return from India, which worried them. They had heard the rumours about Nandini, and Rosalind was very humanly jealous, having been for so long the only woman in K's life. Jealousy led to possessiveness and K could not be possessed, however much he loved. He was back in India again in November. Talking in December at Rajamundy, 350 miles north of Madras, he was asked: 'You say that man is the measure of the world, and that when he transforms himself the world will be at peace. Has your own transformation shown this to be true?' K replied:

You and the world are not two different entities. You *are* the world, not as an ideal, but factually... as the world is yourself, in the transformation of yourself you produce a transformation in society. The questioner implies that since there is no cessation of exploitation, what I am saying is futile. Is that true? I am going around the world trying to point out truth, not doing propaganda. Propaganda is a lie. You can propagate an idea, but you cannot propagate truth. I go around pointing out truth; and it is for you to recognize it or not. One man cannot change the world, but you and I can change the world together. You and I have to find out what is truth; for it is truth that dissolves the sorrows, the miseries of the world.

In January 1950, speaking in Colombo for the first time, K was asked an essentially similar question: 'Why do you waste your time preaching instead of helping the world in a practical way?' K answered this:

You mean bringing about a change in the world, a better economic adjustment, a better distribution of wealth, a better relationship – or, to put it more brutally, helping you to find a better job. You want to see a change in the world, every intelligent man does; and you want a method to bring about that change, and therefore you ask me why I waste my time preaching instead of doing something about it. Now, is what I am actually doing a waste of time? It would be a waste of time, would it not, if I introduced a new set of ideas to replace the old ideology, the old pattern. Instead of pointing out a so-called practical way to act, to live, to get a better job, to create a better world, is it not important to find out what are the impediments which actually prevent a real revolution – not a revolution of the left or the right, but a fundamental, radical revolution not based on ideas? Because, as we have discussed it, ideals, beliefs, ideologies, dogmas prevent action.

At Ojai, in August 1950, K decided to go into retreat for a year. As well as giving no talks, he gave no interviews and spent most of his time going for solitary walks, meditating and 'pottering about in the garden', as he told Lady Emily. In the winter of 1951 he was back in India once more, this time with Rajagopal who had not been there for fourteen years, but he was still in semi-retreat and gave no talks and was very withdrawn. He seemed to be looking very deeply into himself all this time.

The best thing that happened to K outwardly in the early 1950s was the forming of a close friendship with Vanda Scaravelli, née Passigli, whom he had met in Rome in 1937. After staying with her and her husband for two days in Rome in the autumn of 1953, he was taken by her up to Il Leccio,* her large house above Fiesole. There, among olive trees, cypresses and hills, he was at peace. Il Leccio became a refuge for him between his constant journeyings to Ojai and India. Although he would stop in England, and sometimes in Paris and other parts of Europe, it was only at Il Leccio that there was freedom from talks, discussions and interviews.

In May 1954 K spoke and held discussions for a week in New York, at the Washington Irving High School. These talks attracted large crowds, many new people having become interested in him since the recent publication of *The First and Last Freedom*. Anne Morrow Lindbergh, reviewing the American edition of the book, had written: '... the sheer simplicity of what he has to say is breathtaking. The reader is given in one paragraph, even one sentence, enough to keep him exploring, questioning, thinking for days.' When the book was published in

---

*There was a huge ilex tree in the garden from which the house derived its name.

England one reviewer, in the *Observer*, wrote: '... for those who wish to listen it will have a value beyond words', and another in the *Times Literary Supplement*: 'He is an artist both in vision and analysis.' When the American edition of *Commentaries on Living*, impeccably edited by Rajagopal, came out two years later, Francis Hacket, the well-known American author and journalist, wrote about K in the *New Republic*: 'I feel that he has hold of a magic secret ... He is no other than he seems – a free man, one of the first quality, growing older as do diamonds but with the gem-like flame not dating and ever alive.' And the *Times Literary Supplement* reviewer wrote of the English edition: 'The insight, spiritual and poetical, of the commentaries is as simply expressed as it is searching in its demand.'

K never mentioned a published book of his in any of his letters to Lady Emily, though in the 1930s he had mentioned correcting his talks which he had long ceased to do. K had no interest at all in his own published works except, sometimes, to suggest a title for a book when appealed to. Was his lack of memory due to the fact that he never thought of anything once it was over?

After another winter of talks in India, from October 1954 to April 1955, accompanied by Rajagopal, and another visit to Il Leccio and talks in Amsterdam, K came to London in June, where he spoke six times at the Friends' Meeting House. (When he was in London now he stayed with Mrs Jean Bindley, an old friend from the early Star days, since Lady Emily had moved into a small flat and no longer had room for him; nevertheless, he saw her every day.) It was in the third of these London talks that he made his first public reference to entering the house of death while still living – a theme he was often to talk about in future. It came in answer to a question: 'I'm afraid of death. Can you give me any reassurance?' K replied in part:

> You are afraid to let go of all the things you have known ... You are afraid to let all that go, totally, deep down, right from the depths of your being, and be with the unknown – which is, after all, death ... Can you, who are the result of the known, enter into the unknown which is death? If you want to do it, it must be done while living, surely, not at the last moment ... While living, to enter the house of death is not just a morbid idea; it is the only solution. While living a rich, full life – whatever that means – or while living a miserable, impoverished life, can we not know that which is not measurable, that which is only glimpsed by the experiencer in rare moments? ... Can the mind die from moment to moment to *everything* that it experiences, and never accumulate?

K was to express the same idea more simply in the second series of *Commentaries on Living* (1959): 'How necessary it is to die each day, to die each minute to everything, to the many yesterdays and to the moment that has just gone by! Without death there is no renewing, without death there is no creation. The burden of the past gives rise to its own continuity, and the worries of yesterday give new life to the worries of today.'

K went to many places during the next two years in addition to Ojai, India and England, in all of which he gave public talks and private interviews, held gatherings and group discussions – Sydney, Alexandria, Athens, Hamburg, Holland and Brussels. He spent the whole of June 1956 with a Belgian friend, Robert Linnsen, at his villa near Brussels. Monsieur Linnsen arranged six talks for him at the Palais des Beaux-Arts in Brussels and six private talks at the villa. Queen Elisabeth of the Belgians attended every one of these talks and also asked to have a private interview with K.

In the winter of 1956–7 K was in India with Rajagopal and Rosalind, going from place to place with them and his group of Indian followers. In 1956 the twenty-one-year-old Dalai Lama, Tenzin Gyatso, accepted an invitation to visit India and see the sacred places associated with the Buddha. It was the first time that any Dalai Lama had left Tibet and three years before he escaped to India when the Chinese threatened his life. A political officer from Sikkhim, Apa Sahib Pant, who travelled with the Dalai Lama and his huge entourage in a special train, told him about Krishnamurti and the nature of his teaching. In December, when the Dalai Lama reached Madras and heard that Krishnamurti was at Vasanta Vihar, he insisted on meeting him, although it was against all protocol. According to Apa Sahib, as related by Pupul Jayakar, '"Krishnaji received him simply. It was breathtaking to feel the electric affection that instantly flashed between them." The Dalai Lama asked gently but directly, "Sir, what do you believe in?" And then the conversation went on in almost monosyllabic sentences as it was a conversation without rhetoric. The young lama was feeling on familiar ground as Krishnaji made him "co-experience".' The Dalai Lama was to say afterwards, '"A great soul, a great experience"', and expressed the wish to meet Krishnamurti again.[48] A further meeting between them was not arranged until 31 October 1984, in Delhi, but it never took place because, on that very day, Mrs Gandhi was assassinated.

In January 1957, in Colombo, the Government of Sri Lanka allowed all five of K's public talks to be broadcast, which seemed extraordinary to K since they were so subversive. After a last talk in Bombay in March, it so happened that he was to give no more talks anywhere until September 1958. This was dictated by circumstances, not by a decision taken at the time. He was nearing a great change in his outer life.

From Bombay K flew to Rome with Rajagopal on 6 March and from there he went to Il Leccio where he had planned to stay only until end of the month before going on to Helsinki with Rajagopal for a gathering. He had been rather ill in India and suddenly cancelled not only Helsinki but his whole future programme of talks in London, Biarritz, Ojai, New Zealand and Australia. He stayed on at Il Leccio for weeks, doing nothing, hardly even writing a letter. (Vanda Scaravelli's husband died in Florence while he was still there.) It was not until the end of May that he met Rajagopal in Zurich and went with him to Gstaad where they had been invited to stay. This was K's first introduction to a place which he was soon to know intimately. It was probably during this visit that he conceived the idea of having an international annual gathering in Switzerland on the lines of the Ommen camps. It would save him so much travelling. (He never wanted to return to Ommen after it had been a concentration camp.)

On 11 June K and Rajagopal moved on to the Hotel Montesano at Villars where K had first stayed with Nitya in 1921. After a fortnight there Rajagopal returned to Ojai, leaving K alone with only just enough money to pay the hotel bill. Evidently there had been some kind of crisis in their relationship. Tension had been growing between them since K's return from India in 1949. The frailty of an already frayed relationship was exposed when Rajagopal, who did not believe that K had been really ill at Il Leccio, and had made all the arrangements for his tours, suddenly had to cancel everything. It seems that he told K at Villars that he was sick of being his travel agent and that in future his arrangements could be made by Miss Doris Pratt, the secretary of KWINC in London, who had worked for K since the early Ommen days. K's expenses in London and journeys from London were paid out of the dividends on a gift of shares donated for his work and administered by Doris Pratt. Rajagopal's expenses in England were also paid out of this fund. Rajagopal had instructed Doris Pratt to keep an account of everything spent on K. Rajagopal sent funds from Ojai to India for K's expenses there.

Whatever it was that had happened between K and Rajagopal made

K reluctant to return to Ojai. On leaving him at Villars Rajagopal had told him that he would learn what it was to be lonely. But K was never lonely. He remained at Villars by himself for a full month, perfectly happy. He wrote to Lady Emily: 'I am in retreat. I see nobody and the only conversation is with the waiter. It's nice doing nothing but doing other things. There are splendid walks here and hardly anybody on them. Please don't tell anyone where I am.' By 'doing other things' he meant the meditation that went on intensely inside him whenever he was quiet, going deeper and deeper into himself. Doris Pratt knew where he was. She forwarded letters to him which he returned after reading them, telling her he was not going to reply to any of them since he wanted 'a long and complete rest even though I am well'. He sent her instructions on how to answer them without her having to read them.

On 20 July Léon de Vidas and his wife, whom K had known for some time (he had a textile business in Paris), somehow found him at Villars without any money and took him down to their house in the Dordogne. (K could have asked Rajagopal to send him money but apparently he did not want to communicate with him, and it was impossible to send money from England because of exchange controls.) K stayed in the Dordogne until November, writing to Lady Emily at the end of October: 'It's very quiet here and I see no one except my two hosts. It's right away from any town. It has been a complete retirement, walks and solitude. It has been very good. I shall do the same in India.'

Rajagopal went with K to India that winter for the last time but stayed only until January 1958. K remained in retirement until September, first at Rishi Valley, then at Rajghat, and then for a month alone at the northern hill station at Ranikhet. After this he resumed his public talks. At Vasanta Vihar he signed a document on 13 November, attested by the Notary Public, High Court of Jurisdiction in Madras, assigning to KWINC the copyright in all his writings, previous to and from that date, and authorising Rajagopal, the President of KWINC, to make all arrangements for the publication of his books. K did not remember when he had resigned his trusteeship of KWINC nor why he had done so. It seems a strange moment to have signed this document when his relationship with Rajagopal was so uneasy, yet probably it was for this very reason that Rajagopal wanted his position legalised. An alternative reason may have been that this was the year that an international copyright agreement came into force.

The heat was so intense in Delhi, where K was giving talks at the beginning of 1959 and staying there as usual with his old friend Shiva Rao, that a house was taken for him in March at Srinagar in Kashmir, but when it was found to be dirty and rat-infested he moved up to Pahalgam, a valley in Kashmir 7,200 feet above sea level, where he stayed in a Government hut, 'not at all luxurious,' as he told Lady Emily, 'but with marvellous surroundings, snow peaks and miles of pine woods'. Pupul Jayakar and Madhavachari had been with him at Srinagar but at Pahalgam he was alone with Parameshwaran, the head cook at Rishi Valley. In the middle of August he fell ill with a kidney infection again and was taken down to Srinagar with a very high temperature, and from there to Shiva Rao's house in New Delhi where, for the first time, he was given antibiotics. These acted on him so strongly that they temporarily paralysed his legs (he believed he was paralysed for life, as he later admitted, accepting the fact serenely) and he became so weak that Parameshwaran had to feed him like a baby. He was in bed for nearly seven weeks and then recuperated at Rishi Valley before giving more talks in various parts of India. It was not until 11 March 1960 that he at last flew to Rome where Vanda Scaravelli met him and took him up to Il Leccio.

Rajagopal knew nothing of K's plans until he had a letter from him saying that he would stay at Il Leccio for some weeks and then enter the Bircher-Benner Clinic in Zurich. Rajagopal did not know whether K intended to return to Ojai that summer or not. He asked Doris Pratt to send K money for the clinic from the English fund but the continuation of exchange controls prevented this. K told her not to worry; Puerto Rican friends had offered to pay all his expenses at the clinic.

K entered the clinic on 11 April, where he was put on a very strict diet, and stayed until 1 May when he flew to London en route for America. Doris Pratt, who met him at Heathrow, was shocked to see how haggard he looked. He had to order new shoes because his feet had become so thin. In spite of his frailty, 'he positively refused to travel first class by air', Doris Pratt reported to Rajagopal; and again, on the day he left London, she wrote: 'I must tell you, very, very privately, that I feel him to be a very sick man and not at all in a fit state to give talks at Ojai, but he seems determined to do so . . . It has been said that he nearly died in Delhi and I can believe it from his present state. I should think it highly important that the utmost and most loving and gentle care be taken of him at Ojai.'[49]

K broke his journey in New York, where he stayed with a friend who told him that unless he took some steps he would soon find that he had no say at all in the affairs of KWINC. This friend begged him to take more responsibility since the large sums donated to KWINC were for his work. After thirty-five years of running K's affairs with great efficiency and success, Rajagopal saw no reason for K's sudden interference. True, Rajagopal had a vice-president and a board of trustees, but he ruled them autocratically. Unfortunately he refused to give K any of the information he asked for, and when K further requested to be reinstated as a trustee, the request was refused. If only Rajagopal had put K back on the board K would almost certainly have lost interest very quickly. As it was, Rajagopal's intransigence bred suspicion, thus further injuring a relationship based on mutual trust.

One can sympathise with Rajagopal when K, having insisted on giving talks at Ojai, and having undertaken to give eight, announced at the third that he could give only one more. (This third talk was a superb one on how the mind could be 'made innocent through the death of the known' and the urgent need for a radical transformation in the human psyche.) The cancellation of the last four talks created a turmoil and great disappointment in people who had come a long distance for the whole series. Rajagopal was all the more incensed because, as he told Doris Pratt, K had not cancelled them because he was ill but merely because he had not got 'enough energy' to go on with them and yet he had given 'three days to interviews of several hours duration'. One wonders if, in expecting K to give public talks as easily as private interviews, Rajagopal had any understanding of K's real inner life. It seems so obvious that it needed a special energy to talk in public to a large audience.

K had intended to return to the Bircher-Benner Clinic at the end of June but kept on postponing his departure, to Rajagopal's intense annoyance. He gave no interviews now and answered no letters, not even those from Lady Emily and Vanda Scaravelli, so his mail was piling up. In the end he stayed on until he went to India in November, although the atmosphere at Arya Vihara must have been very unpleasant, for not only was there growing tension between him and Rajagopal but Rajagopal and Rosalind were quarrelling and were soon to be divorced.

K did not yet feel up to giving talks in India; he was prepared, however, to address small gatherings. Apparently he wrote to Rajagopal from India asking him to arrange a gathering for him in England the following year, for he received a cable: 'Unable now personally arrange anything. Have discussed with Doris Pratt who will help. Kindly write her. Happy New Year.' Rajagopal had washed his hands of anything to do with K in Europe. He was in London when he sent this cable and had many 'bitter exchanges' with Doris Pratt who found him in a very unhappy state. I myself saw him once and, knowing nothing of his change of relationship with K, I was deeply distressed when he began to abuse him. I had been particularly fond of Rajagopal since he had been at Cambridge where I used often to visit him. He also abused K to my mother who was equally distressed, being equally fond of him. We hoped it was just a temporary phase.

K spoke to small groups in New Delhi at the end of 1960 and in Bombay at the beginning of 1961. He was deeply concerned at this time with the urgency for a change in the human psyche and the creation of a new mind. In the middle of March he left India for Il Leccio again, where he spent several weeks before coming to London in May. Doris Pratt had done the very best she could for him in arranging a gathering. Knowing how he had enjoyed walking on Wimbledon Common in the old days when staying with Miss Dodge at West Side House, she had rented a house for him at Wimbledon and hired the Town Hall there for twelve small meetings and sent out personal invitations to about 150 people. She and a Dutch friend whom K had known for many years, Anneke Korndorffer, looked after him. For the first time at these meetings he allowed his talks to be recorded on tape.

Doris and Anneke, who stayed with him at Wimbledon for eight weeks, were very troubled when they heard him calling out loudly in the night and often at meals dropping his knife and fork and appearing 'transfixed' and about to faint. Doris asked him if there was anything she could do. He replied there was 'nothing except keep quiet, relax and *not* worry, but also *not* touch him'. He said that while he himself knew exactly what was happening, he was unable to explain it to them. On 18 May he was writing to Nandini Mehta in India: 'Strangely the things that happened at Ooty are taking place here, though no one knows about it – it is very strong.'[50]

K left London for Ojai via New York on 14 June, taking with him at Rajagopal's request the tapes of his Wimbledon talks. Next day Doris wrote to Signora Vanda, as K called her, that he was dreading the occasion of his Ojai visit, for there was, she gathered, something to be faced there. He had said that he might return very quickly.

It was on 18 June, the day before he flew to Los Angeles from New York, that K started to write a most extraordinary account of his inner states of consciousness. Written in pencil in exercise books, with not a word crossed out, he continued this journal for seven months. He had never kept such a record before and had no recollection of what prompted him to start it. It is the nearest we shall ever get to knowing what it was like to *be* him. It shows how little the events of his outer life affected his inner being.* One has only to open the book at random to be transfixed by a sense of wonder and mystery. It starts abruptly: 'In the evening it was suddenly there, filling the room, a great sense of beauty, power and gentleness. Others noticed it [the friends he was staying with in New York].' The 'immensity', the 'sacredness', the 'benediction', the 'otherness', the 'other', the 'vastness' were all names by which K referred in the course of the journal to the mysterious 'it' which could not be sought but which came to him every day so strongly that others sometimes noticed it. He wrote also of 'the process', the intense pain in his head and spine that went on at the same time. The whole of his teaching is in this journal as well as very beautiful descriptions of nature. On the 21st, at Ojai, he was writing: 'Woke up at about two and there was a peculiar pressure and the pain was more acute, more in the centre of the head. It lasted over an hour and one woke up several times with the intensity of the pressure. Each time there was a great expanding ecstasy; the joy continued.' And next day: 'The strength and beauty of a tender leaf is its vulnerability to destruction. Like a blade of grass that comes up from the pavement, it has the power than can withstand casual death.' And on the 23rd: 'Just as one was getting into bed, there was the fullness of Il L [Il Leccio]. It was not only in the room but it seemed to cover the earth from horizon to horizon. It was a benediction.' And on the 27th he wrote: 'That presence which was at Il L was there, waiting patiently, but benignly, with great tenderness.' These two last extracts show that whatever was going on had been experienced earlier at Il Leccio. He often found himself shouting in the night but since he was sleeping alone in Pine Cottage he could not be heard at Arya Vihara.

Although K remained nineteen days at Ojai, writing every day in his notebook, he mentioned nothing of what he did there except once visiting the dentist when 'it' was with him while sitting in the chair, and a walk when 'surrounded by these violet, bare, rocky mountains, suddenly there was solitude; it had great unfathomable richness; it had that beauty which is beyond thought and feeling... It was uniquely alone, not isolated but alone, like a drop of water which holds all the

---

*This journal, under the title *Krishnamurti's Notebook*, was published by Gollancz and Harper & Row in 1976.

waters of the earth.' This *Notebook* must be read. No amount of random quotation can begin to do it justice. It is an infinitely precious document, one of the great mystical works of all time which will surely one day be recognised for what it is.

K told Rosalind while he was at Ojai that she could live at Arya Vihara for life. She was still running the Happy Valley school but it had long ceased to be a Krishnamurti school. Rajagopal had moved to a house he had built for himself, not far from the Oak Grove at the western end of the valley. Rosalind was now independent since Robert Logan, whose wife had died, had left her money and property at his own death. (Mr Logan had given two Pathek-Philippe watches to K – a gold one which he never wore and a pocket steel one on a short chain with an ancient Greek coin at the end. This he wore always until his last illness.)

After flying overnight to London on 8 July, K recorded next day in his journal:

> ... amidst all the noise, smoking and loud talking, most unexpectedly, the sense of immensity and that extraordinary benediction which was felt at Il L, that imminent feeling of sacredness, began to take place. The body was nervously tense because of the crowd, noise etc but in spite of all this, it was there. The pressure & the strain were intense & there was acute pain at the back of the head. There was only this state & there was no observer. The whole body was wholly in it and the feeling of sacredness so intense that a groan escaped from the body and passengers were sitting in the next seat. It went on for several hours, late into the night. It was as though one was looking, not with eyes only but with thousand centuries; it was altogether a strange occurance. The brain was completely empty, all reaction had stopped; during all those hours, one was not aware of this emptiness but only in writing it is the thing known, but this knowledge is only descriptive and not real. That the brain could empty itself is an odd phenomenon. As the eyes were closed, the body, the brain seemed to plunge into unfathomable depths, into states of incredible sensitivity and beauty.

115

13

'The ending of sorrow'

After three nights in London K met Vanda Scaravelli at Geneva and went with her to Gstaad where she had rented a house for him for the summer, Chalet Tannegg. A small gathering had been arranged for him at the Town Hall of the neighbouring village of Saanen. Doris Pratt, who had met him at Heathrow, had found him 'absolutely exhausted' as she told Vanda. He had said, 'You don't know what it is like to have someone like Signora Vanda to go to. I have never been treated so wonderfully before.' Doris gathered that he had not had a happy time at Ojai. He had asked her not to give Rajagopal any more information about what was spent on him in England. (His total expenses in May and June, including the Wimbledon house and hire of the Hall, had been £477, while donations had totalled £650.) Whether or not he had spoken to Rajagopal about the affairs of KWINC is unknown; but he was to write to him afterwards asking to be kept informed of its concerns, insisting that his letter be shown to all the trustees and asking again to be reinstated on the board. He received no reply, though some time afterwards, when he was in India, Rajagopal sent him a balance sheet which, of course, he did not understand.

Three hundred and fifty people, all the Town Hall would hold, of nineteen different nationalities, attended this first Saanen gathering. (The Saanen gatherings were to become an international annual event, growing in numbers each year, for the next twenty-four years.) K had almost a fortnight at Chalet Tannegg before the gathering began. On 14 July, the day after his arrival, he wrote in his notebook: 'The urge for the repetition of experience, however pleasant, beautiful, fruitful, is the soil in which sorrow grows.' And two days later:

The whole process went on most of the night; it was rather intense. How much can the body stand! The whole body was quivering and, this morning, woke up with the head shaking.

There was, this morning that peculiar sacredness, filling the room. It had great penetrating power, entering into every corner of one's being, filling, cleansing, making everything of itself. The other felt it too [Vanda]. It's the thing that every human craves for and because they crave for it, it eludes them. The monk, the priest, the sanyasi torture their bodies and their character in their longing for this but it evades them. For it cannot be bought; neither sacrifice, virtue nor prayer can bring this love. This life, this love cannot be if death is the means. All seeking, all asking must wholly cease.

Truth cannot be exact. What can be measured is not truth. That which is not living can be measured and its height be found.

It was on this day that Vanda had her first experience of K's 'process', which she recorded:

We were talking after lunch. No one was in the house. Suddenly K. fainted. What happened then is impossible to describe, as there are no words that can come close to it; but it is also something that is too serious, too extraordinary, too important to be kept in the dark, buried in silence or not mentioned. There was a change in K.'s face. His eyes became larger and wider and deeper, and there was a tremendous look, beyond any possible space. It was as if there were a powerful presence which belonged to another dimension. There was an inexplicable feeling of emptiness and fullness at the same time.

K had evidently 'gone off', for Vanda jotted down the remarks made by the entity left behind: 'Don't leave me till he comes back. He must love you if he lets you touch me, as he is very particular in this. Don't let anyone near me until he returns.' Vanda then added: 'I could not understand at all what was taking place, and I was very astonished.'

The next day, at the same hour, K 'went off' again, and again Vanda noted down what 'the body' said while he was away: 'I feel very strange. Where am I? Don't leave me. Could you kindly stay with me until he returns? Are you comfortable? Take a chair. Do you know him well? Will you look after him?' Vanda continued: 'I still could not fathom what was happening. It was all too unexpected, too incomprehensible. When K regained consciousness he asked me to tell him what had happened, and so I wrote these notes in an attempt to convey some faint idea of what I had seen and felt.'[51]

At the end of July Aldous Huxley and his second wife were at Gstaad and went several times to hear K speak at the Town Hall in Saanen. It was 'among the most impressive things I ever heard,' Huxley wrote. 'It was like listening to a discourse of the Buddha – such power, such intrinsic authority, such an uncompromising refusal to allow the *homme moyen sensuel* any escapes or surrogates, any *gurus*, saviours, *führers*, churches. "I show you sorrow and the ending of sorrow" – and if you don't choose to fulfil the conditions for ending sorrow, be prepared, whatever gurus, churches etc you may believe in, for the indefinite continuance of sorrow.'[52]

Huxley was evidently writing of K's sixth talk on 6 August, in which he spoke of sorrow. 'Time does not wipe away sorrow. We may forget a particular suffering, but sorrow is always there, deep down, and I think it is possible to wipe away sorrow in its entirety. Not tomorrow, not in the course of time, but to see the reality in the present, and go beyond.'

After the last talk, on 15 August, K wrote in his journal: 'On waking this morning, there was again this impenetrable strength whose power is the benediction... During the talk it was there, untouchable and pure.'

In print, this talk is not as powerful as the others. It often happened that people who, at the time, had felt a talk to be particularly revealing were disappointd when reading it afterwards in print. It is quite probable that many times when he was speaking, K had been experiencing this strange benediction, and that it was this which had inspired the audience rather than his words.

That summer a Saanen Committee was formed for making all the arrangements necessary for K to speak there annually. Rajagopal was perturbed when he heard this, fearing that K was going to cut out Ojai altogether. This was not the intention, although, as it happened, he did not return to Ojai for five years.

K remained quietly with Vanda at Chalet Tannegg after the gathering. During that time Vanda herself was constantly aware of the 'benediction', the 'otherness' that K wrote about every day. In September he flew alone to Paris where he stayed with his old friends Carlo and Nadine Suarès in their eighth-floor apartment in the Avenue Labourdonnais. To be in a city after the peace of the mountains he loved was a violent change and yet, as he wrote: 'Sitting quietly... looking over the roof tops, most unexpectedly, that benediction, that otherness came with gentle clarity; it filled the room and remained. It is here as this is being written.'

After giving nine talks in Paris and going again to Il Leccio, K flew to Bombay in October and thence to Rishi Valley for a month, and afterwards to Vasanta Vihar, Rajghat and Delhi. From his descriptions in his notebook one gets to know Rishi Valley and Rajghat as if one had been there oneself. In Delhi, on 23 January 1962, his journal stopped as suddenly as it had begun. It was so intensely cold in Shiva Rao's house that he could no longer hold a pencil. The last entry reads in part:

> ...of a sudden that unknowable immensity was there, not only in the room and beyond but also deep, in the innermost recesses, which was once the mind... that immensity left no mark, it was there, clear, strong, impenetrable and unapproachable whose intensity was fire which left no ash. With it was bliss... The past and the unknown do not meet at any point; they cannot be brought together by any act whatsoever; there is no bridge to cross over nor a path that leads to it. The two have never met and will never meet. The past has to cease for the unknowable, for that immensity to be.

The publication, in 1976, of this extraordinary document passed unnoticed by the press both in England and America except for a paragraph in the American *Publishers' Weekly*, concluding, 'Krishnamurti's teaching is austere, in a sense annihilating.' One or two people who read the manuscript were against its publication. They feared it would dishearten K's followers. He maintained that human beings can transform themselves radically, not in time, not by evolution, but by immediate perception, whereas the *Notebook* shows that Krishnamurti was not an ordinary man transformed but a unique being existing in a different dimension. It was a valid point, and when it was put to him he replied, 'We do not all have to be Edisons to turn on the electric light.' Later he was to say to a journalist in Rome, who suggested that he had been born as he was and that therefore others could not attain to his state of consciousness, 'Christopher Columbus went to America in a sailing ship; we can go by jet.'

K gave twenty-three public talks in India that winter, as well as holding innumerable discussions, so it was not surprising that he was exhausted when he arrived in Rome in the middle of March, where he was met by Vanda. The next day he was ill with fever. In that state he 'went off' as he used to do during 'the process'. Vanda recorded what was said by the being left in charge of the body. But it was no longer a child's voice speaking; the voice sounded quite natural:

Don't leave me. He has gone far away, very far away. It has been told to you to look after him. He should not have gone out. You should have told him. At table he is not all there. You must tell him with a look so that other people don't see it, and he will understand. Nice face to look at. Those eyelashes are wasted for a man. Why don't you take them? That face has been very carefully worked out. They have worked and worked for so long, so many centuries, to produce such a body. Do you know him? You cannot know him. How can you know the running water? You listen. Don't ask questions. He must love you if he lets you come so near him. He is very careful not to allow his body to be touched by other people. You know how he treats you. He wants that nothing should happen to you. Don't do anything extravagant. All that travelling was too much for him. And those people in the plane, smoking, and all that packing all the time, arriving and going, it has been too much for the body. He wanted to arrive in Rome for that lady [Vanda]. Do you know her? He wanted to come quickly for her. He gets affected if she is not well. All that travelling – no, I am not complaining. You see how pure he is. He allows nothing for himself. The body has been all this time on the edge of a precipice. It has been held, it has been watched like mad all these months and if it lets go, he will go very far. Death is near. I told him it was too much. When he is in those airports he is by himself. He is not quite there. All that poverty in India, and the people die. Terrible. This body too would have died had it not been found. And all that dirt everywhere. He is so clean. His body is kept so clean. He washesit with so much care. This morning he wanted to convey something to you. Don't stop him. He must love you. Tell him. Take a pencil, tell him: "Death is always there, very close to you, to protect you. And when you take shelter you will die."

When K felt well enough they moved to Il Leccio, but there he became very ill, with a recurrence of his kidney trouble complicated by a severe attack of mumps. He was so ill that for several nights Vanda slept outside his door. It was not until the middle of May that he came to England where Doris Pratt had rented another furnished house for him at Wimbledon. Lady Emily was now eighty-seven and had practically lost her memory; nevertheless, he would often go and see her and sit holding her hand for an hour or more and chanting to her. She recognised him and loved his presence. She was to die early in 1964. I would go and fetch him from Wimbledon sometimes and drive him down to Sussex to walk in our bluebell woods. We never talked seriously and during the walk we would not speak at all. I knew he relished the silence, the sight and scent of the bluebells, the peace of the wood, the birdsong and the tender young beech leaves. He would often stop and look back through his legs at the blue mist. He was what he had always been to me, not a teacher but a beloved human being, closer than any of my siblings. It pleased me to think that I was perhaps the one person with whom he never had to make an effort.

When I heard that he was speaking at the Friends' Meeting House as well as at Wimbledon, I had a sudden impulse to go and hear him. I had not heard him talk since 1928, at Ommen. The hall was packed; people were standing at the back. I did not see him come on to the platform; at one moment the single hard chair, placed in the middle of the platform, was empty; the next moment he was sitting there on his hands having made no sound on entering, a very slight figure, impeccably dressed in a dark suit, white shirt, dark tie, feet in highly polished brown shoes placed neatly side by side. He was alone on the platform (he was never introduced and, as I have said, he never had any notes). There was complete silence in the hall as a strong vibration of expectancy ran through the audience. He sat there perfectly silent, his body still, assessing his audience with slight movements of his head from side to side. One minute; two minutes; I began to panic for him. Had he broken down altogether? I was prickling all over in an anguish of concern for him when he suddenly began, unhurriedly, in his rather lilting voice with its faint Indian accent, startling the silence.

I discovered later that this long silence at the beginning of a talk was customary. It was immensely impressive but the reason for it was not to impress. He rarely knew what he was going to say before he started speaking and seemed to look to his audience for guidance. This is why a talk frequently began lamely: 'I wonder what the purpose is of a gathering such as this?' he might say, or, 'What do you expect from this?' or he might begin a series of talks, 'I think it would be as well if we could establish a true relationship between the speaker and the audience.' At other times he knew exactly what he wanted to say: 'I want this evening to talk about knowledge, experience and time', but the talk that followed did not necessarily confine itself to those subjects. He was always insistent that he was not speaking didactically, that he and the audience were taking part together in an investigation. He would remind the audience of this two or three times in the course of a talk.

On this particular evening at the Friends' Meeting House he had known just what he wanted to say:

To understand what we are going to consider this evening and on succeeding evenings, needs a clear mind, a mind that is capable of direct perception. Understanding is not something mysterious. It requires a mind that is capable of looking at things directly, without prejudice, without personal inclinations, without opinions. What I want to say this evening concerns the total inward revolution, a destruction of the psychological structure of society, which we are. But the destruction of this psychological structure of society, which is you and me, does not come about through effort; and I think that is one of the most difficult things for most of us to understand.

The meaning behind K's words came for most people, I think, through the physical presence of the man himself – there was an emanation that flashed a meaning direct to one's understanding, bypassing the mind, and whether one found a talk more or less meaningful depended more on one's own state of receptivity than on what he said. Although he would sit on his hands when he first came on to a platform, he gesticulated with one or both of them most expressively in the course of a talk, often spreading his fingers wide. His hands were a joy to watch. At the end of a talk he would slip away as unobtrusively as he had entered. His audiences in India had always been far more demonstrative than in the West, and, speaking out of doors there, it was more difficult for him to leave the platform. He was acutely embarrassed by the demonstrative devotion he received in India, by prostrations and efforts to touch him or his clothes. As he drove away from a meeting in Bombay, hands would reach out to take hold of his hands through the open car window. Once he was horrified when a man seized his hand and engulfed it in his mouth.

The second gathering at Saanen that summer took place in a large tent. (It was not until 1965 that the strip of rented land on which the tent was erected, close to the Saanen river, was bought by KWINC, with funds provided by Rajagopal.) Vanda Scaravelli rented Chalet Tannegg again, as she was to do every summer until 1983, bringing with her a retired cook of her own, Fosca, to run the house. K was not at all well after the meetings at the end of August. He decided to cancel his visit to India that year and remained at Tannegg until Christmas. Rajagopal went over to see him in October in the hope of effecting a reconciliation, but as Rajagopal wanted it to be on his own terms, and K still insisted on being put back on the board of KWINC, they reached a deadlock. Rajagopal also went to London where he abused K to me more virulently than before, accusing him of hypocrisy, for which he gave no evidence, and for caring too much for his appearance before he went on to a platform, making sure in a mirror that every hair was in place. Rajagopal knew as well as I did that K had always cared for outward appearance, both his own and that of others. When one was going to see him one always took the greatest care to look one's best, for he noticed everything. It would have been only courteous to his audience to look as neat as possible when he was on the platform. I urged Rajagopal to stop working for K, feeling as he did about him (he led me to understand that money was no problem), and to settle in Europe where he had many friends, but his real trouble seemed to be that he was locked in a one-sided love–hate relationship which K's aloofness made it all the harder to escape from.

After leaving Tannegg, K went with Vanda to Rome where she introduced him to many prominent people – film directors, writers, and musicians, including Fellini, Pontecorvo, Alberto Moravia, Carlo Levi, Segovia and Casals who played for him. (From Il Leccio she had taken him several times to see Bernard Berenson at I Tatti.)* Huxley was in Rome in March and saw K frequently. It was their last meeting for Huxley was to die in Los Angeles in November. A month after Huxley's death K wrote to me: 'Aldous Huxley told me a couple of years ago that he had cancer of the tongue; he told me he had told no one, not even his wife. I saw him in Rome this spring and he looked fairly well and so it was a shock when I knew that he had gone. I hope he didn't suffer.'

At the end of May K returned to Gstaad. My husband and I stopped a night in Gstaad on our way to Venice by car and went to Tannegg to see him. He was alone there except for Fosca. He was most welcoming and took us for a drive in the Mercedes owned by the Saanen Committee. It was evident that the car was cherished, seldom used, and cleaned and polished by him every time it returned from even the shortest run. Continuing into Italy, we stopped at the Castle Hotel at Pergine where we had stayed in 1924. I sent him a postcard of the round tower which

---

*The entry in Berenson's diary for 7 May 1956, when he was ninety, reads: 'Krishnamurti for tea: affable, responsive, conceding all my objections, and indeed our discussion was scarcely controversial. He insisted nevertheless on a Beyond, and that this was a state of immobile, uneventful existence, no thought, no questioning, no – what? He rejected my contention that such a state was something beyond my Western cast of mind. I went so far as to ask him whether he was not after something merely verbal. He denied it firmly, but without heat.' (*Sunset and Twilight*, Nicky Mariano (ed), Hamish Hamilton, 1964.)

he had occupied. He replied: 'I can't remember a thing about it; it might be any other castle. It's so completely blotted out of my mind.'

There was a newcomer at the Saanen gathering that year who was to play an important part in K's outer life for a few years; this was the thirty-five-year-old Alain Naudé, a professional pianist from South Africa who had studied in Paris and Siena and given concerts in Europe and was at that time a professor at the University of Pretoria. Having been interested from boyhood in the religious life, Alain had heard of Krishnamurti and gone to Saanen in the vacation to hear him speak. He met K personally and was in India that winter when K was there. When he returned to Pretoria, early in 1964, it was to resign his professorship in order to follow his spiritual destiny.

Alain Naudé was at Saanen again in the summer of 1964. Also there that summer was Mary Zimbalist, née Taylor, the widow of Sam Zimbalist, the film producer. She was a gentle, elegant Europeanised American from a New York family well established in the business world. She had first heard K talk at Ojai with her husband in 1944. When her husband died suddenly of a heart attack in 1958 she had gone, still devastated with grief, to hear K speak again at the Ojai gathering of 1960. Afterwards she had had a long private interview with him in which he had talked to her of death in a way she was ready to understand: one could not run away from death by the usual routes of escape; the fact of death had to be understood; it was the escape from loneliness that brought sorrow, not the *fact* of loneliness, of death; grief was self-pity, not love. Mary had hoped to hear him speak again at Ojai but when it seemed unlikely that he was going to return there, she had travelled to Saanen to hear him. There she became friends with Alain Naudé and they were both asked by K to stay on after the gathering to attend some small private discussions at Tannegg. Mary also had another long private interview with him.

The shares held in England for K's expenses had now ceased to pay dividends, and Doris Pratt suggested to Rajagopal that all K's travel costs to India and in Europe should in future be paid by KWINC to the Saanen Committee, which would also receive KWINC's funds raised in Europe; and, for reasons of health, that K should in future travel first class. Rajagopal agreed to the first proposal but gave no answer to the suggestion of K travelling first class. Considering that every penny that went to KWINC, either in the form of donations, bequests or royalties from books, was earned by K himself, it seems extraordinary that Rajagopal's permission had to be asked as to how the money might be spent for K's personal comfort; and that when K, having seen Alain Naudé again in the winter of 1964–5, wanted him to become his secretary and travelling companion, Rajagopal's consent had again to be obtained to pay him a modest salary. It was so obvious that, at the age of seventy, travelling alone had become too much for K, especially after his many illnesses.

I met Alain Naudé with K in London in the spring of 1965 at K's tailor, Huntsman in Savile Row. Alain was staying with K and Doris Pratt in yet another furnished house in Wimbledon and had taken charge of the recording of K's Wimbledon talks. When K went with me for our usual bluebell walk he seemed in higher spirits than he had been for years. He told me how much difference Alain had made to his life, travelling with him and looking after the luggage. He felt a natural affinity with him; he was light hearted, though serious minded, energetic and cosmopolitan, with a flair for languages. Mary Zimbalist was also in London, but I did not meet her until the following year. She hired a car and took K and Alain to places of beauty in England, and when the three of them went to Paris after London, Mary drove them to Versailles, Chartres, Rambouillet and other places, the kind of pleasant trips that K had been denied for years in his outwardly dull life.

14

'Ideals are brutal things'

Mary Zimbalist and Alain Naudé went to India with K that winter and travelled round with him and his Indian friends to all the usual places where he gave talks and held discussions. In December 1965, still in India, K received an unexpected invitation from Rajagopal, which he accepted, to speak at Ojai in October 1966. The Indian Prime Minister, Lal Bahadur Shastri, died on 11 January 1966 and Indira Gandhi, Pupul Jayakar's close friend, became Prime Minister.

In the spring of 1966, in England, I met Mary Zimbalist. One afternoon she drove up unexpectedly with K and Alain to the door of our country house. They had had a picnic lunch and K had guided them to us. When the three of them eventually drove away I remember thinking what a wonderfully happy and companionable trio they seemed and how beneficial their companionship was to K's health and spirits. It had been a visit full of laughter. My friendship with these new friends of K's grew rapidly. Thereafter, K wanted to stay with them wherever he went. They were at Gstaad that summer, though staying at another chalet; in New York K stayed with them in the apartment of Mary's brother and then, in California, at Mary's beautiful house on a cliff above the sea at Malibu. On 28 October the three of them moved to Ojai and the next day K gave the first of six talks in the Oak Grove, where he had not spoken since 1960. Before the third talk a television crew arrived, and for the first time a talk of K's was filmed. This talk was concerned with what all his talks were fundamentally concerned with – the bringing about of a radical transformation in the human mind. Without such a transformation there

127

could be no real change in society, no real joy, no peace in the world. He repeated what he had said several times before – his words were a mirror in which people could see what was actually taking place within themselves.

Unfortunately, the hoped-for reconciliation between K and Rajagopal did not take place although they met alone several times. K still insisted on being put back on the board of KWINC; Rajagopal denied that K had any responsibility for the organisation. K also talked to the Vice-President of KWINC and to one of the trustees, both of whom he had known well for years, but they were unable or unwilling to help. Jealousy of K's two new friends did not improve the situation.

K flew alone to Delhi that December. (Alain Naudé had returned to Pretoria to see his parents.) K's talks in India that year were the last ever to be published by KWINC. Mary and Alain rejoined him in Rome in March 1967 and went with him to Paris to a house which Mary had rented. He was never again to stay with the Suarès; they drifted out of his life after some kind of quarrel with Léon de Vidas over arrangements for his Paris talks. After Paris, K, with Mary and Alain, went to Holland where K spoke in Amsterdam for the first time for eleven years. They stayed at a farmhouse at Huizen, the town where Wedgwood had had his community, but K had no memory of this. My husband and I, happening to be in Holland at the time, went to visit them. Just as we were leaving K asked me out of the blue if I would write a book for him. I was flabbergasted as I heard myself saying, 'Yes. What kind of book?' He answered, 'Something based on the talks. I leave it to you.' I believe it was Alain who had suggested it. I had never spoken to K of my writing and I do not think he had realised, until Alain told him, that I was a professional author. But neither of them could have known that I had not read a word of K's since 1928. The rest of the summer was overshadowed for me by the enormity of what I had undertaken, yet I never considered going back on it. I knew it was a tremendous challenge. When I returned to London I asked Doris Pratt, whom I had known since the Ommen days, what she considered to be the best talks of the last two years. She recommended those of 1963–4 and sent me the four paperback volumes of authentic reports of talks in India and Europe for those years.

I read these volumes with intense excitement. It was as if I had been living in a room with many windows, all of them covered with dark spring-blinds, and as I read blind after blind sprang up. Such pronouncements as 'ideals are brutal things' and 'I will try is the most dreadful statement one can make' revolutionised my thinking. K covered the same basic subjects in each talk and therefore there was a great deal of repetition, though never in exactly the same words, so I indexed these themes under about a hundred headings – Awareness, Conditioning,Consciousness,Death, Fear, Freedom, God, Love, Meditation, etc – and chose from them those passages in which I thought he had expressed himself most clearly and beautifully and wove them into a book of 124 pages. I did not alter one word of K's, nor add a word, yet this book is not an anthology. Rather it is a Krishnamurti primer. I have never had a harder, more concentrated or more thrilling task. One sentence which I learnt by heart was: 'To be free of authority, of your own and that of another, is to die to everything of yesterday, so that your mind is always fresh, always young, innocent, full of vigour and passion.' This little book, under the title, chosen by K himself, of *Freedom from the Known*, was published in 1969.

To me the most moving and beautiful chapter in it is the one on love. Many people find Krishnamurti's teaching negative because sometimes he could only discover what something was by saying what it was not. Love is a prime example of this. Love is not jealousy, love is not possessiveness, love does not demand to be loved, love is not fear, love is not sexual pleasure; dependence on another is not love, thought cannot cultivate love, love is not beauty, love is not self-pity. (This makes one understand a later pronouncement of K's: 'There is no such thing as unhappy love.') 'Don't you know what it means really to love,' he asks, ' – to love without hate, without jealousy, without anger, without wanting to interfere with what he is thinking or doing, without condemning, without comparing – don't you know what it means? When you love somebody with all your heart, with all your mind, with all your body, with your entire being, is there comparison?'

The concept I found most difficult to understand was that of 'the observer is the observed'. I finally came to an interpretation of this: the self looks at all its inner states of being with its own conditioned mind and therefore what it sees is a replica of itself; what we are is what we see. The conception of a superior self which can direct one's other selves is an illusion, for there is only one self. When K said in other talks 'The experience is the experiencer' and 'The thinker is the thought', he was merely using different words to express the same idea.

Mary Zimbalist drove K and Alain Naudé to Gstaad at the beginning of June 1967, where they stayed together at another villa before Vanda arrived to open up Tannegg for K. A few days before K moved to Tannegg, he was in bed with fever. Mary noted in her diary that she believed he was delirious when he looked at her without recognition and said in his child's voice, 'Krishna has gone away.' He asked her whether she had 'questioned Krishna', and added, 'He doesn't like to be questioned. After all these years I'm not used to him.' Mary had evidently not heard about 'the process'. Although she was from now onwards to be with him more than anyone else until his death, this seems to have been the only time that 'the process' manifested itself to her. He had, however, warned her that he sometimes fainted even when he was being driven; she must take no notice and drive on slowly. This did happen several times. He would collapse on to her lap or shoulder in a faint, but would soon recover and feel no worse for it.

There was much talk that summer at Gstaad about a school which K wanted to start in Europe. An old friend had offered him £50,000 to build a house for himself for when he retired. Intending never to retire, he asked if he might spend the money on a school, a request that was immediately granted. He had recently met the ideal person to become its Principal – Dorothy Simmons who, with her husband Montague, had just retired from running a Government school after eighteen years. It was soon decided that the new school should be in England because Mrs Simmons would not be able to run it efficiently in a foreign language. Eventually Brockwood Park, a large Georgian house in Hampshire with thirty-six acres of park and garden, was bought for £42,000, and the Simmonses, Doris Pratt and one pupil moved in there at the end of 1968.

K had decided to start the school against the advice of his then financial adviser, Gérard Blitz, founder of the Club Méditerranée who told him it was quite impossible to do this until more funds had been collected to equip it. However, K's policy all through his life was to do what he felt was right and the money would come in somehow. And it usually did.

But before that, a complete break had taken place with Rajagopal and K had set up a new trust for the dissemination of his teachings, the trust deed ensuring that the Rajagopal situation could never arise again. At the Saanen gathering of 1968 it was announced:

Krishnamurti wishes it to be known that he has completely disassociated himself from Krishnamurti Writings Incorporated of Ojai, California.

He hopes that, as a result of this public announcement, those who wish to be associated with his work and teachings will give support to the new, international, Krishnamurti Foundation of London, England, whose activities will include a school. The Deed which establishes the Foundation ensures that Krishnamurti's intentions will be respected.

Doris Pratt retired to Brockwood Park after forty years of the most devoted voluntary service, and a married woman with a daughter, Mary Cadogan, who had helped Doris Pratt since 1958, became the Secretary of the new Foundation. Before her marriage Mary Cadogan had worked for the BBC, and her qualifications were of the highest. (She has since published five successful books while remaining Secretary of the Foundation.)

A difficult period followed until donations for the new Foundation started to come in. The KWINC assets were frozen but, fortunately, Doris Pratt and Mary Cadogan had built up a small fund which enabled the new Foundation to carry on. At this time K formed a publications committee under the chairmanship of George Wingfield-Digby, then Curator of Textiles at the Victoria and Albert Museum, an expert on oriental porcelain and author of a life of William Blake. This committee was in future to be responsible for editing K's talks and seeing them through the press and bringing out a Bulletin. The authentic reports of the talks were thereafter printed in Holland instead of in India.

An American Krishnamurti Foundation was set up in 1969, and an Indian Foundation in 1970. An inevitable lawsuit between KWINC and the American Foundation followed, which dragged on until 1974 when it was settled out of court. The main terms of the settlement were that KWINC should be dissolved and another organisation, K & R Foundation, of which Rajagopal had control, should hold the copyright in Krishnamurti's writings prior to 1 July 1968; that 150 acres of land at the western end of the Ojai valley, including the Oak Grove, and eleven acres at the upper end on which Pine Cottage and Arya Vihara stood, should be conveyed to the Krishnamurti Foundation of America (KFA); that the cash assets of KWINC should be transferred to KFA after the deduction of certain sums for pensions and Rajagopal's legal costs, and that Rajagopal should retain possession of his house for life.

While the case was going on, K continued his rounds of travelling. The differences were that he now stayed at Brockwood Park when he came to England and that when in California he stayed with Mary Zimbalist at Malibu instead of at Ojai, and spoke at Santa Monica instead of in the Oak Grove. In the autumn of 1969 Alain Naudé ceased to work for K and went to live in San Francisco where he taught music. He sometimes stayed at Malibu and K saw him whenever he went to San Francisco. He had done a great deal for K in bringing him in touch with young people in America by arranging for him to talk at several universities, including Harvard and Berkeley. 'Quite naturally,' Alain wrote, 'yet a little surprisingly, Krishnamurti is suddenly the hero and friend of these students, for long before they met him the things he talks about had become for them as important as eating or breathing. They love what he says and feel for him a very familiar affection without awe or fear.'[53]

While K was staying at Brockwood in the spring of 1970 he asked me to write an account of his early life. He had first asked his old friend, Shiva Rao, to write it but after gathering a mass of material from the Theosophical Archives at Adyar, Shiva Rao fell very ill and knew he would never recover sufficiently to complete the book. (He died the following year.) He offered, therefore, to put all his documentation at my disposal. I had known him since 1923, when I first went to India, and we had remained close friends ever since. K said he would bring the papers with him when he came from India early the following year. Of course I was delighted to be asked to write this account but made the stipulation before accepting that I should not be required to show the text to anyone. After agreeing to this, K gave me written permission to quote his letters and the accounts of his Ojai experience in 1922 which had never been published. Although I did not intend to start the book until I had received Shiva Rao's material, I went to Brockwood in June to have my first interview with K about it. He seemed keenly interested in 'the boy', as he referred to himself, and wondered why he had been picked out by Leadbeater. What was the quality of the boy's mind? What had protected him all these years? Why was it that the boy, subjected to all that adulation, had not been corrupted or conditioned? He might have become 'an abomination'. This curiosity about the boy, though intense, was quite impersonal. It was as if he hoped that the written record of the true story might reveal something to explain the phenomenon of the man in whom he had an equally impersonal interest. He could not have been more co-operative, but, alas, he remembered nothing of his early life except what Shiva Rao and others had told him.

A book of K's was published in 1970 called *The Urgency of Change* which consists of probing questions put to him by Alain Naudé at Malibu and his replies. Alain would take down both questions and answers in longhand, dictate them on to a tape recorder and read them back to K in the evening to make any corrections. This book, therefore, has a value beyond the books of edited talks which K never revised or even looked at. There is a passage in it on one of K's most frequently recurring themes and one of the hardest to grasp – the ending of thought:

> *Questioner*: I wonder what you really mean by ending thought. I talked to a friend about it and he said it is some kind of oriental nonsense. To him thought is the highest form of intelligence and action, indispensable. It has created civilization and all relationship is based on it. All of us accept this . . . When we don't think we sleep, vegetate or daydream; we are vacant, dull and unproductive, whereas when we are awake we are thinking, doing, living, quarrelling: these are the only two states we know. You say, be beyond both – beyond thought and vacant inactivity. What do you mean by this?
>
> *Krishnamurti*: Very simply put, thought is the response of memory, the past. When thought acts it is this past which is acting as memory, as experience, as knowledge, as opportunity. When thought is functioning it is the past, therefore there is no new living at all; it is the past living in the present, modifying itself and the present. So there is nothing new in life that way, and when something new is to be found there must be the absence of the past, the mind must not be cluttered up with thought, fear, pleasure, and everything else. Only when the mind is uncluttered can the new come into being, and for this reason we say that thought must be still, operating only when it has to – objectively, efficiently. All continuity is thought; when there is continuity there is nothing new. Do you see how important it is? It's really a question of life itself. Either you live in the past, or you live totally differently: that is the whole point.

In his *Notebook* K had written: 'There is a sacredness which is not of thought, nor of a feeling resuscitated by thought. It is not recognizable by thought nor can it be utilized by thought. Thought cannot formulate it. But there's a sacredness, untouched by any symbol or word. It is not communicable.' This is the whole difficulty of such a concept as the ending of thought – it cannot be communicated except through thought.

Later K was to say: 'Thought contaminates' and 'Thought is corruption'. These bald statements without any explanation are incomprehensible. Thought was corrupt because it was 'broken up', 'fragmented'. What he was talking about was, of course, psychological thought. Thought is necessary for all practicable purposes, just as memory is.

K also stated his attitude to sex in *The Urgency of Change*, in answer
to the question: 'Can there be sex without this desire of thought?'

You have to find out for yourself. Sex plays an extraordinarily important
part in our lives because it is perhaps the only deep, first-hand experience
we have. Intellectually and emotionally we can imitate, follow, obey. There
is pain and strife in all our relationships, except in the act of sex. This act,
being so different and beautiful, we become addicted to, so it in turn becomes
a bondage. The bondage is the demand for its continuation – again the
action of the centre which is divisive. One is so hedged about – intellectually,
in the family, in the community, through social morality, through religious
sanctions – so hedged about that there is only this one relationship left
in which there is freedom and intensity. Therefore we give tremendous
importance to it. But if there were freedom all around then this would not
be such a craving and such a problem. We make it a problem because we
can't get enough of it, or because we feel guilty at having got it, or
because in getting it we break the rules which society has laid down. It is
the old society which calls the new society permissive because for the new
society sex is a part of life. In freeing the mind from the bondage of imitation,
authority, conformity and religious prescriptions, sex has its own place, but
it won't be all-consuming. From this one can see that freedom is essential
for love – not the freedom of revolt, not the freedom of doing what one likes
nor of indulging openly or secretly one's cravings, but rather the freedom
which comes in the understanding of this whole structure and nature of the
centre. Then freedom is love.[54]

K decided not to go to India in the winter of 1971, not because of
the threat of war between India and Pakistan, but because, as he told
Mary Zimbalist, his body was 'bone tired' and he needed a chance to
catch up with his mind which was 'bursting with energy'. For the next
few weeks, therefore, from 20 November, he relaxed completely at
Mary's house at Malibu, going to cinemas, walking on the beach,
watching television and reading whodunits. But as always when resting
quietly, his head was bad; he was often awake for hours in the night
with the intensity of his meditation and several times he would wake
after sleeping with a sense of 'special joy', feeling that the room was full
of 'eminent holy beings'. Evidently 'the process' was going on in a mild
form without his 'going off'. He felt that something was happening to
expand his brain, for there was 'an extraordinary light burning in his
mind'. He declared all the same that he had not felt so rested since the
war. Yet his body had become so sensitive that one evening, when the
television was on and he was 'far away', he had such a shock when
Mary spoke to him that he began to shake and felt the shock effects all

134

night.* These meditations, so intense that they kept him awake for hours, continued until he went to New York in May 1972 to give talks.

This year saw the publication of the first Krishnamurti book from India, *Tradition and Revolution*, edited by Pupul Jayakar and Sunanda Patwardhan, and published by Orient Longman. It comprised thirty dialogues held during 1970–1 in New Delhi, Madras, Rishi Valley and Bombay with a small group of people – artists, politicians, *sanyasis* and pundits – whom K had been meeting since returning to India in 1947. Although nothing new was said in these discussions, the approach was new and refreshingly different in having a glossary of Indian words. There is one particularly memorable passage: 'There is only one way of meeting sorrow. The escapes with which we are all familiar are really ways of avoiding the greatness of sorrow. The only way to avoid sorrow is to be without any resistance, to be without any movement away from sorrow, outwardly or inwardly, to remain totally with sorrow without wanting to go beyond it.'

There had always been a tendency among K's Indian followers to regard him as an Indian since he was born in an Indian body, whereas he himself protested that he belonged to no race or nationality any more than to any religion. His Indian passport made it difficult to get visas for Europe and America so he was thankful when, in 1977, he obtained a so-called Green Card which enabled him to enter America without a visa.

K stopped at Brockwood for a few days in February 1973 on his way from Bombay to Los Angeles. I was now deeply absorbed in writing the account of his early life which was to become the first volume of a three-volume biography, but I had misgivings as to the advisability of publishing it, the story was at once so crazy and yet somehow so sacred; therefore I went to Brockwood for the day to talk it over with him. Alone with him after lunch in the large drawing room of the West Wing, that part of the house that had become his home when in England (he sitting in a hard chair as he always preferred to do, drawn up close to the sofa where I sat), I put my doubts to him. He replied instantly, 'Can't you feel it in the room? Well, that is your answer.' I am not in the least psychic but at that moment I did feel a slight throbbing in the room which might easily have been imagination. He evidently felt it coming from outside himself and giving its approval. 'What is this thing?' I demanded. 'This power? What is behind you? I

*Quotations from Mary's diary.

know you have always felt protected but what or who is it that protects you?' 'It's there, as if it were behind a curtain,' he answered, stretching out a hand behind him as if to feel an invisible curtain. 'I *could* lift it but I don't feel it's my business to.'

When I left that afternoon K had gone up to his room to rest, and my daughter, who had driven me from London, was waiting impatiently in the car outside. Having said goodbye to people in the school, I had to return to the West Wing to get my coat from the cloakroom. As I passed the open door of the drawing room, with no thought in my head but to hurry, a great power rushed out at me, terrifying in its force. Was it hostile to me? One thing I do know is that it was *not* imaginary or auto-suggestive. I came to the conclusion that it was not personally hostile. It was as I imagine it would be like to be caught in the whirlwind of a propeller. Was this the source, the energy, that went through K so frequently? I did not know at the time that the year before, at Ojai, K had been questioned on this same subject of the power behind him by a group of trustees of the American Foundation, of whom Erna Lilliefelt and her husband, Theodor, who lived at Ojai, were the most prominent; indeed, the Foundation could hardly have been started without Erna. K had said on that occasion, speaking of himself in the third person:

First of all we are enquiring into something which K himself has never enquired into. He has never said, 'Who am I?' I feel we are delving into something which the conscious mind can never understand, which doesn't mean I am making a mystery of it. There is something. Much too vast to put into words. There is a tremendous reservoir, as it were, which if the human mind can touch can reveal something which no intellectual mythology, invention, dogma, can ever reveal. I am not making a mystery of it – that would be a stupid childish trick, a most blackguardly thing to do because that would be exploiting people. Either one creates a mystery when there isn't one or there is a mystery which you have to approach with extraordinary delicacy and hesitancy. And the conscious mind can't do that. It is there. It is there but you cannot come to it, you cannot invite it. It's not progressive achievement. There is something but the brain can't understand it.

K was most indignant when it was suggested at this same meeting that he might be a medium. 'Of course I'm not a medium; that's obvious. That [explanation] would be too childish, too immature.' Was he aware, he was asked, that he was being used? 'No. That would be like a petrol station which is being used by others.' He then asked in his turn: 'Is something going on in the brain uninvited by me – the various experiences like at Ojai and other times? For instance, I woke up at 3.30 and there was a tremendous sense of energy, bursting energy, great beauty, all kinds of things happened. This kind of experience is going on all the time when the body isn't too tired.'[55]

At this time K described more fully to Mary Zimbalist this waking in the night. She noted it down and passed it on to me in a letter: 'I woke at three with a sense of extraordinary power, light burning in the mind. There was no observer. The testing was from the outside but the observer didn't exist. There was only that and nothing else. The power penetrated the whole being. I sat up and it lasted three hours.' He told Mary that he often woke with some extraordinary feeling of new and vast energy. A few years later, he asked her to write down another experience he had had, which was again relayed to me in a letter:

Before beginning *asanas,** he [K] generally sits very quietly, thinking about nothing. But this morning a strange thing took place, most unexpected and in no way invited – and besides you cannot invite these things. Suddenly it appeared as though in the very centre of his brain, head, right inside, there was a vast space in which was unimaginable energy. It was there, but nothing whatever is registered, for that which is registered is a waste of energy. If one can so call it, it was pure energy in a limitless state, a space that had nothing but this sense of immensity. One doesn't know how long it lasted but all during the morning it was there, and as this is being written it is as though it was taking root and becoming firm. These words are not really the thing itself.

K's descriptions of the energy that entered him should be carefully noted in view of the tape recording he made shortly before his death, the last he ever made.

---

*Yoga positions. K had first been taught yoga exercises by B. K. S. Iyengar, but from 1965 for many years he had been taught by Iyengar's nephew T. K. B. Desikachar, at Vasanta Vihar and Chalet Tannegg. He practised yoga as a form of physical exercise only.

15

'The future is now'

Two more books written by K came out in 1973, by which time his books had practically ceased to be reviewed in the press, though they continued to sell very well. One can understand the difficulty of reviewing them, yet John Stewart Collis, who was unknown to K, took up the challenge when he reviewed the first short one, *Beyond Violence*, for the *Sunday Telegraph* in March 1973:

> To be refreshing it is necessary to be fresh. This is rare enough in the arts. In the field of religious-philosophical-ethical thought it is hardly ever found. J. Krishnamurti is always fresh, he is always surprising. I doubt if a cliché has ever passed his lips.
>
> He is also very difficult. Not because he ever uses a long word but because he doesn't believe in 'belief'. This must be appalling for those who rely upon *isms* and *ologies*. He believes in Religion, in the fundamental meaning of the word, but not in religions or in any systems of thought whatever.
>
> The sub-title of *Beyond Violence* is 'Authentic Reports of Talks and Discussions in Santa Monica, San Diego, London, Brockwood Park, Rome'. First of all Krishnamurti gives a talk and then answers questions. The questions are ordinary, the answers are never ordinary. 'Is not the belief in the unity of all things just as human as the belief in the division of all things?'
>
> 'Why do you want to believe in the unity of all human beings? – We are not united, that is a fact. Why do you want to believe in something that is non-factual? There is this whole question of belief; just think, you have your beliefs and another has his beliefs; and we fight and kill each other for a belief.'
>
> Again;
>
> 'When should we have psychic experiences?'
>
> 'Never! Do you know what it means to have psychic experiences? To have

extra-sensory experience, you must be extraordinarily mature, extra-ordinarily sensitive, and extraordinarily intelligent; and if you are extra-ordinarily intelligent, you do not want psychic experience.'

This volume is chiefly concerned with changing *ourselves*, so as to go beyond the violence so widespread everywhere:

'To be free from violence implies freedom from everything that man has put to another man, belief, dogma, ritual, my country, your country, your god, my god, my opinion, your opinion.'

How to achieve this freedom? I'm awfully sorry, but I can't give Krishnamurti's message in a neat sentence. He has to be read. The act of reading him alone works a change in the reader. One clue: substitute for thinking the act of *attention* – the power to *look*.

The second book, *The Awakening of Intelligence*, was a very long one, edited by George and Cornelia Wingfield-Digby with seventeen photographs of K by Mark Edwards. From the early 1930s for over thirty years, K had refused to have any photographs taken of himself. When he relented in 1968 a young freelance photographer, Mark Edwards, just out of art school, happened to have asked if he might photograph him. Since then Mark has made a name for himself with pictures of the Third World and has done a great deal of photographic work for the Krishnamurti Foundation. (K was later photographed by Cecil Beaton and by Karsh of Ottawa.)

The Awakening of Intelligence contains interviews with several different people, including 'Conversations between Krishnamurti and Jacob Needleman', Professor of Philosphy at San Francisco State College, 'Conversations between Krishnamurti and Swami Ventakesananda', 'Conversations with Alain Naudé' and a conversation with Professor David Bohm, who was at that time Professor of Theoretical Physics at Birkbeck College, London University. David Bohm had been a friend of Einstein at Princeton in the 1940s. He had first become interested in K after finding by chance *The First and Last Freedom* in a library. He had attended K's talks at Wimbledon in 1961 and since then had frequently been to Saanen and Brockwood where he had held discussions with K. He was the author of several books on the quantum theory, and in 1980 he was to publish *Wholeness and the Implicate Order*, propounding a revolutionary theory of physics akin to K's teaching of the wholeness of life.

In his first conversation with Professor Needleman, K emphasised the importance of getting rid of all religious conditioning: 'One has to discard all the promises, all the experiences, all the mystical assertions. I think one has to start as if one knew absolutely nothing.' Needleman interposed, 'That is very hard.' 'No, Sir, I do not think that is hard. I think it is only hard for those who have filled themselves with other peoples' knowledge.' And, later in the discussion, K said, 'I don't read any religious, philosophical, psychological books: one can go into oneself at tremendous depth and find out everything.' That is fundamental to K's teaching – that the whole understanding of life can be discovered in oneself, for, as he said in one of his conversations with Alain Naudé: 'The world is me and I am the world; my consciousness is the consciousness of the world, and the consciousness of the world is me. So when there is order in the human being there is order in the world.'

In his conversations with the Swami, K defined his attitude to gurus. In answer to the Swami's question, 'Now what, according to you, is the rôle of the *guru*, a preceptor or an awakener?', K replied, 'Sir, if you are using the word *guru* in its classical sense which is the dispeller of darkness, of ignorance, can another, whoever he be, enlightened or stupid, really help to dispel the darkness in oneself?' The Swami then asked, 'But would you, Krishnaji, accept that pointing out was necessary?' This K answered, 'Yes, of course. I point out. I do that. We all do that. I ask a man on the road, "Will you please tell me which is the road to Saanen", and he tells me; but I do not spend time and expect devotion and say, "My God, you are the greatest of men." That is too childish.'

As a result of K's discussions with David Bohm, which went on at intervals for several years, he spoke more and more about the ending of time as well as the ending of thought. He was excited and stimulated by these discussions, feeling that a bridge had been opened between the religious and the scientific minds. It might be called the intellectual rather than the intuitive approach to his teaching. David Bohm liked to start a discussion by giving the root meaning of a word as a help to understanding, and K came sometimes to adopt this practice himself in his later talks, not adding to their lucidity and in one case causing some confusion. Bohm had pointed out to K that the word 'reality' was derived from 'res', a thing, a fact, and K thereafter would sometimes use the word to mean the ultimate or truth, as he had done for years, or, after talking to Bohm, to mean a fact, like the chair we sit on, the pen we hold, the clothes we wear, the toothache we feel. To know that the word 'communicate' is derived from the Latin for 'make common' did not help K to communicate the incommunicable which he was for ever trying to do. Yet many people responded more to K's new intellectual approach than to his poetic mysticism or his descriptions of nature such as: 'The evening sun was on the new grass and there was splendour in every blade. The spring leaves were just overhead, so delicate that when you touched them you could not feel them.'

Several conferences of scientists and psychologists were organised at Brockwood and Ojai by David Bohm, at K's request, and seminars of psychologists were arranged in New York by Dr David Shainberg in which K took part. These meetings were, on the whole, disappointing. K was not really interested in the psychological ideas and conclusions reached by scientists and philosophers; what he liked was the stimulation of other minds in order to delve more deeply into himself, whereas those attending the conferences naturally wanted to read aloud their own papers. But K eagerly grasped any factual information about the new scientific developments going on in the world. Thus he learnt as much as he could about genetic engineering from Professor Maurice Wilkins, a Nobel prize winner for medicine, who attended two of the Brockwood conferences, and later on he became fascinated in learning about computers from Asit Chandmal, Pupul Jayakar's nephew, who had worked on computers with the great Indian Tata group. In the same way K had, in the past, wanted to learn all about the internal combustion engine and other mechanical devices such as clocks and cameras. When one day at Brockwood someone asked Mark Edwards in K's presence a technical question about photography, Mark was astonished when K promptly gave the answer himself, clearly and concisely.

One of the remarkable things about K was the equal ease with which he talked seriously to a swami, a Buddhist monk, a Western scientist, an industrial millionaire, a prime minister or a queen. Although shy and diffident, and having read so little and with no intellectual pretensions, he had no apprehension in discussing in public the most abstruse psychological problems with the world's greatest philosophers, scientists and religious teachers. The explanation of this was, I think, that while others discoursed and argued about the theories of x, K saw x as clearly as if it was his own hand.

In June 1973 there was an international meeting in Brockwood of representatives of all three Foundations, who met for the first time. K was concerned with the problems which would arise after his death and the deaths of the existing trustees. He could not see how the Foundations could be carried on. His attitude to the future had changed completely from what it had been in August 1968 when, during a walk in Epping Forest, my husband had asked him what would happen to his new English Foundation and all his work after his death, and he had replied with a sweeping gesture, 'It will all disappear.' His teachings would remain and his books and tapes; everything else could go.

When it was suggested now, at this international meeting, that he should choose some young people to carry on, he replied: 'Most of the young people put a shield between themselves and me. It is the responsibility of the Foundations to find young people. You may find it easier than I, because people fall in love with me, with my face, they are attracted to me personally, or they want to advance spiritually... but the schools have to go on definitely because they may produce a different kind of human being.'[56]

To produce a different kind of human being was the purpose of K's teaching. His main theme at the Saanen gathering that year was how to bring about 'a fundamental, revolutionary, psychological change in the mind'. He had now begun to say, moreover, that the change must be instantaneous. It was useless to say, 'I will try to change', or, 'I will be different tomorrow', for what you were today you would be tomorrow. 'The future is now' is a phrase he was to use.

After Saanen, K returned to Brockwood for the annual gathering that had taken place there for the last four years, and stayed on until he went to India in October. Whenever he was at Brockwood now, he would come up to London about once a week with Mary Zimbalist, sometimes to go to the dentist or the barber, Truefitt & Hill in Bond Street – but always to visit his tailor, Huntsman, usually just to take them a pair of trousers to be altered or have the umpteenth fitting for a suit that never quite reached his standard of perfection. He rarely ordered a new suit. He seemed to love the atmosphere of the shop, lingering to examine with complete attention the bales of cloth lying on the counters. I would lunch with them whenever they came to London, in the fourth-floor restaurant at Fortnum & Mason, a conveniently short walk from Savile Row through the Burlington Arcade and next door to Hatchards' book shop where K would replenish his stock of paperback crime stories. The menu in this restaurant was very limited for vegetarians but the room was quiet and spacious, the tables sufficiently far apart for conversations not to be overheard. K would keenly observe the people round him, what they wore, what they ate, how they ate and behaved. At one time there was a model girl going round the tables. K would nudge Mary and me: 'Look at her, look at her. She wants to be looked at,' but it was he who was much more interested in what she was wearing than we were. He always took a great interest in clothes, not only in his own. Occasionally at lunch I would ask him to wear my ring, a turquoise set in baguette diamonds, which he knew well because my mother had always worn it. He would put it on his little finger. When he returned it as we were leaving the restaurant the diamonds would be sparkling as if they had just been cleaned by a jeweller. This was not imagination. One day, when I met one of my granddaughters after lunch she said to me, 'How wonderful your ring looks. Have you just had it cleaned?'

In the 1970s a friend of K's described him thus:

> When one meets him what does one see? Truly, to a superlative degree, there is nobility, power, grace and elegance. There is an exquisite breeding, a heightened aesthetic sense, enormous sensitivity and penetrating insight into any problems that one might bring to him. Nowhere in Krishnamurti is there the slightest trace of anything vulgar, mean or commonplace. One may understand his teaching or not understand it; one may perhaps criticize this or that in his accent or his words. But it is not conceivable that anybody could deny the enormous nobility and grace that flow from his person. One could perhaps say that he has a style or a class quite above, quite beyond, the common run of man.
>
> No doubt these words would embarrass him. But there you are. His dress, bearing, manners, movement and speech are, in the highest sense of the word, princely. When he enters a room someone quite extraordinary is there.

K's interest in good clothes and cars, and his taste for escapist books and films, have seemed anomalous to some: it did not occur to him either to change his inclinations in such trivial matters or to pretend they were other than they were.

One day, when K was in London that autumn, I suggested that he should start writing a journal as he had done in 1961. He jumped at the idea, bought notebooks and a new fountain pen with a broad nib that very afternoon and began to write it the next morning, 14 September. He continued to write every day for the next six weeks, mostly at Brockwood but continuing when he went to Rome in October. These daily writings, published early in 1982 under the title of *Krishnamurti's Journal*, reveal more about him personally than any of his other works. Referring to himself in the third person, he wrote on 15 September: 'He only discovered recently that there was not a single thought during these long walks . . . ever since he was a boy it had been like that, no thoughts entered his mind. He was watching and listening and nothing else. Thought with its associations never arose. There was no image-making. One day he was suddenly aware how extraordinary it was; he attempted often to think but no thought would come. On these walks, with people or without them, any movement of thought was absent. This is to be alone.' And on the 17th: 'He always had this strange lack of distance between himself and the trees, rivers and mountains. It wasn't cultivated: you can't cultivate a thing like that. There was never a wall between him and another. What they did to him, what they said to him never seemed to wound him, nor flattery to touch him. Somehow he was altogether untouched. He was not withdrawn, aloof, but like the waters of a river. He had so few thoughts; no thoughts at all when he was alone.' And on the 21st: 'He has never been hurt though many things happened to him, flattery and insult, threat and security. It was not that he was insensitive, unaware; he had no image of himself, no conclusion, no ideology. Image is resistance and when that is not, there is vulnerability but no hurt.' Two days later he was to write:

He was standing by himself on the low bank of the river . . . he was standing there with no one around, alone, unattached and far away. He was about fourteen or less. They had found his brother and himself quite recently and all the fuss and sudden importance given to him was around him. He was the centre of respect and devotion and in the years to come he would be the head of organizations and great properties. All that and the dissolution of them still lay ahead. Standing there alone, lost and strangely aloof, was his first and lasting remembrance of those days and events. He doesn't remember his childhood, the schools and the caning. He was told later by the very teacher who hurt him that he used to cane him practically every day; he would cry and be put out on the verandah until the school closed and the teacher would come out and ask him to go home, otherwise he would still be on the verandah. He was caned, this man said, because he couldn't study or remember anything he had read or been told. Later the teacher couldn't believe that that boy was the man who had given the talk he had heard. He was greatly surprised and unnecessarily respectful. All those years passed without leaving scars, memories, on his mind; his friendships, his affections, even those years with those who had ill-treated him – somehow none of these events, friendly or brutal have left marks on him. In recent years a writer asked if he could recall all those rather strange events and happenings, and when he replied that he could not remember them and could only repeat what others had told him, the man openly, with a sneer, stated that he was putting it on and pretending. He never consciously blocked any happening, pleasant or unpleasant, entering into his mind. They came, leaving no mark, and passed away.

16

'A dialogue with death'

For the past few years K had not been able to stay at Vasanta Vihar when he was in Madras because Rajagopal was claiming it as part of the assets of KWINC, so he stayed instead with an Indian lady close by in Greenways Road. (It was not until 1975 that Vasanta Vihar was ceded to the Indian Foundation.) K was now obliged to part company from Madhavachari, Rajagopal's right-hand man, whose loyalties K found were still with Rajagopal. In that winter of 1973–4, an Indian doctor from the hospital in the compound of the Rajghat school at Varanasi, as Benares is now called, Dr T. K. Parchure, began to travel with K wherever he went in India, as did also Parameshwaran, the head cook at Rishi Valley, who had looked after him when he nearly died in Kashmir in 1959. As well as the free hospital in the grounds of Rajghat, catering for the needs of twenty surrounding villages, there is a womens' college with a hostel attached, a farm and an agricultural school. The school itself has about 300 boys and girls, from the ages of seven to eighteen.

At Rishi Valley, also, there is more than a school; there is a free rural centre where seventy children from adjacent villages are educated and given medical care. In talking to the teachers at Rishi Valley that year K said something in answer to the question, 'Does not suffering dull the mind?' that struck me with great force when I read it afterwards: 'I should have thought rather that the continuation of suffering dulls the mind, not the impact of suffering... Unless you resolve suffering immediately it must inevitably dull the mind.' A Krishnamurti co-educational day school had just been started in Madras. Called simply

147

The School, it accommodated 112 children from the ages of three to twelve.

K was now very anxious to start a school at Ojai without waiting for the settlement with KWINC. An architect was consulted and a Principal chosen, to the dismay of the trustees of the American Foundation who had no funds or land for such a venture, but K never let such considerations stand in the way of what he really wanted to do. Fortunately the case was settled in September before suitable land had been found. Meanwhile K had been with Mary Zimbalist in May to San Diego where a series of eighteen dialogues on different subjects between him and Dr Allan Anderson, Professor of Religious Education at the San Diego State College, were video taped in colour.[57] The last two discussions were on meditation. In the course of them K emphasised three times that meditation covered the 'whole field of existence' and that all effort to meditate was a denial of meditation. One of his most beautiful passages on meditation came in a talk he had given a few years earlier:

> Meditation is one of the greatest arts in life – perhaps *the* greatest, and one cannot possibly learn it from anybody. That is the beauty of it. It has no technique and therefore no authority. When you learn about yourself, watch yourself, watch the way you walk, how you eat, what you say, the gossip, the hate, the jealousy, if you are aware of all that in yourself, without any choice, that is part of meditation. So meditation can take place when you are sitting in a bus or walking in the woods full of light and shadows, or listening to the singing of birds or looking at the face of your wife or child.[58]

Shortly after San Diego, K spoke at Santa Monica for the last time. At one of these talks he was asked: 'I have been listening to you for some time now but no change has come about. What is wrong?' To this K replied:

> Is it that you are not serious? Is it that you don't care? Is it that you have so many problems that you are caught up in them, no time, no leisure to stop, so that you never look at that flower? ... Sir, you have not given your life to it. We are talking about life, not ideas, not about theories, practices, technologies – but looking at the whole of life which is your life.

K told Mary at this time that he had to live another ten or fifteen years because there was still so much to be done. His body, he said, was deteriorating (he was seventy-nine), though his 'brain was untouched'. A few mornings after arriving at Chalet Tannegg that summer, he woke saying that 'something extraordinary had happened to him, something spreading out to take in the universe'. That same morning he dictated a letter to Mary about the new school at Ojai: 'It must produce people so religiously based that they would carry that quality with them whatever they did, wherever they went, whatever career they took up.' It was very hot at Gstaad, and at the Saanen gathering K was often 'very far away' and his head was bad. He had become even more sensitive and could not bear to be touched, but he was having 'marvellous meditations'. 'My mind,' he told Mary, 'feels as if it had been washed out, clean, healthy – and much more than that – a tremendous sense of joy, of ecstasy.'

Flying alone to Delhi in November, K found himself on the same plane as the Maharishi (Mahesh Yogi) who came along beamingly to talk to him, carrying a flower. K's abhorrence of gurus and systems of meditation soon put a stop to their conversation. (K told us afterwards that he would have liked to see his balance sheet.)

At Rajghat in November, K was asked to define his own teaching. He answered in surprise, 'Are you asking me? You are asking me what is the Teaching? I don't know myself. I cannot put it in a few words, can I? I think the idea of the teacher and the taught is basically wrong, at least for me it is. I think it is a matter of sharing rather than being taught.'[59]

Wanting to ask K the same question myself when writing the second volume of his biography, I wrote out a short statement beginning, 'The revolutionary core of Krishnamurti's teaching...' and sent it to him for approval. As I had hoped, he rewrote it entirely, leaving in the single word 'core'. Below is what he wrote:

The core of Krishnamurti's teaching is contained in the statement he made in 1929 when he said 'Truth is a pathless Land'. Man cannot come to it through any organisation, through any creed, through any dogma, priest or ritual, not through any philosophical knowledge or psychological technique. He has to find it through the mirror of relationship, through the understanding of the contents of his own mind, through observation and not through intellectual analysis or introspective dissection. Man has built in himself images as a sense of security – religious, political, personal. These manifest as symbols, ideas, beliefs. The burden of these dominates man's thinking, relationships and daily life. These are the causes of our problems for they divide man from man in every relationship. His perception of life is shaped by the concepts already established in his mind. The content of his consciousness *is* this consciousness. This content is common to all

149

humanity. The individuality is the name, the form and superficial culture he acquires from his environment. The uniqueness of the individual does not lie in the superficial but in the total freedom from the content of consciousness.

Freedom is not a reaction; freedom is not choice. It is man's pretence that because he has choice he is free. Freedom is pure observation without direction, without fear of punishment and reward. Freedom is without motive; freedom is not at the end of the evolution of man but lies in the first step of his existence. In observation one begins to discover the lack of freedom. Freedom is found in the choiceless awareness of our daily existence.

Thought is time. Thought is born of experience, of knowledge, which are inseparable from time. Time is the psychological enemy of man. Our action is based on knowledge and therefore time, so man is always a slave to the past.

When man becomes aware of the movement of his own consciousness he will see the division between the thinker and the thought, the observer and the observed, the experiencer and the experience. He will discover that this division is an illusion. Then only is there pure observation which is insight without any shadow of the past. This timeless insight brings about a deep radical change in the mind.

Total negation is the essence of the positive. When there is negation of all those things which are not love – desire, pleasure – then love is, with its compassion and intelligence.

This is more than a short statement, but could it be more concisely worded or more clearly stated? Perhaps he has not stressed enough in this resumé the concept of image-making. We all make images about ourselves and about each other and it is these images that meet, react and get hurt. It is these images that interfere with true relationships between human beings – even the closest relationships.

Returning to Malibu from India in February 1975, K went with Mary Zimbalist for the day to look at Arya Vihara and Pine Cottage which, since the settling of the lawsuit, had become the property of the American Foundation; they also walked with the Lilliefelts on land near the Oak Grove where the school was to be built. When K went back a fortnight later, he felt that the atmosphere of the cottage, which had repelled him at his first visit, had already changed. On 1 April he took up again the journal which he had begun at Brockwood in 1973 and wrote in it daily for three weeks. On 12 April, a beautiful cloudless day, he gave the first of four talks in the Oak Grove where he had not spoken since October 1966.

When K came with Mary to Brockwood again in May, I took down to show him an advance copy of the first volume of his biography, an account of his life up to the dissolution of the Order of the Star. Naturally he looked first at the illustrations, gazing a long time at photographs of Nitya. He then kept asking me how the book would strike a complete outsider; what would 'an ordinary stockbroker think of it?' I could only answer that I did not imagine 'an ordinary stockbroker' was likely to read it. Judging from the reviews, however, the strange story seemed to fascinate a great many people one would not have expected to have any interest at all, and the many letters I received showed that it had helped dozens of people to a better understanding of K, although it was a great shock to some who had had no idea of his Theosophical upbringing. When Mary Zimbalist, after reading it, asked him why, if the Masters existed, they had spoken then but not now, he suggested, 'There is no need of them now the Lord is here.' One would have had to have heard his tone of voice before knowing whether this was a serious reply or not.

K's eightieth birthday fell on 11 or 12 May. On the 11th Dr Parchure arrived at Brockwood from India to spend several weeks in Europe monitoring K's health. In the middle of the month David Bohm was there and held four of what were to be twelve discussions with K. Bohm had just read the biography and asked K whether there had been a particular moment of change for him. K said no; physical pain during 'the process' had made him more sensitive and so had suffering over his brother's death but 'meeting that fully had left no marks'.

K devoted one of his talks at the Saanen gathering that year to what he called a very serious matter – can there be total freedom from psychological fear? 'If one is to be free of fear,' he pointed out, 'one must be free of time. If there were no time one would have no fear. I wonder if you see that? If there were no tomorrow, only the now, fear, as a movement of thought, ends.' Fear arises from the desire for security. 'If there is complete psychological security there is no fear', but there can never be psychological security 'if one is wanting, desiring, pursuing, becoming'. He went on:

... thought is always trying to find a place where it can abide, abide in the sense of hold. What thought creates, being fragmentary, is total insecurity. Therefore there is complete security in being absolutely nothing – which means not a thing created by thought. To be *absolutely nothing* means a total contradiction of everything you have learnt ... You know what it means to be nothing? No ambition – which does not mean that you vegetate – no aggression, no resistance, no barriers built by hurt?... The security that thought has created is no security. That is an absolute truth.

K was persuaded not to go to India that winter because of the state of emergency which had been declared by Mrs Gandhi in June; during this, nothing could be published or publicly spoken without submission to the Censorship Committee. The last thing K was prepared to do was to water down his denunciation of authority and tyranny; there was no point in going if he did not speak and a real danger of imprisonment if he did. After the Brockwood gathering, therefore, he returned to Malibu, spending every weekend at Pine Cottage, talking to the parents and teachers of the prospective Oak Grove school.

Although Mrs Gandhi's state of emergency was still in force the following winter, K decided to go to India after an assurance from Pupul Jayakar, Mrs Gandhi's closest friend, that he would be allowed to say anything he liked in his talks. He stayed in New Delhi with Pupul, who now lived in the same road as Mrs Gandhi. Soon after his arrival he had a long private talk with Mrs Gandhi. One cannot help wondering whether there was any connection between this talk and her surprise decision to hold a general election in 1977. K himself thought there might have been.

At K's request representatives of the Krishnamurti Foundations met at Ojai in March 1977. He wanted as many of them as possible to be with him all the time now. He particularly wanted the Americans and Europeans who had never been to India to be there with him in future years. He was convinced that the more people saw of each other the closer and more affectionate they would become. Jealousy and competition were so alien to him that he never really understood them in others. At one of these trustees' meetings at Ojai he said, 'If people come here and ask, "What was it like to live with this man?" would you be able to convey it to them? If any of the Buddha's disciples were alive would one not travel to the end of the earth to see them, to find out from them what it had been like to live in his presence?' This mention of the Buddha and his disciples was the nearest K ever came to associating himself with the Buddha, yet it is difficult to convey to anyone who did not know him how totally without self-importance this comparison was made. When the self is absent there can be no conceit. 'This man' he spoke of was not his own personality. All the same, how does one reconcile this with his constant reiteration that no one had any authority to represent him after his death and that the guru–disciple relationship was an abomination? Is it not quite simple? In asking the trustees to be with him as much as possible surely he was hoping that at least one or two of them might be granted the depth of perception to bring about a total psychological transformation in themselves which would free them from him as well as from all other crutches? This is very different from the guru-worship of disciples. If anyone ever claims authority to speak for K, one will know that he or she has not been transformed.

It had been decided by this time that Mary should sell her house at Malibu and build an addition to Pine Cottage which would revert to the American Foundation at her death. At Pine Cottage, K would be close to the school, whereas the Malibu house was some sixty miles from Ojai.

On 9 May K underwent a prostate operation at the Cedars-Sinai Medical Center in Los Angeles. He warned Mary beforehand that she must be watchful and not let him 'slip away', and also to remind him to be watchful himself; otherwise, after 'fifty-two years [of public speaking] he might feel enough is enough'. He told her that he had 'always lived with a very thin line between living and dying'. He found it easier to die than to stay alive. A fortnight before the operation he had been to the hospital to give a pint of his own blood in case a transfusion was needed. He refused to have a general anaesthetic, convinced that 'the body would never stand it'. Even a local anaesthetic, causing a spinal block, might be too much for 'the body'. K always had this sense of complete detachment between himself and his body.

When the day came Mary went with him to the hospital and stayed in a room next door. He went round both rooms, touching the walls, something he did to any new room he stayed in and which he was evidently doing for Mary too. Why he did this was never revealed. It seems to have been a means of purification, of banishing some alien, though not necessarily evil, influence and filling the room with his own. Mary asked the anaesthetist to talk to him during the operation to keep him alert so that he would not 'slip away'. He was wheeled back to his room after two hours looking very cheerful and asking for a detective story, but by the evening he was in great pain. He was given a child's dose of a strong pain killer which could not be continued because it produced giddiness and nausea. He 'went off' for about an hour and talked of Nitya and later had what he called 'a dialogue with death'. The next day he dictated to Mary an account of this experience:

153

It was a short operation and not worth talking about, though there was considerable pain. While the pain continued I saw or discovered that the body was almost floating in the air. It may have been an illusion, some kind of hallucination, but a few minutes later there was the personification – not a person – but the personification of death. Watching this peculiar phenomenon between the body and death, there seemed to be a sort of dialogue between them. Death seemed to be talking to the body with great insistence and the body reluctantly was not yielding to what death wanted. Though there were people in the room this phenomenon went on, death inviting, the body refusing.

It was not a fear of death making the body deny the demands of death but the body realised that it was not responsible for itself, there was another entity that was dominating, much stronger, more vital than death itself. Death was more and more demanding, insisting and so the other interfered. Then there was a conversation or a dialogue between not only the body, but this other and death. So there were three entities in conversation.

He had warned, before he went to the hospital, that there might be a disassociation with the body and so death might intervene. Though the person [Mary] was sitting there and a nurse came and went, it was not a self-deception or kind of hallucination. Lying in the bed he saw the clouds full of rain and the window lighted up, the town below stretching for miles. There was spattering of rain on the window pane and he saw clearly the saline solution dripping, drop by drop, into the organism. One felt very strongly and clearly that if the other had not interfered death would have won.

This dialogue began in words with thought operating very clearly. There was thunder and lightning and the conversation went on. Since there was no fear at all, neither on the part of the body or the other – absolutely no fear – one could converse freely and profoundly. It is always difficult to put a conversation of that kind into words. Strangely, as there was no fear, death was not enchaining the mind to the things of the past. What came out of the conversation was very clear. The body was in considerable pain and not apprehensive or anxious and the other was discernibly beyond both. It was as though the other was acting as an umpire in a dangerous game of which the body was not fully aware.

Death seemed to be always present but death cannot be invited. That would be suicide which would be utterly foolish.

During this conversation there was no sense of time. Probably the whole dialogue lasted about an hour and time by the watch did not exist. Words ceased to exist but there was an immediate insight into what each one was saying. Of course if one is attached to anything – ideas, beliefs, property or person, death would not come to have a conversation with you. Death in the sense of ending is absolute freedom.

The quality of conversation was urbane. There was nothing whatsoever of sentiment, emotional extravagance, no distortion of the absolute fact of time coming to an end and the vastness without any border when death is part of your daily life. There was a feeling that the body would go on for many years but death and the other would always be together until the organism could no longer be active. There was a great sense of humour amongst the three of them and one could almost hear the laughter. And the beauty of it was with the clouds and the rain.

The sound of this conversation was expanding endlessly and the sound was the same at the beginning and was without end. It was a song without a beginning or an end. Death and life are very close together, like love and death. As love is not a remembrance, so death had no past. Fear never entered this conversation for fear is darkness and death is light.

This dialogue was not illusory or fanciful. It was like a whisper in the wind but the whisper was very clear and if you listened you could hear it; you could then be part of it. Then we would share it together. But you won't listen to it. As you are too identified with your own body, your own thoughts and your own direction. One must abandon all this to enter into the light and love of death.

The only addition to K's usual programme that summer was that before flying alone to India in November he went with Mary to the Janker Clinic at Bonn for three nights to consult a Dr Scheef. Various tests showed, according to the doctor, that he was 'fantastic' for his age.

Some of the trustees of the English and American Foundations joined him in Madras at the beginning of 1978 and then went with him to Rishi Valley where a few changes had been made in the school. G. Narayan, the eldest son of K's eldest brother, had now become Principal after the resignation of Dr Balasundaram. Narayan had been teaching for twenty-five years, first at Rishi Valley and then at a Rudolph Steiner school in England. His wife had been a teacher at Brockwood almost from the beginning and their only child, Natasha, was a pupil at Brockwood. K took no account of his blood relationship with Narayan and seemed no more nor less fond of Natasha than of any other bright young girl. He loved all children and most young people. Pupils from Rishi Valley had been encouraged to go to Brockwood for a time; now K was questioning the wisdom of this. It was so easy to be corrupted by the West. The young in India still showed respect for their elders and an eagerness to learn, regarding education as a privilege.

When K returned to Ojai the extension to Pine Cottage was finished and he and Mary moved in there. It had been hard for Mary to give up her beautiful home at Malibu, which K also missed, but she had transformed Pine Cottage into an equally lovely house, keeping intact the cottage where K slept and joining it to an extension by a passage. K and Mary both came to love this new house. K took pleasure in polishing the electric kettle and the counter tops in the kitchen, as he did in the West Wing at Brockwood, and in helping to create a new small garden. He always enjoyed doing the watering and would try to help in the house by carrying his breakfast tray into the kitchen and stacking and unstacking the dishwasher. He was afraid that Mary was exhausting herself both at Ojai and Brockwood. She acted as his secretary and chauffeur, did all the shopping and washed and ironed his clothes. When she returned with baskets of groceries he was eager to see what she had bought. However, he would never allow anyone to do his packing on which he prided himself. In those years when Mary did not go with him to India, she had three months' rest in California.

On his way to Gstaad in June, K went with Mary to the Janker Clinic again, where all the tests he underwent proved satisfactory. Back at Brockwood in September, after the Saanen gathering, he began to dictate to Mary fortnightly letters to his schools, which he continued to do on and off until March 1980 – thirty-seven letters altogether, of about three pages each. Mostly dictated in batches, but sent out fortnightly, these letters bore the date of their despatch, not that of the day on which they were dictated.[60] It was a way of keeping in touch with all his schools. In his first letter he clearly stated what his intention was for them: 'They are to be concerned with the cultivation of the whole human being. These centres of education must help the students and educators to flower naturally.' And in a later letter: 'It is the concern of these schools to bring about a new generation of human beings who are free from self-centred action. No other educational centres are concerned with this and it is our responsibility, as educators, to bring about a mind that has no conflict within itself.'

A copy of each letter was given to every teacher and pupil. What K expected the teachers to do seems impossible – to see that fear in any form did not arise in the students (and for this it was necessary that the teachers should uncover the root of their own fear) and to help the student 'never to be psychologically wounded, not only while he was part of the school but throughout life'. Competition was one of the greatest evils in education: 'When in your school you compare B with A you are destroying them both.'

In these letters K reiterated that teaching was the highest calling and that 'the Schools exist primarily to bring about a profound transformation in human beings'. He also went very deeply into the difference between learning and the accumulation of knowledge; the latter merely dulls the mind: 'to know is not to know and the understanding of this fact that knowledge can never solve our human problems is intelligence.'

In a book published the following year K explained what he meant by the phrase 'never to be psychologically wounded'. He had been enlarging on 'living with sorrow' and then continued:

> We are seeing the fact, the 'what is', which is suffering... I suffer and the mind is doing everything it can to run away from it... So, don't escape from sorrow, which does not mean that you become morbid. Live with it... What takes place? Watch. The mind is very clear, sharp. It is faced with the fact. The very suffering transformed into passion is enormous. From that arises a mind that can never be hurt. Full stop. That is the secret.[61]

In his letter to the schools dated 1 May 1979, K began one paragraph: 'God is disorder.' If one goes on reading, his meaning becomes perfectly clear: 'Consider the innumerable gods that man has invented... and observe the confusion that this has created in the world, the wars it has brought about.' The parents of one Brockwood pupil who took this letter home in the holidays, read the bare statement 'God is disorder' and were so outraged that they considered removing the girl from the school. So many of K's bald statements puzzled people: 'Ideals are brutal things' (this has the same meaning as 'God is disorder'); 'There is no such thing as unhappy love'; 'If you really loved your children there would be no wars'; 'All thought corrupts' or 'is corruption'. The last is the only one that it is hard to explain to oneself. He often explained it at length in his talks. He said, for instance, in one: 'We are using the word mind to imply the senses, the capacity to think, and the brain that stores all the memories as experience, as knowledge... Knowledge corrupts the mind. Knowledge is the movement of the past, and when the past overshadows the actual, corruption takes place... We are using the word corruption to mean that which is broken up, that which is not taken as a whole.'[62]

Mary Zimbalist went to India with K in October 1978, and later in the year several members of the English and American Foundations again joined K and the trustees of the Indian Foundation in Madras. On 8 January 1979, Mrs Gandhi went to Vasanta Vihar to see K. In December she had been jailed for four days which had caused riots in many parts of India. It was apparent that talking to K meant a great deal to her. He gained the impression that she was a very unhappy woman who could 'never get off the tiger', as he put it.

Another Krishnamurti school, the last of the Indian schools, had been opened that summer in a valley ten miles from the centre of Bangalore. The building and land of a hundred acres had been made possible by the gift of one man. Called the Valley School, it is a co-educational day and boarding school for over a hundred children, between the ages of six and thirteen. K visited it before he left India.

17

'The vacant mind'

K had asked me in 1974 to write a second volume of his biography.
I wanted to do so but hesitated for a long time before starting it,
knowing how much more difficult it would be to write than the first
volume which had an enthralling, if at times crazy, story to tell. Not
much had happened to K outwardly in the last forty years, though he
had lived a thrilling inner life. It was not for five years that I felt ready
to tackle the book and one of the first steps was to make another attempt
to uncover the mystery of who and what he was. Reading the *Notebook*
had not helped to elucidate my mystification.

When K came to Brockwood, therefore, in June 1979, I went down
there and had two long conversations with him. Mary Zimbalist, who
was present, took notes. I made no notes myself at the time and did not
like the idea of using a tape recorder which might inhibit spontaneity.
The first conversation took place one morning in K's large bedroom,
looking south over the lawn and fields beyond, while he sat up in bed,
straight-backed and cross-legged in a pale blue bath robe. There was
a faint smell of sandalwood in the room which I always associated with
him. Even his writing paper smelt of it. He was very alert that morning
and seemed eager to make some new discovery.

I started by asking him if he could explain what had made him what
he was. He countered this by asking me what explanation I thought
there could be. The most plausible explanation, I said, was of course
the Besant–Leadbeater theory of the Lord Maitreya taking over a body
specially prepared for his occupation, the ego having evolved through
a series of incarnations until it was born in a Brahmin body, which was
purer than any other, not having touched meat or alcohol for countless

generations. This explanation would also account for 'the process' – the body being 'tuned' as it were, rendered more and more sensitive to accommodate its divine occupant, thus ultimately blending the consciousness of the Lord Maitreya with that of Krishnamurti. In other words, everything Mrs Besant and Leadbeater had predicted had come to pass. K agreed that this theory was the most likely but he did not think it was that. Another possible explanation I put forward was that there was a huge reservoir of goodness in the world which could be tapped, and had been tapped by many great artists, geniuses and saints. K dismissed this out of hand. The only other theory I could suggest was that Krishnamurti himself had evolved through many lives to become what he was, though this I found hard to accept because the young Krishna I had known had been quite vacant, childish, almost moronic, interested in nothing really except golf and motor bicycles. I could not see how this being could ever have developed the brain to expound Krishnamurti's subtle teaching.

I now quote from Mary Zimbalist's notes:

ML: The teachings are not simple. How did they come out of that vacant boy?

K: You admit a mystery. The boy was affectionate, vacant, not intellectual, enjoyed athletic games. What is important in this is the vacant mind. How could that vacant mind come to this? Was vacancy necessary for this to manifest? Does this thing that manifests come out of the universal pool as genius comes out of it in other fields? The religious spirit has nothing to do with genius. How is it that the vacant mind was not filled with Theosophy etc.? Was the vacancy intended for the manifestation? The boy must have been strange from the beginning. What made him that way? Was the body prepared through many lives or did this force pick out the vacant body? Why didn't he become an abomination with all that adulation? Why didn't he become cynical, bitter? What kept him from that? This vacancy was guarded. By what?

ML: That is what we are trying to find out.

K: Right through life it has been guarded, protected. When I get into an aeroplane I know nothing will happen. But I don't do anything that will cause danger. I would have loved to go up in a glider [the opportunity had been offered to him at Gstaad] but I felt, 'No, I mustn't.' Always I have felt protected. Or does the impression I am protected come because Amma [Mrs Besant] always saw that I was – always saw that there were two initiates to guard me. I don't think it is that.

ML: No, because the other thing – 'the process' – came for the first time when you were away from them all – all alone at Ojai with Nitya.

K: Yes, the vacancy has never gone away. At the dentist for four hours not a single thought came into my head. Only when talking and writing does '*this*' come into play. I am amazed. The vacancy is still there. From that age till now – eighty or so – to keep a mind that is vacant. What does it? You can feel it in the room now. It is happening in this room now because we are touching something very, very serious and it comes pouring in. The mind of this man from childhood till now is constantly vacant. I don't want to make a mystery: why can't it happen to everyone?

ML: When you give talks is your mind vacant?

K: Oh, yes, completely. But I'm not interested in that but in why it stays vacant. Because it is vacant it has no problems.

ML: Is it unique?

K: No. If a thing is unique then others cannot get it. I want to avoid any mystery. I see that the boy's mind is the same now. The other thing is here now. Don't you feel it? It is like throbbing.

ML: The essence of your teaching is that everyone can have it. [I did feel the throbbing but was not sure it was not imagination.]

K: Yes, if it is unique it is not worth anything. But this isn't like that. Is it kept vacant for this thing to say, 'Though I am vacant, you – X – can also have it'?

ML: You mean it is vacant in order to be able to say that this can happen to everyone?

K: That's right. That's right. But did that thing keep the mind vacant? How did it remain vacant all these years? It is extraordinary. I never thought of it before. It would not be that way if it weren't detached. Why was he not attached? That thing must have said, 'There must be vacancy or I – it – cannot function.' This is admitting all sorts of mystical things. So what is *that* that keeps it vacant in order to say all these things? Did it find a boy that was most likely to remain vacant? This boy apparently didn't have any fear of going against Leadbeater, going against Theosophy, against authority. Amma, Leadbeater – they had great authority. That thing must have been operating. This must be possible for all mankind. If not, what is the point of it?

The conversation broke off here; K had to get up to be in time for lunch in the school dining room. After lunch we resumed talking, in the kitchen of the West Wing:

K: We haven't discovered why this boy was kept vacant from then till now. Is the vacancy a lack of selfishness – the self – *my* house, attachment? But how did the vacancy with its non-self come about? It would be simple if we said that the Lord Maitreya prepared this body and kept it vacant. That would be the simplest explanation but the simplest is suspect. Another explanation is that K's ego might have been in touch with the Lord Maitreya and the Buddha and said, 'I withdraw; *that* is more important than my

161

beastly self.' It doesn't feel clean, right. The Lord Maitreya saw this body with the least ego, wanted to manifest through it and so it was kept uncontaminated. Amma said the face of K was very important because it represented *that*. It was prepared for *that*. This means everyone cannot have it. K is a biological freak. An easy way out. So what is the truth? I don't know. I really don't know. What is the truth of all this? It is not self-delusion, deception, an induced state, a wish produced – I don't know what to wish for. Another peculiar thing in all this is that K has always been attracted to the Buddha. Was this an influence? I don't think so. Is that reservoir the Buddha? the Maitreya? What is the truth? Is it something we can never find out?

Mary Zimbalist: Do you ever feel used, feel something coming into you?

K: I wouldn't say that. It comes into the room when we are talking seriously.

ML: How is it related to the pain?

K: Pain comes when I am quiet, not talking. It comes slowly until the body says, 'That is enough.' After reaching a crisis the body faints; the pain peters out or there is some interruption and it goes.

ML: Can we rule out something from outside?

K: I don't. But what is the truth? There is an element in all this which is not man-made, thought-made, not self-induced. I am not like that. Is this something which we cannot discover, mustn't touch, is not penetrable? I am wondering. I have often felt it is not my business, that we will never find out. When we say it comes into being because the mind is vacant, I don't think it is that either. We have come to an impasse. I have talked to you, to her [Mary], to Subba Rao [who had known K since the early days]. He said: 'You have been as you are since the beginning.' I ask myself: 'Is this true?' If it is, there is no hope for others. Is it all something which we cannot touch? We are trying with our minds to touch *that*. Try to find out what *that* is when your mind is completely quiet. To find out the truth of the matter you have to have your mind empty. Not *my* mind which *is* in emptiness. But there is a factor we are missing. We have come to a point where our brains, our instruments of investigation, have no meaning.

ML: Might someone else be able to find out? And would it be right to enquire?

K: *You* might be able to because you are writing about it. I cannot. If you and Maria* sat down and said, 'Let us enquire', I'm pretty sure you could find out. Or do it alone. I see something; what I said is true – I can never find out. Water can never find out what water is. That is quite right. If you find out I'll corroborate it.

ML: You would know if it were right?

---

*K always called Mary 'Maria', pronounced 'Mareea', to distinguish her from me.

K: Can you feel it in the room? It is getting stronger and stronger. My head is starting. If you asked the question and said: 'I don't know', you might find it. If I was writing it I would state all this. I would begin with the boy completely vacant.

ML: Do you mind it said that you want it explained?

K: I don't care. Say what you like. I'm sure if others put their minds to this they can do it. I'm absolutely sure of this. Absolutely, absolutely. Also, I am sure *I* can't find it.

ML: What if one could understand it but not be able to put it into words?

K: You could. You would find a way. The moment you discover something you have words for it. Like a poem. If you are open to enquire, put your brain in condition, someone could find out. But the moment you find it, it will be right. No mystery.

ML: Will the mystery mind being found?

K: No, the mystery will be gone.

Mary Zimbalist: But the mystery is something sacred.

K: The sacredness will remain.

Here the conversation ended because K's head had become so bad that he had to go and lie down. It was not only when he was quiet that the pain came on but also when he was talking about such matters as we had been discussing. I returned to London awed by the responsibility he had put on us: he was 'absolutely sure' that we could find out the truth about him if we tried, but I was still reluctant to believe that he himself could not help more towards discovering the truth, so three weeks later I talked to him again at Brockwood before he left for Gstaad. It was after lunch in the kitchen of the West Wing again, and again Mary was present and took notes from which I quote:

ML: Your teaching is very complicated.

K: Very complicated.

ML: If you read it would you understand it?

K: Oh, yes, yes.

ML: Who made the teachings? You? The mystery?

K: A good question. Who made the teachings?

ML: Knowing you as K, the man, it is hard for me to think of you making the teachings.

K: You mean without study, did you or some other person make them?

ML: Something manifests in you which does not seem to be part of your own brain.

K: Are the teachings extraordinary?

ML: Yes. Different. Original.

K: Let us be clear. If I deliberately sat down to write it, I doubt if I could produce it. I'll tell you something that happens: I said yesterday, 'Thinking about something is different from thinking.' I said, 'I don't quite understand it, let me look at it,' and when I did I saw something clearly. There is a sense of vacuity and then something comes. But if I sat down to it I might not be able to. Schopenhauer, Lenin, Bertrand Russell etc. had all read tremendously. Here is the phenomenon of this chap who isn't trained, who has had no discipline. How did he get all this? What is it? If it were only K – he is uneducated, gentle – so where does it come from? This person hasn't thought out the teaching.

ML: He hasn't come to it through thought?

K: It is like – what – what is the biblical term? – revelation. It happens all the time when I'm talking.

ML: Does the audience create something towards the revelation?

K: No. Let's begin again. The deeper question would be: the boy was found, conditioning took no hold – neither the Theosophy, nor the adulation, nor the World Teacher, the property, the enormous sums of money – none of it affected him. Why? Who protected him?

ML: It is difficult for me not to personify a power – protection by *someone*. A *power* to protect is too vast a conception for our limited brains but perhaps it's like a lightning conductor. The lightning, the electricity, finds a conductor – the most direct way to earth. This power, which I think is really love, found a conductor in the vacant mind.

K: It must be a special body. How did that body come about and remain uncorrupted? It would have been so easy to corrupt it. It means that the power was guarding it.

ML: And training it – opening it up with 'the process'?

K: That comes later.

ML: It started as soon as the body was strong enough.

K: Yes, but if you admit all this, it is a freak, in the kindly sense. The freak was kept for the teaching, the freak is totally unimportant. Anyone can accept the teaching, see the truth of it. If you make the freak important it rules out everything else.

Mary Zimbalist: The freak is necessary to give out the teaching but non-freaks can receive it?

K: Yes, yes. So we are asking, how was it maintained as a freak? An awful word.

ML: Say a power was waiting...

K: Amma and Leadbeater maintained that a Bodhisattva was to manifest and they must find a body – the tradition of the Avatar manifesting. The Buddha went through all that, the suffering, etc., then threw it aside and became enlightened. What he taught was original but he went through all that. But here is a freak who didn't go through any of it. Jesus may have been a freak too. The power must have watched over this body from the moment it was born. Why? How did it happen? A boy from a family that was nothing special. How did that boy happen to be there? Was it the power wanting to manifest that created the boy or was it that the power saw a Brahminical family, an eighth child, and said, 'That is the boy'? That thing is in the room. If you ask it what it is, it wouldn't answer. It would say, 'You are too small.' I think we said the other day that there is a reservoir of good that must manifest. But then we are back where we began. How would you describe this without talking of a biological freak? But all this is sacred and I don't know how you will convey not only the sacredness but everything else we have talked about. It is really quite extraordinary why this boy was not corrupted. They did everything to dominate me. Why was he put through the Ojai experience? Was it because the body wasn't sufficiently tuned?

Mary Zimbalist: You never tried to escape pain.

K: Of course not. You see it has begun – the pain – about half an hour ago. Suppose you put all this on paper; what would a sane man, a thinking man, like Joe [my husband], say about it? Would they say it isn't anything? It happens to every genius? If you said, 'Criticize this,' what would be their reaction? Would they say that it is all made up? Or that it is a mystery? Are we trying to touch a mystery? The moment you understand it, it is no longer a mystery. But the sacredness is not a mystery. So we are trying to remove the mystery leading to the source. What would they say? That you are making a mystery where there is none? That he was born that way? The sacred is there and because it is sacred it is vast. What happens when I die? What happens here? Is it all depending on one man? Or are there people who will carry on?

ML: There has been a change from what you said about ten years ago in Epping Forest that it could all go after your death.

K: I'm not sure there is a change. There are the books but they are not enough. If they [the people round him] really had it they would be freaks like K. The freak is saying, 'Are there people who have drunk the waters and will carry on?' I would go to someone who had known him and through them get a feeling of what he was like. I would walk many miles to talk to someone who had been with him: 'You have drunk the waters, what is it like?'

This was the end of the conversation, for again K had to go and lie down because of the pain in his head and neck. I was left with the feeling that K would love to have been on the outside for once, which he had never been. I recalled what he had said on 28 December 1925, after the first manifestation, as we believed, of the Lord Maitreya speaking through him at Adyar. My mother had told him that his face had altered as well as his words and had shone with a glorious radiance as he suddenly changed from the third to the first person singular. 'I wish I could have seen it,' he had replied wistfully. And he had made the same answer to Mrs Kirby when she had told him at the Ommen camp, in 1927, how his face had changed.

I went back to London with a feeling of huge compassion for him. 'Water can never find out what water is,' he had said during our previous conversation. He would never get outside; he would never know what he was; he would never see how transfigured his face became in moments of special inspiration or revelation. *Could* I find out for him? He had told us it was possible, told us to try to find out, whereas in 1972 he had said to the group of American trustees at Ojai that no one could ever understand – that it was something 'much too vast to be put into words.' Now he was saying, 'The moment you discover something you must have words for it.' Could I find out? The sense of protection he had always felt, and his repeated insistence on his vacant mind, were clues to go upon. Could I find out? The challenge was thrilling, intoxicating.

I was able to talk to K again in the autumn at Brockwood, after the Saanen and Brockwood gatherings and after a seminar of scientists, also held at Brockwood. I wanted to try to discover whether the 'revelation' he had spoken of came from inside or outside himself. He began by saying that when he first started speaking he had used the language of Theosophy but that from 1922 (the year of his experience at Ojai) he had found his own language. He then commented again on his vacant mind and said, 'When the mind is empty, it only knows it was empty afterwards.' I now quote once again from Mary Zimbalist's notes:

ML: When does it cease to be empty?

K: When it is necessary to use thought, to communicate. Otherwise it is empty. During the seminar – while I am talking it comes out.

ML: Do you *see* something?

K: No, it comes out. I don't see something and translate. It comes out without my thinking about it. As it comes out, it becomes logical, rational. If I think it out carefully, write it down, repeat it, nothing happens.

ML: Does it come from somewhere outside yourself?

K: With artists and poets it is different because they build up to it. Perception of his [K's] revolutionary teaching must have come slowly, gradually. It was not changing parallel to the language. [He now repeated how he had been invited to go gliding at Gstaad.] I would have gone like a shot – it would have been fun. But I realised I shouldn't do it. I mustn't do anything that is irrelevant for the body. I feel it because of what K has to do in the world. I mustn't get ill because I couldn't talk, so I take as much care as possible. The body is here to talk; it has been brought up that way and its purpose is to talk. Anything else is irrelevant, so the body has to be protected. Another aspect of this is that I feel that there is another kind of protection which is not mine. There is a separate form of protection as if the future is more or less laid down. A different kind of protection, not only of the body. The boy was born with that peculiarity – he must have been protected to survive all he did. Somehow the body is protected to survive. Some element is watching over it. Something is protecting it. It would be speculating to say what. The Maitreya is too concrete, is not simple enough. But I can't look behind the curtain. I can't do it. I tried with Pupul [Jayakar] and various Indian scholars who pressed me. I have said it isn't the Maitreya, the Bodhisattva. That protection is too concrete, too worked-out. But I've always felt protection.

I was inclined to believe that K was being used, and had been used since 1922, by something from outside. This did not mean that he was a medium. A medium is separate from what he or she 'brings through', whereas K and whatever it was that manifested through him were for the most part one. His consciousness was as permeated with this other thing as a sponge with water. There were times, however, when the water seemed to drain away, leaving him very much as he used to be when I first remember him – vague, gentle, fallible, shy, simple-minded, compliant, affectionate, delighting to laugh at the silliest jokes, yet unique in his complete absence of vanity and self-assertiveness. But then I turned to the *Notebook* and found in it a state of consciousness that seemed to be entirely K's own and the wellspring of his teaching, and it was difficult to accept the theory that he was being used.

Before the year was out, K was to undergo another psychic experience, while he was in India. On 21 February 1980, at Ojai, he dictated an account of it to Mary, who had not accompanied him to India that winter, referring to himself in the third person:

K went from Brockwood to India on 1 November 1979. He went after a few days in Madras straight to Rishi Valley. For a long time he had been awakening in the middle of the night with that peculiar meditation which has been pursuing him for very many years. This has been a normal thing in his life. It is not a conscious, deliberate pursuit of meditation or an unconscious desire to achieve something. It is very clearly uninvited and unsought. He has been adroitly watchful of thought making a memory of these meditations. And so each meditation has a quality of something new and fresh in it. There is a sense of accumulating drive, unsought and uninvited. Sometimes it is so intense that there is pain in the head, sometimes

167

a sense of vast emptiness with fathomless energy. Sometimes he wakes up with laughter and measureless joy. These peculiar meditations, which naturally were unpremeditated, grew with intensity. Only on the days he travelled or arrived late in the evening did they stop; or when he had to wake early and travel.

With the arrival in Rishi Valley in the middle of November 1979 the momentum increased and one night in the strange stillness of that part of the world, with the silence undisturbed by the hoot of owls, he woke up to find something totally different and new. The movement had reached the source of all energy.

This must in no way be confused with, or even thought of, as god or the highest principle, the Brahman, which are the projections of the human mind out of fear and longing, the unyielding desire for total security. It is none of those things. Desire cannot possibly reach it, words cannot fathom it, nor can the string of thought wind itself around it. One may ask with what assurance do you state that it is the source of all energy? One can only reply with complete humility that it is so.

All the time that K was in India until the end of January 1980 every night he would wake up with this sense of the absolute. It is not a state, a thing that is static, fixed, immovable. The whole universe is in it, measureless to man. When he returned to Ojai in February 1980, after the body had somewhat rested, there was the perception that there was nothing beyond this. This is the ultimate, the beginning and the ending and the absolute. There is only a sense of incredible vastness and immense beauty.

18

'Ending of the known'

When K returned to Ojai in February, with his tremendous new energy, he felt he was 'not being used' enough. 'What am I to do here for two months?' he asked Mary. 'I am being wasted.' As it happened, he had plenty to do in connection with the new Oak Grove School, talking to the staff and parents. Many parents had moved to the Ojai Valley so that their children might attend the school and they played a much greater part in the running of it than if it had been a boarding school. Mark Lee, an American, who had taught at Rishi Valley and had an Indian wife, was the first Director of the school.

K was certainly not wasted when David Bohm came to stay in March and held eight long discussions with him. These, together with five others which later took place at Brockwood, were published in 1985 under the title *The Ending of Time*, one of K's most important books since it awakened the interest of a new public. The conversations, with their quick questions and responses, do not lend themselves to quotation. The development of the ideas expressed in them is very slow. They deal with the ending of thought as well as with the ending of time – that is, psychological time and thought which are the past. All that we have learnt, all that we are, the whole content of our consciousness, is the past, stored in our memory as thought, and the cluttering up of the brain with the past means that there is no true insight because everything is seen through a cloud of thought which must always be limited by the self. 'Is it possible,' K asked, 'for time to end – the whole idea of time as the past so that there is no tomorrow at all?' If the brain remains in self-centred darkness it wears itself out with the resulting conflict. Can the deterioration of the brain cells and senility be prevented? K suggested that through insight it was possible for the brain cells to change physically, and to act in an orderly way which would lead to a healing of the damage caused by all the years of wrong-functioning.

In the foreword to a booklet containing two dialogues of a later date between K and Bohm, Bohm illuminates this:

> ...it is worth remarking that modern research into the brain and nervous system actually gives considerable support to Krishnamurti's statement that insight may change the brain cells. Thus, for example, it is now well known that there are important substances in the body, the hormones and neurotransmitters, that fundamentally affect the entire functioning of the brain and the nervous system. These substances respond from moment to moment, to what a person knows, to what he thinks, and to what all this means to him. It is by now fairly well established that in this way the brain cells and their functioning are profoundly affected by knowledge and passions. It is thus quite plausible that insight, which must arise in a state of mental energy and passion, could affect the brain cells in an even more profound way.[63]

On the way to Gstaad that summer, K went to the Janker Clinic for the third year. An X-ray showed that a lump he felt under his diaphragm was due to a hernia and was of no consequence. At the Brockwood gathering after Saanen, K was asked why he went on speaking at his age. He answered: 'That has often been asked: "Why do you go on using your energy after fifty years when nobody seems to change?" I think when one sees something true and beautiful one wants to tell people about it, out of affection, out of compassion, out of love. And if there are those who are not interested that is all right. Can you ask the flower why it grows, why it has perfume? It is for the same reason that the speaker talks.'

For the last six years of his life K was to continue his rounds of travelling, talks and discussions, though he had practically given up private interviews. In July 1980 Mrs Radha Burnier, whom K had known well for many years and was extremely fond of, was elected president of the Theosophical Society. She was the daughter of N. Sri Ram, a former president, and a niece of Rukmini Arundale who had contested the election. For her sake K agreed to visit the Theosophical Society when he was in Madras that winter. On 3 November, therefore, Radha Burnier went to Vasanta Vihar to fetch him, and for the first time for forty-seven years he entered the gates of the Theosophical compound, where a crowd was gathered to welcome him, and walked through the grounds to Radha's house on the beach. He remembered hardly anything of the place. Thereafter, for the rest of his life when he was at Vasanta Vihar, he would drive to Radha's house every evening and walk along the beach where he had been 'discovered'.

The next day K flew to Sri Lanka where he had been invited to give talks and where he had not been since 1957. It was a triumphant visit; he met the Prime Minister, was interviewed for television by the Minister of State and talked privately for an hour with the President. He also gave four public talks attended by great crowds.

Later, at Rishi Valley, K was joined by trustees from all three Foundations, and on 20 December Mrs Gandhi, with Rajiv and his wife, came to stay for the night, arriving at Madanapalle by helicopter. Pupul Jayakar was joint host with K. K and Mrs Gandhi took a long walk alone together, with armed guards hidden in the bushes.

When K broke his journey at Brockwood early in 1981, on his way from India to Ojai, he told us excitedly about this visit from Mrs Gandhi and his VIP treatment in Sri Lanka. He seemed really impressed that the President of Sri Lanka should have wanted to see him. This was one of the strange anomalies in K, his respect for wordly success and academic honours in others; yet he was repelled by anyone who boasted of his fame or showed signs of self-importance. He never seemed to consider that the donations given for his work might have originated from some ruthlessly competitive business which he would have deplored had he known about it. If, however, there had not been these contradictions in his nature, he would have been much less interesting and certainly less personally lovable.

At the Saanen gathering of 1981, K suffered a great deal from stomach ache, but tests at the Saanen hospital showed nothing to account for the pain. All the same, it was arranged before he went to India again that he should have a hernia operation when he returned to Ojai the following year. On the way to Gstaad he had suddenly asked Mary Zimbalist, who was with him, to write a book about him – what it was like to be with him. Twice more, in the course of the next few years, he would ask her to do this – even if it was only a hundred pages, writing a little bit each day. One must hope that she will write this one day because since 1966 she had been with him more than anyone else. She was always with him at Gstaad, Brockwood and Ojai now. Vanda Scaravelli would still open up Tannegg for him with Fosca, but she would go back to Florence during the gathering, to return later to close the chalet.

In September, K was to vary his annual programme somewhat by giving two talks in Amsterdam where he had not spoken for ten years. The great RAI Hall was packed, the audience flowing into an adjoining hall with closed circuit television. A few friends from England were with him. On the way to the first talk he asked us in the car what he was going to talk about. I said to him, 'Have you no idea?' He replied, 'No, none.' When his small figure appeared, to sit alone on the huge platform on a hard chair without even a table in front of him, it was somehow intensely moving. As always he remained quite silent for a few minutes, looking from side to side at his audience while they remained dead quiet and tensely expectant. At last he began: 'Most unfortunately there are only two talks and so it is necessary to condense what we have to say about the whole of existence.' More and more he was emphasising at this time that the difference between human beings was only superficial. He explained this in the first talk:

> The content of our consciousness is the common ground of all humanity...a human being living in any part of the world suffers, not only physically but also inwardly. He is uncertain, fearful, confused, anxious, without any sense of deep security. So our consciousness is common to all mankind...and therefore we are not individuals. Please do consider this. We have been trained, educated, religiously as well as scholastically, to think that we are individuals, separate souls, striving for ourselves, but this is an illusion.... We are not separate entities with separate psychological content, struggling for results; we are, each one of us, actually the rest of mankind.

In this same talk he dwelt on another theme about which he had spoken before and was often to speak about again in his last years – living with death:

> Death means the ending of the known. It means the ending of the physical organism, the ending of all the memory which I am, for I am nothing but memory. And I am frightened to let all that go, which means death. Death means the ending of attachments, that is dying while living, not separated by fifty years or so, waiting for some disease to finish you off. It is living with all your vitality, energy, intellectual capacity and with great feeling, and at the same time, for certain conclusions, certain idiosyncrasies, experiences, attachments, hurts, to end, to die. That is, while living, also live with death. Then death is not something far away, death is not something which is at the end of one's life, brought about by some accident, disease or old

...city and that extraordinary benediction which was felt at il d., that immense feeling of sacredness, began to take place. The body was nervously tense because of the crowd, noise etc but in spite of all this, it was there. The pressure & the strain were intense & there was acute pain at the back of the head. There was only this state & there was no other. The whole body was wholly in it and the feeling of sacredness so intense that a groan escaped from the body and passengers were sitting in the next seat. It went on for several hours, late into the night. It was as though one was looking, not with eyes only but with thousand centuries; it was altogether a strange occurrence. The brain was completely empty; all reaction had stopped. During those hours, one was not aware of this emptiness but only

15 Page of K's notebook (actual size), 9 July 1961

17 Nandini Mehta and Pupul Jayakar at Rajghat, 1969

18 K and Friedrich Grohe at Rishi Valley, 1983

posite: 16 K listening to a concert at Rajghat School, 1969

19 K at Brockwood School, 1972

26 K talking to students at Brockwood School, 1975

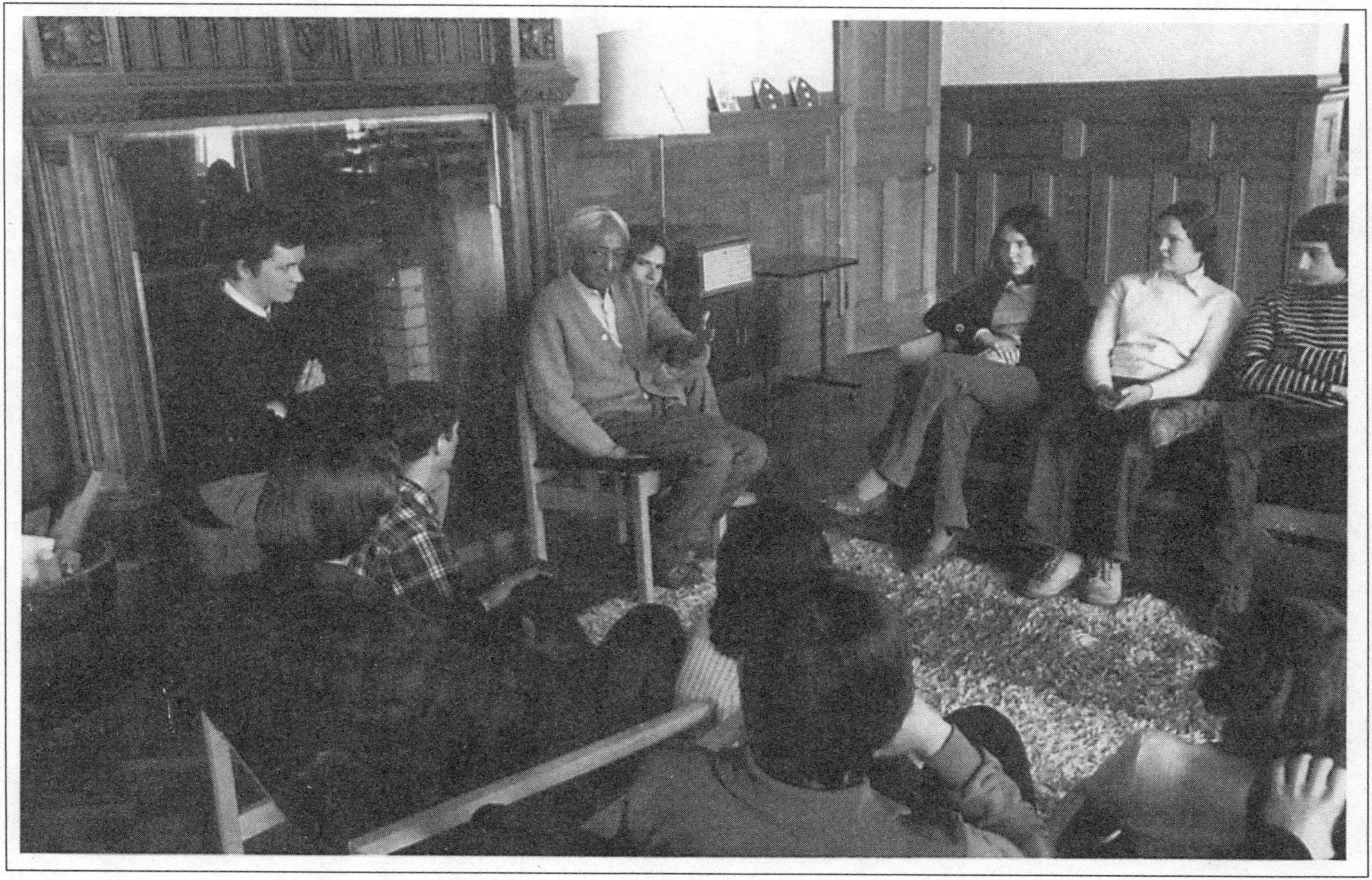

21 K in the Oak Grove at Ojai, 1972

22 K at the Lilliefelts' house, Ojai, 1972

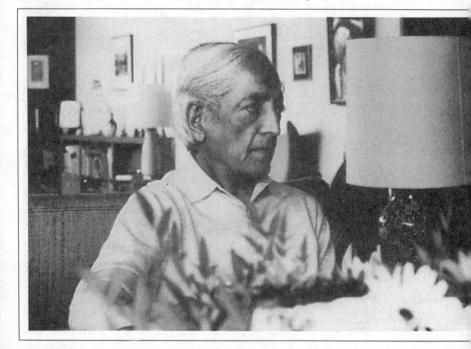

23 K and Scott Forbes at Rougemont, 1985

24 K speaking in Amsterdam, 1981

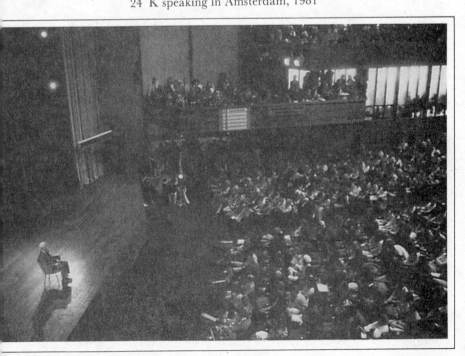

25 K's last talk, Vasanta Vihar, 4 January 1986

age, but rather an ending to all the things of memory – that is death, a death not separate from living.[64]

What he was really asking his listeners to do was to give up all human attachments. How many wanted to do so even if they could? Yet more and more people throughout the world went on attending his talks.

K was very happy to be in Holland where he had spent so much time when he was young. One afternoon he drove to see Castle Eerde again, which was now a school, and where he had not been since 1929. Driving through the beautiful beech woods he wondered, half seriously, why he had ever given back the estate. When he reached the castle, however, he refused to get out of the car for fear of being recognised.

Returning to Ojai at the beginning of 1982, after his usual strenuous months in India, K went in February into the University of California Los Angeles Medical Center for the hernia operation. This was not an urgent operation, but it was felt that if the condition suddenly worsened while he was travelling it might become dangerous. Mary Zimbalist stayed on a couch in his room during the four nights that he was in hospital. This operation also took place under a spinal anaesthetic. It was a great ordeal for him, and as the anaesthetic wore off the pain became intense and he spoke of the 'open door'. Mary asked him to close it. That evening he said to her, 'It was very close. I didn't know whether I had the strength to close the door,' but by that time he was sitting up in bed, reading a thriller.

A later check up at the UCLA Medical Center found that K's blood sugar count was too high, and he was put on a diabetic diet; a visit to the oculist soon afterwards diagnosed the beginnings of cataracts in both eyes and a threat of glaucoma in the left eye, for which he was given drops. On the whole, though, he was declared to be very fit for his age.

At the end of March, K gave two talks in New York, where he had last spoken in 1974, but this time they were given at the Carnegie Hall which held nearly 3,000 people. Every seat was taken. Interviewed by Paul L. Montgomery for the *New York Times* on 26 March at the Hotel Parker-Meridien where he was staying, K told Montgomery: 'You see, I never accepted authority, and I never exercised authority over others. I'll tell you a funny story. During Mussolini's time, one of his chief workers asked me to speak in Stresa, by Lago Maggiore [this was in the summer of 1933]. When I got to the hall, there were in front of me cardinals, bishops, generals. They probably thought I was a guest of Mussolini. I talked about authority, how pernicious it was, how destructive it was. The next day, when I spoke again, there was only one old woman in the audience.' On being asked by Montgomery if he thought his lifetime of work had made any difference to the way people lived, he replied, 'A little, sir, But not much.'

When K had to compress what he had to say into two talks he was more effective now than when he gave a series of talks as at the Ojai, Saanen and Brockwood gatherings and at the places where he spoke regularly in India. In the first of these New York talks, he spoke about psychoanalysis, so much a part of American life: 'If there is any trouble we trot off to the analyst – he's the modern priest – we think he's going to solve all our stupid little problems. Analysis implies that there is an analyser and the analysed. Who is the analyser? Is he separate from the analysed? Or is he the analysed?' K was saying about the analyst and the analysed what he had said for years about the observer and the observed, the thinker and his thought. There was no difference between them. This was true, he maintained, of all inward fragmentation. 'When you're angry,' he said, 'anger is you. You are not different from anger. When you are greedy, envious, you are that.'

He pleaded with the New York audience not to clap before or after a talk: 'If you clap you are clapping for your understanding... The speaker is not interested in any way in being a leader, in being a guru – all that stupid nonsense. We are together understanding something in life, life which has become so extraordinarily complex.'

At the end of the second talk he asked if he might get up and leave and was evidently rather dismayed when questions were put to him. He begged for no more than two. The last one was: 'Sir, could you describe to me God? Does God exist?' To this K replied:

We have invented God. Thought has invented God, that is we, out of misery, despair, loneliness, anxiety, have invented that thing called God. God has not made us in his image – I wish he had. Personally I have no belief in anything. The speaker only faces what is, what are facts, the realisation of the nature of every fact, every thought, all the reactions – he is totally aware of all that. If you are free from fear, from sorrow, there is no need for a god.[65]

There was applause when he stood up, in spite of his plea for no clapping.

*

At Ojai, in April, four hour-long discussions took place on 'The Nature of the Mind' between K, David Bohm, Dr John Hidley, a psychiatrist in private practice in Ojai, and Rupert Sheldrake, who was at that time a consultant to the International Crops Institute in Hyderabad. These discussions, video taped in colour, had been sponsored by the Robert E. Simon Foundation, a private body which gave substantial grants towards the furthering of mental health. There were immediate requests for these tapes from various universities and training centres throughout the country, who could either buy or borrow them to show. They were also shown on several cable TV stations, including New York.[66]

K seemed to be particularly well and energetic on his eighty-seventh birthday in May. He told Mary, 'Every night now meditation wakes me.' It was during his meditation that 'the other' was always present with him. He had described in his *Notebook* (p. 121) what it was like to be woken in the night by this meditation:

> Meditation at that hour was freedom and it was like entering into an unknown world of beauty and quietness; it was a world without image, symbol or word, without waves of memory. Love was in the death of every minute and each death was the returning of love. It was not attachment, it had no roots; it flowered without pause and it was a flame which burnt away the borders, the carefully built fences of consciousness. Meditation was joy and with it came benediction.

In June K was to give two talks at the Barbican Hall in London – the first time he had spoken in England in any hall larger than the Friends' Meeting House – but, although the hall overflowed, the talks were not a success. In the first one, the loudspeaker failed to work; in the second K, disliking the atmosphere of the place, was by no means at his best. There was no separate entrance for the artists, who had to pass through the main vestibule to reach the hall. Unable to face this, K had to be taken up in the service lift.

Dr Parchure, from Rajghat, usually travelled with K now wherever he went, and this year Dr Dagmar Liechti, retired from the Bircher-Benner Clinic in Zurich, started by her uncle and which K had attended in 1960, was at the Saanen gathering and went up to Tannegg to discuss K's health with Dr Parchure; his sugar count was still too high. They suggested that K should cancel the seminar of scientists to be held at Brockwood after the gathering there and take a real holiday in some place where he was not known. He agreed to this. He was beginning to realise himself that he ought to space out his activities more. In spite of feeling tired after the Saanen gathering, he dictated another batch of Letters to the Schools, one a day between 1 and 12 August. Then, in September, he went with Mary to France, to an hotel near Blois where they stayed for over a fortnight. Dorothy Simmons stayed with them for a week. It was the last real holiday of K's life – no talks, no discussions, no interviews and, for once, when he was resting his head did not bother him.

Before he went to India at the end of October I begged him to continue with his Journal. I felt that he was talking too much and not writing at all. It was so much easier to talk than to write, and in his talks one missed his beautiful descriptions of nature. He said that writing was very difficult now because his hands had become so shaky. Then why, I suggested, did he not dictate when alone into a cassette recorder? He liked this idea but said that he would not have time while he was in India.

In India there were not only all the talks in the usual places, with the addition this year of four very successful talks in Calcutta, where he had never spoken before, but also endless discussions with the group of people whom he had surrounded himself with for years, including Pupul Jayakar, Sunanda and Pama Patwardhan and Pama's elder brother Achyut, and an eminent Pandit, Jagannath Upadhyaya.[67] In Europe and America K would have breakfast in bed and not get up until midday unless he had an appointment, whereas in India he came down to breakfast with his friends and the talk began then. Discussions, with several people taking part and asking questions, was the favoured way in India of delving into philosophical or religious teaching. This was no doubt the best way for intellectual understanding but it seemed to preclude those intuitive leaps by which some people more readily perceived what K was talking about. K himself was stimulated by these discussions in India. He liked to go slowly, logically, step by step into his philosophy. It was also the Indian way to question everything that was said. This K thoroughly approved of, since faith, unquestioningly accepting the words of another, was to him an insurmountable barrier to the discovery of truth through self-understanding.

At the Rishi Valley School, Pupul Jayakar's daughter, Rahdika, who had a PhD in Sanskrit and Buddhist studies from an American university and was married to a Canadian professor, Hans Herzberger, was now Director of Studies, working closely with Narayan who was still Principal. K was delighted by the way the school was going. There

were 340 fee-paying students, drawn from different pa
third of them girls and ten per cent receiving scholarshi
had the reputation of being one of the best schools in I...

On K's return to Ojai in February 1983, he began to dictate the
continuation of his Journal. He dictated the first piece into a new
recorder while alone in his room after breakfasting in bed, and continued these dictations, though not daily, until the beginning of April.
Most of the pieces begin with a description of nature, showing that
every day was indeed a new day to him, a day such as had never been
before. For many, these descriptions quicken the whole being, making
it intuitively receptive to the teaching that follows. In March the
following year, again at Ojai, he dictated three more pieces while alone
in his room. Coming two years before his death, these were the last we
were to have of his private reflections and, as it happened, the last one
of all is about death. He described how, while walking on a beautiful
sunny morning in spring, he had seen a dead leaf, 'yellow and bright
red', lying on the path. 'How beautiful that leaf was,' he said, 'so
simple in its death, so lively, full of the beauty and vitality of the
whole tree and the summer. Strange that it had not withered.' He
continued:

Why do human beings die so miserably, so unhappily, with a disease, old
age, senility, the body shrunk, ugly? Why can't they die naturally and as
beautifully as this leaf? What is wrong with us? In spite of all the doctors,
medicines and hospitals, operations and all the agony of life, and the
pleasures too, we don't seem able to die with dignity, simplicity, and with
a smile ... As you teach children mathematics, writing, reading and all the
business of acquiring knowledge, they should also be taught the great dignity
of death, not as a morbid unhappy thing that one has to face eventually,
but as something of daily life – the daily life of looking at the blue sky and
the grasshopper on a leaf. It is part of learning, as you grow teeth and
have all the discomforts of childish illnesses. Children have extraordinary
curiosity. If you see the nature of death, you don't explain that everything
dies, dust to dust and so on, but without any fear you explain it to them
gently and make them feel that the living and the dying are one ...
    There is no resurrection, that is superstition, a dogmatic belief. Everything
on earth, on this beautiful earth, lives, dies, comes into being and withers
away. To grasp this whole movement of life requires intelligence, not the
intelligence of thought, or books, or knowledge, but the intelligence of love
and compassion with its sensitivity ... As one looked at that dead leaf with
all its beauty and colour, maybe one would very deeply comprehend, be

177

aware of, what one's own death must be, not at the very end but at the beginning. Death isn't some horrific thing, something to be avoided, something to be postponed, but rather something to be with day in and day out. And out of that comes an extraordinary sense of immensity.[68]

19

'You must hurry to understand'

In April 1983 K went to New York again, giving talks this time at the Felt Forum in Madison Square Garden which held an even larger audience than Carnegie Hall. Two reporters who interviewed him for the *East West Journal* commented: 'We met a polite and shy man who seemed to have infinite patience, yet at the same time exhibited a fierceness and sense of mission... His clarity and insightful comments put us on the spot many times, leaving us with the feeling that here was a truly free man who, without trying, had achieved what I feel is a type of spiritual anarchy – a deeply moral and sacred outlook completely independent of orthodox ideologies or religions.'

At the Ojai gathering, which followed the New York talks, a full-length colour film of K's life was shown, which had taken Evelyne Blau, one of the trustees of the American Foundation, five years to make. Called *The Challenge of Change* and directed by Michael Mendizza, with readings by the American actor Richard Chamberlain, K sat through the whole of it, something very rare with him, for he never wanted to see himself on television or hear his radio interviews any more than to look at any of his own books. He evidently enjoyed this film, with its beautiful shots of Switzerland and India. It has had some very successful public showings in various towns in America.

Soon after K and Mary arrived at Brockwood in June, Dorothy Simmons had a heart attack. Although she recovered well, she was no longer able to carry the whole burden of the school as she had been doing so magnificently for fourteen years. She retired,but continued to live at Brockwood with her husband, who had himself retired some years earlier.* Eventually, a young American, Scott Forbes, married to a girl from South Africa, Kathy, who taught dancing at the school, was appointed the new Principal. A dynamic young man who had been working at Brockwood for some ten years, mostly in charge of the video (which now had colour equipment), Scott was widely travelled, had lived for a time in Paris and run a small antique business in Geneva before coming across K when he went, by chance, one summer to Saanen. He had listened to a talk and been captivated. In going to work for K, he entirely changed his style of living, while retaining all his vitality. His wife took over responsibility for the video after his appointment as Principal.

Still at Gstaad, after the Saanen gathering of 1983, K was to meet a man who made it possible for him to fulfil what was now his most cherished wish – to build an adult centre at Brockwood, quite independent of the school, where people could go for the sole purpose of studying his teaching. This middle-aged man was Friedrich Grohe, a German living in Switzerland, who four years earlier had retired from the family business, known internationally for its manufacture of bathroom and kitchen taps. Reading one of K's books in 1980 (*The Impossible Question*) determined the course of his life from that time onwards, to use his own words. He came to see K at Tannegg because he was anxious to start a Krishnamurti school in Switzerland. K dissuaded him from taking this step, saying how hard it was to find teachers. (When K asked him whether he was married and he replied no, he was divorced, K grabbed his arm and said 'Good'.)† The following year, on a visit to Brockwood, Friedrich Grohe suggested that, instead of starting a school, he should finance the building of the study centre. K welcomed this proposal enthusiastically. A beautiful site was chosen, close to, but invisible from the school building, with uninterrupted views to the south over fields that could never be built on. K entrusted Scott Forbes with the task of finding an architect and obtaining outline planning permission.

After a full programme in India in that winter of 1983–4, K returned, rather exhausted, to Ojai in February, to deal with problems arising from the opening of a secondary school at Ojai, adjoining the primary

---

*Montague Simmons died in 1986, and Dorothy in 1989. Doris Pratt also died in 1989.

†Friedrich Grohe was subsequently made a trustee of both the English and Indian Foundations.

Oak Grove School. In March he was invited by Dr M. R. Raju of the National Laboratory Research Center at Los Alamos in New Mexico to take part in a symposium on 'Creativity in Science'. This centre for atomic research in America provided a stimulating new audience for K. At 8 am on 19 March, he spoke for over an hour to about 700 scientists, on the theme that knowledge could never be creative because it was incomplete. He ended:

> Surely creation can take place only when thought is silent... Science is the movement of knowledge gathering more and more and more. The 'more' is the measurement, and thought can be measured because it is a material process. Knowledge has its own limited insight, its own limited creation, but this brings conflict. We are talking about holistic perception in which the ego, the 'me', the personality, does not enter at all. Then only is there this thing called creativity. That is it.

The next morning K answered questions to a smaller audience, confined to Fellows of the Los Alamos National Laboratory. Of the fifteen questions handed to him, he answered only the first and last. The answer to the first question 'What is creativity? What is meditation?' took up almost the whole of the allotted hour and a half and he repeated much of what he had said the day before. About meditation he said: 'Meditation is not conscious meditation. What we have been taught is conscious, deliberate meditation, sitting cross-legged or lying down or repeating certain phrases, which is a deliberate, conscious effort to meditate. The speaker says such meditation is nonsense. It is part of desire. Desiring to have a peaceful mind is the same as desiring a good house or a good dress. Conscious meditation destroys, prevents the other form of meditation.'

The last question was: 'If you were Director of the Laboratory with the responsibility for the defence of the country and recognizing the way things are, how would you direct the activities of the Laboratory and the research?' K answered this in part:

> If I have a group of people who say, let's forget all nationalism, all religion, let's, as human beings, solve this problem – try to live together without destruction; if we gave time to all that as a group of absolutely dedicated people who have gathered together at Los Alamos for one purpose and are concerned with all the things we have been talking about, then perhaps there is something new that can take place... Nobody has a global outlook – a global feeling for all humanity – not *my* country – for God's sake. If you went around the world, as the speaker does, you would cry for the rest of your life. Pacifism is a reaction to militarism, that's all. The speaker is not

a pacifist. Instead, let's look at the cause of all this – if we all seek together the causation, then the thing is solved. But each one has different opinions about the causation and sticks to his opinions, his historical directories. So, sir, there it is.

Member of audience: Sir, if I may say so – I think you have convinced us.

Krishnamurti: I'm not convincing anything.

Member of audience: What I mean is, that when we really try to understand this and do something in that direction, somehow we seem to lack the necessary energy... What is it that is really holding us back? We can see the house is on fire, but still we are not able to do anything about stopping the fire.

Krishnamurti: The house on fire, which we think is over there, is here. We have to put our house in order first, sir.[69]

K gave talks again at the Felt Forum in New York in April, after which he was a guest speaker at the Pacem in Terris Society in the Dag Hammarskjöld Library Auditorium of the United Nations. He said nothing on this occasion that he had not said in previous talks, though he never repeated himself in quite the same words.[70]

When K arrived at Brockwood that spring, he found a compact disc player installed in his room which was a great joy to him. Beethoven was the composer he played most often, with Mozart a close second. But he loved most classical music as well as Indian music, especially chanting. Scott Forbes was to write to me after K's death:

For several years I had often gone up to his [K's] bedroom while he was eating breakfast, which was when he listened to music. He would sit in his bed with a tray on his lap, and his feet would ever so gently – almost invisibly – dance to the music under the sheets. And I would either listen just to a part of what he was listening to or, in later years, listen to the whole piece with him. It did not have to do with the fact that it was a marvellous stereo system; rather, with a quality of listening which was beyond what I was used to and which just seemed to happen naturally when I was listening to the music with him.

Chalet Tannegg had now, unfortunately, been sold so it could no longer be rented for the Saanen gathering. A chalet at Schönried, just above Gstaad, was taken instead and opened up for K, as Tannegg had always been, by Vanda Scaravelli and Fosca. K did not like it nearly as much as Tannegg; he continued to take his usual afternoon walks through a wood to the river, but now he had to drive to Tannegg before beginning the walk. Each time they came to the wood, he would call out, 'May we come in?'

Some of the trustees from India and America were at Brockwood in September that year, for an international meeting. Scott Forbes had found an architect while K was in America who had now not only produced plans but had had a model made because K could not read architectural plans. When K saw the model he instantly disliked it; he said it looked like a motel. The trustees staying there agreed with him. Rather than continuing with the same architect, Scott decided to look for another. The specification was a challenge to any architect to move away from the look of a motel: twenty small bedrooms, each with its own shower and lavatory, a drawing room, dining room, library, staff quarters and kitchen, and, more important than anything, a 'quiet' room. K had written: 'There should be a room where you go to be quiet. That room is only used for that... It is like a furnace that heats the whole place... If you don't have that, the Centre becomes just a passage, people coming and going, work and activity.' K insisted that all the material used for the building should be of the very best quality; he wanted the highest standard of excellence throughout.

After trying several other architects, Scott Forbes heard of Keith Critchlow by reading an article on him by chance. No building of his existed in England but he showed Scott photographs of his work abroad, which was mostly for religious buildings. In June the following year, Critchlow was asked to Brockwood to meet K, who felt immediately that he was the right man – more from his personality and conversation than from his sketches. Although an Englishman and a Fellow of the Royal College of Art, where he taught, Critchlow was not qualified to practise in England, so the English firm of Triad was brought in to implement his plans.

An application for outline planning permission was turned down in February 1985. When it came to the appeal, in March, it was found that the application had been faulty, so that both application and rejection were invalid. Another application, therefore, was made in May and granted in August, but it was not until 26 February 1986 that the detailed application was granted.

Mary Zimbalist had to go from Brockwood to Rome for two nights in the autumn of 1984 to see an old Italian maid who had worked for her at Malibu. On her return, K said to her: 'When you are away it is much harder for me. You must hurry to understand everything. I may live another ten years but you must understand.' He was frequently saying to her at this time, 'You must outlive me in order to look after this person,' referring completely objectively to himself. He naturally felt a great urgency now to bring forward and train young people to carry on after his death.

K arrived in Delhi with Mary Zimbalist on 28 October 1984, to stay with Pupul Jayakar for a week. Three days later Mrs Gandhi, who lived in the same road, was assassinated. This horrific event coloured the rest of K's stay in India that winter, though it did not prevent him from giving his usual talks at Rajghat, Madras and Bombay, nor from talking every day to the teachers and students at Rishi Valley during the three weeks he stayed there. As was his wont, he broke his journey from Bombay to Ojai at Brockwood for four days in February 1985. When he flew on to Los Angeles on 17 February he had only a year to live to the very day.

In March he had his annual check up from a new young doctor, Dr Gary Deutsch, at Santa Paula, sixteen miles from Ojai. This doctor had been recommended by a friend of Mary's when K's former doctor in Los Angeles advised him to have a practitioner nearer Ojai. K took to Dr Deutsch at once. This was the doctor who was to attend him in his last illness.

20

'My life has been planned'

K did not speak in New York in 1985 because Milton Friedman, author and, at one time, White House speechwriter, had arranged for him to give two talks in April at the Kennedy Center in Washington, DC. Before that, however, he spoke again for the Pacem in Terris Society at the United Nations on the occasion of their fortieth anniversary. This time the audience was poor and he was kept waiting for half an hour due to some muddle about the hall in which he was to speak. As he left the building at the end of the talk, he said to Mary, 'No more United Nations.'

This was the first and only time that K spoke in Washington. There was not an empty seat in the hall. Addressing a new, seriously interested and intelligent audience, he attained again to the height of his powers. It was not that he said anything new; rather, it was the radiance that came from him, the strength and conviction in his voice, the resonance of his language. In the second talk there was a particularly beautiful passage on sorrow:

> When there is sorrow there is no love. When you are suffering, concerned with your own suffering, how can there be love?... What is sorrow? Is sorrow self-pity? Please investigate. We are not saying it is or it is not... Is sorrow brought about by loneliness – feeling desperately alone, isolated?... Can we look at sorrow as it actually is in us, and remain with it, hold it, and not move away from it? Sorrow is not different from the one who suffers. The person who suffers wants to run away, escape, do all kinds of things. But to look at it as you look at a child, a beautiful child, to hold it, never escape from it – then you will see for yourself, if you really look deeply, that

185

there is an end to sorrow. And when there is an end to sorrow there is passion; not lust, not sensory stimulation, but passion.[71]

Two days before the first talk a long interview with K by Michael Kernan appeared prominently in the *Washington Post*. Kernan, as well as giving a brief account of K's early life, quoted some of his remarks such as 'When you end attachment completely, then love is,' and, 'To learn about, to understand, oneself, all authority must be set aside... There is nothing to be learnt from anybody, including the speaker... The speaker has nothing to teach you. The speaker is merely acting as a mirror in which you can see yourself. Then when you can see yourself clearly you can discard the mirror.'

In another interview K was asked: 'What if a listener takes your suggestions to heart and does indeed change, what can one person do?' to which K replied: 'That is the wrong question. Change... and see what happens.' And in a radio broadcast for 'The Voice of America', on 18 April, when asked what he thought of the religious revival in America, he replied: 'It's not religious revival at all. What's revival? To revive something that's gone, that's dead, isn't it? I mean, you can revive a half-dying body, pump a lot of religious medicine into it, but the body after its revival will be the same old body. That's not religion.' Later in the interview he said:

If man doesn't radically change, fundamentally bring about a mutation in himself, not through God, not through prayers – all that stuff is too infantile, too immature – we will destroy ourselves. A psychological revolution is possible now, not a thousand years later. We've already lived thousands of years and we're still barbarians. So if we don't change now we'll still be barbarians tomorrow or a thousand tomorrows... If I don't stop war today I'll go to war tomorrow. So the future is now, very simply put.

It was a pity that K had to go on with his usual annual talks after the apogee of Washington. Ojai, Saanen, Brockwood, India: there was some deterioration in his talks this year, not surprising at ninety. Since he had so disliked Schönried the year before, Friedrich Grohe had lent him his own flat at Rougemont, about five miles from Gstaad, in the same valley, for the gathering that year. He stayed here with Mary while Vanda and Dr Parchure occupied a larger, rented flat in the same chalet. Fosca had at last had to give up work (she died in August, aged ninety), so Raman Patel, who was in charge of the kitchen at Brockwood, looked after them. From Rougemont, as from Schönried, K drove to Tannegg for the start of his afternoon walks. On his first walk that year he went ahead alone into the wood 'to see if we are welcome'.

K was not at all well during the gathering, which took place in perfect weather. One evening he felt so ill that he said to Mary, 'I wondered if my time had come.' In order to cut down his travelling, he suggested at the international trustees' meeting, held during the talks, that after one more summer at Saanen the gatherings should be held at Brockwood. But, before the end of the talks, some of the trustees went to Rougemont and strongly urged him not to hold even one more gathering at Saanen. K considered the suggestion carefully and then agreed to it. Dr Liechti, who was there again, and Dr Parchure greatly approved of this decision on medical grounds and it was announced next day in the tent.

At the last talk, on 25 July, K said with great feeling: 'We have had the most marvellous days, lovely mornings, beautiful evenings, long shadows and deep blue valleys and clear blue sky and snow. A whole summer has never been like this. So the mountains, the valleys, the trees and the river, tell us good-bye.'

Quite by chance Mark Edwards had been asked to go to Saanen that summer, to take photographs of the gathering, from the setting up of the tents to the last of the talks, so it was a fortunate coincidence that he was there to record this final gathering after twenty-four years.[72] When Mark went to the chalet at Rougemont to take a photograph, K noticed immediately that he had a new camera, a Nikon SA instead of a Leica. As there was no film in the new camera Mark opened the back and showed K the newly designed shutter. K held the camera and asked if he could take it to the window. There he gazed at the beautiful mechanism with complete attention for a long time before handing it back.

For the rest of the summer K was faced with a dilemma as he lingered on at Rougemont after the gathering. Travelling was becoming too tiring for him, yet he could not stay long in one place. He had become so sensitive that he felt people were focusing on him if he stayed too long, a pressure he could no longer stand. And he must go on talking. To talk was his *raison d'être*. He badly needed someone to challenge him so that he could find new inspiration to delve even deeper into himself. No one could do it any more, he said. He could get no further with David Bohm or with Pandit Jagannath Upadhyaya in India. The seminars with psychologists, arranged for him by Dr Shainberg every time he went to New York, had begun to pall as had the conferences.

with scientists at Brockwood. In the last few years he had had discussions with Dr Jonas Salk, discoverer of the polio vaccine, Professor Maurice Wilkins, the writer Iris Murdoch and others, and had been interviewed by innumerable people, including Bernard Levin, on television, but none of them had provided fresh inspiration. The more learned a person was, the more he had read, the better his memory, the fuller his head was stuffed with second-hand knowledge, the harder K found it to get through to him. His interviewers sought to compare him with other religious teachers, other philosophers, to pigeon-hole him in some way. They seemed incapable of listening to what he had to say without screening it through their own prejudices and knowingness.

K intended to cut down his programme in India that winter and give only one series of talks in America in 1986. He considered giving talks in Toronto, where he had never been, but was afraid he might have to cancel them if his health failed. He talked at length to Mary at Rougemont, trying to find an answer to his problem. A letter had just come from a Greek couple asking him and Mary to stay with them on a Greek island. K was tempted and found the island on the map, then wondered whether there would be enough shade (he had once had sunstroke and could not bear walking or sitting in the sun).

He said one day to Mary while they were still at Rougemont, '*It* is watching.' Mary noted: 'He speaks as if something is deciding what happens to him. "It" will decide when his work is done and hence by implication his life.' On another day she wrote down an exchange she had with him when discussing travel plans:

K: It is not the physical effect on the brain. It is something else. My life has been planned. It will tell me when to die, say it is over. That will settle my life. But I must be careful that 'that' is not interfered with by saying: 'I will give only two more talks.'
M: Do you feel how much more time it gives?
K: I think ten more years.
M: Do you mean ten years of talking?
K: When I don't talk it will be over. But I don't want to strain the body. I need a certain amount of rest but no more. A quiet place where nobody knows me. But unfortunately people get to know me.

He told Mary once again at this time that she should write a book about him – what it was like being with him, what he said. He also asked her to make a note: 'If anyone gets hurt by what I am about to say they haven't listened to the teaching.'

Before Erna Lilliefelt, who had been at the international meeting, left to return to California, K told her and Mary that they must see that he had things to do while he was at Ojai. He wasn't just going to sit there, but they must not arrange things in order to please him: 'It must be something you think is necessary.' Walking in the woods the next afternoon he said, 'The spirit has left Saanen, probably that's why I feel so uncomfortable. It has moved to Brockwood.'

When Vanda Scaravelli, who had as usual been back to Florence during the gathering, returned on the eve of K's departure from Rougemont, she advised him to have a long rest and to go to Italy next summer instead of Switzerland. K suddenly became cheerful and excited. 'We can go to the French Alps or the Italian mountains,' he said to Mary. He would also like to go to Florence, Venice and Rome. On 12 August, the day he left for England, he said goodbye to Vanda for the last time.

K was very tired after he reached Brockwood, too tired one day even to do his exercises, an extremely rare occurrence. He told Mary that since the Saanen gathering something had been going on in him and that, 'If something decides everything that happens to K it is extraordinary.' Mary asked him whether he was aware of certain changes in himself – in his manner – 'a little roughness that is unlike you'. 'Am I rough to others?' he asked her. 'No.' 'Just to you?' 'Yes.' He said he never did anything unawares, that she had to hasten to change, that was why he had been rough. 'I want to give you a new brain,' he said. But a fortnight later he told her that he had been looking into his irritability. 'Either I am getting old or I've fallen into a habit [of picking on her] and it is my fault and it must stop. My body has become hypersensitive. Most of the time I want to go away and I mustn't do that. I'm going to deal with this. It is unforgivable.' Another day he said to her, 'I mustn't be seriously ill. The body exists to talk.' His physical strength was undoubtedly failing. His walks were getting shorter. But he was having 'remarkable meditations' which always meant that 'the other', whatever 'the other' was, was with him.

The gathering at Brockwood began on 24 August in superb weather. A professional camera crew was there for the third talk to make a film. They had a crane so they could photograph the whole scene. The film, called *The Role of the Flower*, was shown on Thames Television on 19 January 1986. It could not have been a better film of the gathering as a whole but the interview with K at the end, which promised to be a particularly good one, was too short.

K now felt that he had 'put the house in order' at Brockwood, but that a similar 'putting in order' awaited him in India, and he was half dreading it and half 'burning to get there'. Waiting on the station platform at Petersfield on the way to London one morning, he told Mary that Scott Forbes had asked him how long he was going to live. He had answered that he knew but would not tell. 'Do you really know?' Mary asked:

K: I think I know. I have intimations.
M: Are you willing to tell me?
K: No that would not be right. I can't tell anyone.
M: Could one at least have some vague idea of time?
K: Scott asked me if I would still be here when the Centre was built at Brockwood. I said I would. [The Centre could not be completed before September 1987.]
M: Is one to live thinking that at any moment K might leave?
K: No, it's not like that; it won't happen for quite a while.
M: How long have you known?
K: About two years.

At lunch that day, at Fortnum's, K told me also that he knew when he was going to die but could tell no one. I gathered it might be in two or three years, though he looked so young and spry and agelessly beautiful that day that ten years seemed more likely. He did not appear as an old man at all but as an immortal sprite. He was as observant as ever, looking round the restaurant at the people with the same eager interest.

That autumn, at Brockwood, K started teaching Scott Forbes some of his yoga exercises. He was a stern teacher. Scott would have found his suppleness extraordinary even in a much younger man. He no longer stood on his head, however, as he had done for years. K also had a tape-recorded conversation with Scott which showed what he expected of a teacher at one of his schools. He began by asking Scott if the group of teachers chiefly responsible for the school knew, even intellectually, what he was talking about? Scott replied that they responded to the 'otherness' which was there. Then K wanted to know what was taking place in Scott himself; what was his feeling about K? What was his attitude to K's teaching and to all the work that was going on in America and India and at Brockwood? Why was he, Scott, at Brockwood? Was his contact with the teaching only because of K himself? Was he dependent on K? Supposing K died tomorrow? Having come in contact with K, 'with that whiff, that breath, or that feeling, will that die after

K's death or will that flower grow, multiply? . . . Will it flower by itself?
Not be dependent on circumstances? Nothing can corrupt it once it is
there. It may pass through different circumstances but is always there.'
Scott replied that it was 'not solid yet'.

'Don't use the word "yet",' K admonished him. 'Yet means time.
Will you allow it to become solid, strong and take deep roots, and
flower? Or will it depend on circumstances?' They continued the conversation:

> S: No, sir. One would do everything . . .
> K: No, no, no, sir. Not you do anything. The thing itself, the seed itself –
> like in a womb, you have nothing to do. It grows. It is there. It is bound to
> grow. It is bound to flourish – that is a better word . . . Is Scott aware that
> the seed is there? Is Scott preventing the flowering of it by too much activity,
> too much organization, not giving it sufficient air to flower? What generally
> happens is that organizations smother that thing . . . You must be quite sure
> that the seed is there, not invented by thought. If the seed is strong you
> really have nothing to do with it. . . . There can be no conflict at all in you.
> They [the students] can have conflict but you cannot . . . They may offer
> opinions. You can't have opinions. . . . You have to listen to them, see what
> they are saying, listen to each one, not react to it as Scott or from your
> background, but listen to them very, very carefully . . . Can you be free of
> your background? That's very difficult . . . That really demands all your
> energy . . . Background being all your American training, your American
> education and so-called culture . . . Discuss with it, weigh it, take counsel
> together. Not say, 'Well, I must get rid of my background' – that you can
> never do . . . You can be aware of the background and not let it react, not
> let it interfere. I think there a deliberate act is necessary because you are
> going to run this place. You have got the energy, you have got the drive.
> Keep it. Don't let it gradually wither because of this burden.[73]

K was very concerned at this time that the organisation and busy-ness
of the schools might be swamping the teaching. It was not organisations
that would keep the Foundations together. 'The unifying factor should
be intelligence,' he told Mary and Scott. 'To be free in the real sense
and that freedom is intelligence. Intelligence is common to all of us and
that will bring us together, not organisation. If you see the importance
that each one of us is free and that freedom implies love, consideration,
attention, co-operation, compassion – that intelligence is the factor to
keep us together.' He also asked Mary to note down: 'Independence
without freedom is meaningless. If you have freedom you don't need
independence.'

On 21 September K asked at a staff meeting: 'How do you instantly, without time, make the students see that self-interest is the root of conflict? Not only see it but instantly be transformed?' He went on to say that of all the hundreds of students who had passed through Rishi Valley, his oldest school, not one had been changed. After the meeting, when they were alone, Mary asked him what was the point of having students if none of them in all these years had been changed? If, with all his influence, no student had been transformed, how could the rest of us, who had apparently not changed either, bring about change in the students? 'If you haven't done it, is there any likelihood that we can?' she asked. 'I don't know,' he replied, but he said this rather jokingly, evidently not wanting to continue with a serious subject.

The Brockwood school has continued to flourish since K's death. It is much smaller than the Indian schools with room for only sixty students, an equal number of girls and boys, of twenty different nationalities, aged from fourteen to twenty, and there is a special scholarship fund. A few of the students take Open University courses while living and working at Brockwood.

Keith Critchlow was at Brockwood again in October with detailed plans of the Centre and samples of the two different-coloured hand-made bricks he wanted to use and of the hand-made roof tiles. These met with general approval. K had recently stated on video what he wanted to Centre to be:

> It should be a religious centre, a centre where people feel there is something not cooked-up, not imaginative, not some kind of 'holy' atmosphere. A religious centre, not in the orthodox sense of the word; a centre where a flame is living, not the ashes of it. A flame is alive, and if you come to that house you might take light, the flame, with you, or you might light your candle or be the most extraordinary human being, not broken up, a person who is really whole, has no shadow of sorrow, pain, all that kind of thing. So, that is a religious centre.[74]

K also said about the quiet room: 'That is the source of K. Sorry, I am being quite impersonal about this. That is the source of truth, it shines, living there.'[75] K told Critchlow that he did not want the building to look '*nouveau riche*' or like 'a country hotel'. 'Will it make me want to dress properly – be clean?' he asked. Critchlow replied that if the building was 'respectful' to the people, the people would be respectful to the building. This sense of mutual respect has been magnificently achieved in the finished Centre, which was opened in December 1987. It shows what can still be accomplished by dedicated craftsmen when inspired by the project in which they were encouraged to participate. When entering the building one immediately enters into Krishnamurti's unique atmosphere.

21

'The world of creation'

K would not allow Mary Zimbalist to go with him to India that winter because she had been ill there the year before. She wondered whether she would ever see him again, he had become so frail. 'If I'm going to die I'll telephone to you right away,' he assured her. 'I won't die all of a sudden. I'm in good health, my heart, everything is all right. It is all decided by someone else. I can't talk about it. I'm not allowed to, do you understand? It is much more serious. There are things you don't know. Enormous, and I can't tell you. It is very hard to find a brain like this and it must keep on as long as the body can; until something says enough.'

When Mark Edwards photographed K on 19 October, four days before he left for India, he found him looking remarkably well. However, during the week K spent in New Delhi, he slept very little and ate hardly anything so that when he arrived at Rajghat on 2 November Dr Parchure, who awaited him, found him dreadfully weak. From that day the doctor never left him until his death and kept a daily record of his health.

While he was at Rajghat K accomplished one of his main tasks in India, that of finding a new Head ('Rector' as the position was called) for the Rajghat School. This was Dr P. Krishna, a nephew of Radha Burnier and Professor of Physics at Benares Hindu University, who agreed, with the consent of his Vice-Chancellor, to give up that post and take up his new duties at Rajghat in February.

Instead of writing daily letters to Mary Zimbalist, as K had done on previous visits to India when she had not been with him, he now dictated much longer letters almost every day on to cassettes which he

195

posted to her. This was because of his shaky hand. He told her from Rajghat, on 9 November, that his blood pressure had gone down considerably and that his legs were so 'wobbly' that he could hardly walk; the day before he had fallen down on some steps because he could not get up them. Dr Parchure was giving him some exercises to do and massaging his legs with oil, and he was sure they would soon get stronger. He no longer felt he could eat with people and was having all his meals in bed. People came to see him all the time in his room and he held discussions there. Pupul Jayakar, Nandini Mehta, Radhika Herzberger, Sunanda and Pama Patwardhan were all at Rajghat. By the 11th his legs were better and he was getting stronger altogether. He spoke about the beauty of the river when the sun rose at about 6.15. He was reading Gore Vidal's *Lincoln* and called it 'really marvellous'.

In spite of his weakness K gave two public talks at Rajghat and took part in a series of discussions with the Indian Trustees and some Buddhist scholars, including Jagannath Upadhyaya.[76] The Indian Government had given an Arts grant to G. Aravindan, a well-known producer, to make a full-length film based on K's life, *The Seer who Walks Alone*. The film had been started the year before and the last sequences were shot at Rajghat during this final visit of K's.

When K went on to Rishi Valley at the end of November he showed his feebleness, according to Dr Parchure, in his afternoon walks when he 'leaned on the right so much that he might fall'. He was also feeling the cold very badly, probably because he had lost weight. He told Mary that blankets and a hot-water bottle could not keep him warm at night; the temperature was down to 48° even in the mornings. He was having his meals alone in his room as he had done at Rajghat and also intended to do in Madras. But he still seemed to have no idea how ill he was, for, on 4 December, he told Mary that he would be going to Bombay from Madras on 20 January, leaving Bombay for London on 12 February and, after four days at Brockwood, would fly on to Los Angeles so that he would see her again on 17 February. (That, in fact, was the day on which he was to die.) On the 11th he said he was feeling very much stronger; his legs were becoming 'a little more firm'.

In the middle of December, teachers gathered at Rishi Valley from all the Krishnamurti schools for a conference. Scott Forbes, one of those who came from England, was painfully struck by the physical deterioration in K. He was to write later:

The people at Rishi Valley were very conscious of his frailty, and all the students and the staff were very gentle and cautious with him. There was a sense of foreboding in the air. People were not openly speaking about it – at least not to me – but there were lots of broad hints that they did not expect Krishnamurti ever to come back to Rishi Valley. Krishnamurti must have been preparing the people for this because gradually it became accepted that he would probably not come back to India.

Radhika was playing hostess to everyone, running this conference and trying to take care of Krishnaji as well as meeting her continuing responsibilities in the school. I remember several times thinking to myself that she did this very well and was handling a very, very difficult situation as well as it could be done.[77]

To everyone's surprise, K took part in the teachers' conference, speaking at it three times and 'setting the whole thing on a different footing and radiating greatness', according to one of the English teachers. On the last occasion, K asked whether there was an intelligence not born of knowledge and therefore free of self-interest. He drew a distinction between mind and brain, the latter being a physical mechanism, essentially the seat of thought. Mind was entirely different from this and had no involvement in thought as time. He asked, 'Is time involved in goodness?' and proposed that, contrary to the human experience, the good was not related to the bad, either as a reaction to it or as a primary state. He brought back to the conference, which had been discussing such issues as curricula, what, to K, was the whole purpose of the schools – how to bring about a new brain and what it meant to flower in goodness.[78]

K also spoke alone to the children while he was at Rishi Valley. He emphasised, as he had done to us in 1924 at Pergine, that the worst thing was to grow up mediocre. You could attain the highest position in the land and still be mediocre. It was a question of *being*, not of accomplishment.

There was some discussion between Radhika Herzberger and Scott about a small study centre that was to be built at Rishi Valley, financed by Friedrich Grohe. Small centres were also to be built at Rajghat and at Uttar Kashi in the Himalayas near Dehradoon, on a piece of land that had been presented to the Indian Foundation and was inaccessible in winter. Friedrich financed these buildings as well.

A hoopoe – a bird with a long beak and a high crest – would sit on the windowsill of K's bedroom during these discussions, pecking at the glass, wanting to get in. It had done this on several other visits. K had never fed it and it seemed to have no reason for wanting to get in, yet it was nearly always there. K talked to it and said that it liked the sound of his voice. It was there as usual, pecking at the glass during this last visit of K's. One can hear it very distinctly when listening to the cassette of the discussion.[79]

On 19 December, two days before he left for Madras, K was telling Mary on his daily cassette:

> I'm losing a lot of weight. I seem to get so quickly tired. By the middle of January you will know whether I don't go to Bombay and/or I take the Singapore Airline from Madras to Singapore, from Singapore to LA. That appeals to me – not to get off at Heathrow-London and then take, five days afterward, another plane to LA . . . we'll see how it goes. I'm really very well as a matter of fact, no heart trouble, no head trouble; my brain is good, the brain is functioning very well and the liver and everything is all right, but I don't seem to be able to continue gaining weight. I'm losing, so it may be the wise thing to go to Singapore and straight over the Pacific . . . but as I write to you every day, talk to you every day, you will know. We'll see what happens. The less I travel the better; everything tires me now.

There were interruptions in this recording as K talked to what was evidently the hoopoe bird: 'Come in here. I'm here, come on. Come on old girl, I'm on this side. Come and sit down. (Sorry, I'm talking to the birds.) You have very sharp eyes, haven't you!'

By the 21st, as he told Mary, K had cancelled his Bombay talks and decided to fly to Los Angeles via Singapore. 'I can't lose weight,' he went on, 'I've lost considerably and any more losing weight will make me so weak I won't be able to walk. That wouldn't do at all.'

He had now asked Scott Forbes to go with him to Ojai instead of returning to Europe with the other teachers and to change his and Dr Parchure's tickets to travel with Singapore Airlines and to get one for himself. Fortunately, Scott had an American Express card with which to make these arrangements. K could not face the cold of Europe. He wanted to leave directly the Madras talks, and the meetings of the Indian Trustees that were to follow, were over.

Dr Parchure arranged for K to have a consultation with an eminent doctor as soon as he got to Madras. He now weighed only 97 lbs and was running a temperature. The doctor, suspecting some malignancy, wanted to carry out tests, but K refused to have anything done which would disturb him during the talks. In the event he gave three instead of four public talks, in the evenings in the garden of Vasanta Vihar, and asked Scott to bring forward the date of his departure from 17 January to the 10th. ('He was almost rushing back to Ojai to hand himself over to Dr Deutsch's care', Dr Parchure recorded.) Ill as he was, he continued to walk every day in the late afternoons on the beach from Radha Burnier's house.

At the beginning of January all those staying at Vasanta Vihar, except K, went to the première of the Aravindan film in Madras which had been finished in a remarkably short time. There are some beautiful shots in the film, though it is a pity that the places where we see K walking and speaking are not identified.[80]

K ended his third talk on 4 January 1986 – the last talk he ever gave – with the words:

Creation is something that is most holy. That's the most sacred thing in life and if you have made a mess of your life, change it. Change it today, not tomorrow. If you are uncertain find out why and be *certain*. If your thinking is not straight, think straight, logically. Unless all that is prepared, all that is settled, you can't enter into this world of creation.

It ends. [These two words are hardly audible, breathed rather than spoken. They can just be heard on the cassette. They could not have been heard by the audience.]

Then, after a long pause, he added. 'This is the last talk. Do you want to sit together quietly for a while? All right, sirs, sit quietly for a while.'[81]

At the Indian Foundation meeting following the talks, K insisted that the houses where he had lived should not become places of pilgrimage, that no cult should grow up around him. And he asked for the following memorandum to be inserted in the rules and regulations of the Foundation:

Under no circumstances will the Foundation or any of the institutions under its auspices, or any of its members set themselves up as authorities on Krishnamurti's teachings. This is in accordance with Krishnamurti's declaration that no one anywhere should set himself up as an authority on him or his teachings.[82]

22

'That vast emptiness'

K was very ill with acute stomach ache on the twenty-four hour flight to Los Angeles, with short stops at Singapore, where they changed planes, and Tokyo. Mary Zimbalist met him at the airport and, as soon as they were alone, driving away from the airport (they left the others to bring on the luggage), he told her that for the next two or three days she must not leave him or he might 'slip away'. He said, '*It* doesn't want to inhabit a sick body, one that couldn't function.' He had a temperature of 101° that night.*

On 13 January, K had a consultation with Dr Deutsch at Santa Paula and, as a result of tests carried out right away at the Santa Paula Community Hospital, the doctor arranged for him to have a sonogram on his liver, gall-bladder and pancreas at the Ojai Hospital on the 20th. This, when carried out, showed 'a mass on the liver', so a CAT scan was ordered for the 22nd. But on the morning of the 22nd K woke at 1 a.m. with pain in the stomach which could not be alleviated. Dr Deutsch, when called on the telephone, said that he was unable to deal with the case out of hospital. K agreed after careful thought to be moved, and later that day he was admitted to a private room in the intensive care unit of the Santa Paula Hospital. An X-ray showed an obstruction of the bowel, and a tube was passed through his nose to

---

*The last volume of my biography of K, *The Open Door*, gives a detailed account of his last illness and death, which is taken from three independent sources – Mary Zimbalist's entries in her diary, Dr Parchure's daily medical report and Scott Forbes's recollections written after K's death. Dr Deutsch afterwards confirmed that the accounts were accurate. The same sources have been used in this book, in an abridged form.

201

pump out the fluid and a hyper-alimentation given intravenously when he was found to be seriously undernourished. His weight had dropped to 94 lbs. After all these unpleasant things had been done to him, he said to Scott, 'I must accept. I have accepted so much.' (When I read these words after his death I thought at once of what Mrs Kirby had written about him at the Ommen camp in 1926: 'What a life, poor Krishnaji! There is no doubt about his being *the Sacrifice*.') What he was thankful to accept, however, was the morphine which was given to him when all other forms of pain killer had failed to act. Since he had never taken any form of pain killer during all the agony he had suffered from 'the process', he must have recognised that this pain from disease was not spiritually necessary; indeed, he was to say that 'the other' could not 'get through' when the pain was there.

K was in hospital for eight nights during which Mary, Dr Parachure and Scott took it in turns to sleep on a reclining chair in his room while Erna and Theodor Lilliefelt spent the days there. The 23rd was a critical day because there was a danger of his falling into a coma from hepatitis. Dr Parchure told him that he probably had cancer, for which there was no treatment. This upset Mary and Scott, who thought it premature, until Dr Parchure explained to them that he had promised K a long time ago to tell him immediately if ever he saw any danger of death and, because of a fear of a coma, he felt it right to fulfil his promise. When Mary and Scott next went into K's room, he said, 'It seems I'm going to die,' as if he had not expected it so soon but accepted the fact like so much else. Later he said, 'I wonder why "the other" doesn't let the body go?' He also told Mary, 'I am watching it. It's most curious. "The other"and death are having a struggle.' After cancer had been diagnosed definitely, he said to Mary wonderingly, 'What have I done wrong?' as if he had in some way failed to look after the body entrusted by 'the other' to his charge. He asked Mary and Scott to stay with him until the end because he wanted 'the body' looked after as he had looked after it himself. He made this request without the slightest sentimentality or self-pity.

On the 24th the stomach obstruction began to disperse and the signs of jaundice to recede. The surgeon changed the intravenous connection from the vein in his hand to a larger tube inserted into his collar bone so that more fluid could get through; this released both hands which was a relief, and when next day the nose tube was taken out, he 'felt like a new man'. He also accepted a blood transfusion to give him strength. On the 27th he had a CAT scan in a large van that travelled round the local hospitals. He was, characteristically, intensely interested in the mechanics of the proceedings – how the stretcher was lifted into the van, etc. The scan confirmed that there was a mass on the liver, with calcification of the pancreas, suggesting that the latter was the primary source of the malignancy. When Dr Deutsch told this to K, K asked to be allowed to return to Pine Cottage; he did not want to die in hospital.

While he was in hospital he asked Scott to make a recording of what he wanted done with his ashes. They were to be divided into three parts to go to Ojai, Brockwood and India. He did not want any ceremonies or 'all that nonsense', and the ground where his ashes were buried 'shouldn't become a holy place where people come and worship and all that rot'. (In India, his ashes were scattered on the Ganges.) Nevertheless, he wanted, purely out of curiosity, to know from Pandit Jagannath Upadhyaya what was the traditional way of treating the dead body of a 'holy' man in India, and a letter was sent asking for this information.

On the morning of the 30th, free from pain and having gained an almost unbelievable 14 lbs in weight from the super-alimentation, K returned to Pine Cottage. A hospital bed had been put in his room in place of his own bed, which had been moved into his dressing room, and twenty-four-hour nursing was arranged. So elated was he to be back that he asked Mary to put on a record of Pavarotti singing Neapolitan songs and for a tomato sandwich and some ice cream. One mouthful of the sandwich made him sick (it was his last food by mouth); the pain returned in the evening and he was given morphine again.

As soon as K knew that he was going to die, and while he was still in hospital, he had asked for four people to be sent for from India – Radhika Herzberger, Dr Krishna (the new Rector of Rajghat), Mahesh Saxena, whom he had appointed in Madras as the new Secretary of the Indian Foundation, and R. Upasani, the Principal of the Agricultural College at Rajghat.* These were members of the younger generation who he hoped would carry on his work in India, and he still had things he wanted to say to them. All the same, others went to Ojai, uninvited by him, when they heard he was dying, including Pupul Jayakar and her nephew, Asit Chandmal, in whose flat K had often stayed in Bombay, Mary Cadogan, the Secretary of the English Foundation and a trustee of the Brockwood Educational Trust, Dorothy Simmons, Jane Hammond, an English trustee who had worked for K for many years,

---

*Upasani did not come because he was unable to get a passport in time.

and my husband and myself. It seemed impossible to keep away, and although K welcomed us he certainly did not need us and our vibrations probably did him more harm than good; we must also have been a burden to the kind people at Ojai who had to feed and generally look after us. Friedrich Grohe, who now had a house at Ojai, was also there.

Those from India and England arrived on 31 January. During the week my husband and I were there, K had a remission and one could not help hoping that a miracle had occurred and that he was going to recover. He told Dr Deutsch that the pain, jaundice, morphine and other drugs had left no effect on his brain. He was also having 'wonderful meditations' at night which showed that 'the other' was still with him. Dr Parchure confirmed all this in his report. K held two meetings in his bedroom during that period which were tape recorded by Scott Forbes. The first, on 4 February, was attended only by those of us who had anything to do with the editing and publication of his books (Radhika and Dr Krishna had just been made the Indian members of the recently formed International Publications Committee). K made his wishes over publications unequivocably clear: he wanted his talks and writings to continue to be edited in England while those in India concentrated on translating his works into the vernacular languages. Towards the end of the meeting he said that the Indian Foundation felt they understood him better than the others because he had been born in an Indian body. 'You see, Dr Krishna, I am not an Indian,' he said. 'Nor am I an Indian,' Radhika interposed, 'in that sense I don't think I am an Indian either.' 'Nor am I English,' Mary Cadogan put in.[83]

That afternoon K felt well enough to go out. He was carried down the steps of the verandah in a wheelchair and, since it was a fine day, he asked to be left alone under the pepper tree, now grown huge, from where he could see across the valley to the hills. Scott, however, stood some distance behind the chair for fear he would tip backwards because he was perched cross-legged on the seat. He remained there, perfectly still, for some time before asking to be wheeled back again. It was the last time he went out.

The next day, when Dr Deutsch came to see him, K asked whether he would be able to travel again and give talks. Not as before, the doctor replied, though he might be able to write or dictate or hold private discussions. The doctor had already become a friend and was visiting him almost every day.

On the morning of the 5th K called another meeting which he asked

Scott to record. There were fourteen of us present on this occasion. K started by telling us what the doctor had told him the day before, that there would be no more talks, no more travel. At the moment he had no pain, he said, and his brain was 'very, very, very clear'. He might go on in that condition for months. 'As long as this body is living,' he went on, 'I am still the teacher. K is here as he is on the platform ... I am still the *head* of it. I want to make this very, very clear. As long as the body is living K is there. I know this because I have marvellous dreams all the time – not dreams but whatever happens.' He wanted to be informed in detail, he said, of what was happening in India and Brockwood: 'Don't tell me everything is all right.'

He then requested, as politely as possible, that all the visitors should leave. When he was dead he did not want people to come and 'salute the body'. He then asked Scott not to change the words being recorded. He made Scott, who was standing by the bed holding the microphone, turn to us and say, 'I swear nothing will be altered on any of the tapes. Nothing has been and nothing will be.'[84]

It came as rather a shock to hear K say, 'I am still the teacher. K is here as he is on the platform.' Could one have doubted it? Although from time to time he had broken down at this meeting from sheer physical weakness, he was overwhelmingly himself. No one could ever truthfully say that he was not 'all there' during this time of remission.

My husband and I left next day in compliance with K's wishes. After I had said goodbye to him, not really believing that I would never see him again, he characteristically sent Mary out to see what kind of car we had ordered to take us to the airport; he was satisfied when he heard it was a good car. The other visitors went soon afterwards. Asit Chandmal also left but was to return and stay until K's death. What K looked forward to were Dr Deutsch's visits, though he was worried by the amount of time he was taking from the doctor's other patients. The doctor accepted, as a friend, not as a doctor, the beautiful Patek-Philippe clock which K gave him. (He never sent in a bill for his treatment of K during his final illness.) Finding that K was a Clint Eastwood fan, as he was himself, he brought him some Eastwood films that he had videoed and also slides of the Yosemite, knowing how much K loved trees and mountains.

On the morning of the 7th, Mary Zimbalist asked K if he felt like answering a question which Mary Cadogan had written down for him. He asked Mary to read it to him. It was: 'When Krishnaji dies what *really* happens to that extraordinary focus of understanding and energy that is K?' K's immediate reply, which Mary scribbled down on the paper, was: 'It is gone. If someone goes wholly into the teachings perhaps they might touch that; but one cannot *try* to touch it.' Then, after a moment, he added, 'If you all only knew what you have missed – that vast emptiness.'

Mary Cadogan's question was probably still in K's mind when, in the middle of the morning, he sent for Scott and asked him to tape record something he wanted to say. 'His voice was weak,' Mary noted, 'but he spoke with intent emphasis.' There were pauses between most of his words as if it was an effort for him to bring them out:

I was telling them this morning – for seventy years that super-energy – no – that immense energy, immense intelligence, has been using this body. I don't think people realise what tremendous energy and intelligence went through this body – there's twelve-cylinder engine. And for seventy years – was a pretty long time – and now the body can't stand any more. Nobody, unless the body has been prepared, very carefully, protected and so on – nobody can understand what went through this body. Nobody. Don't anybody pretend. Nobody. I repeat this: nobody amongst us or the public, know what went on. I know they don't. And now after seventy years it has come to an end. Not that that intelligence and energy – it's somewhat here, every day, and especially at night. And after seventy years the body can't stand it – can't stand any more. It can't. The Indians have a lot of damned superstitions about this – that you will and the body goes – and all that kind of nonsense. You won't find another body like this, or that supreme intelligence, operating in a body for many hundred years. You won't see it again. When he goes, it goes. There is no consciousness left behind of *that* consciousness, of *that* state. They'll all pretend or try to imagine they can get into touch with that. Perhaps they will somewhat if they live the teachings. But nobody has done it. Nobody. And so that's that.[85]

When Scott asked him to clarify some of what he had said for fear it might be misunderstood, he became 'very upset' with him and said, 'You have no right to interfere in this.' In telling Scott not to interfere, it seems evident that K wanted this statement known to all who were interested.

K had only nine more days to live. He wanted to die and asked what would happen if the feeding tube was removed. He was told that the body would quickly dehydrate. He knew he had a legal right to have the tube taken out but he did not want to make possible trouble for Mary or the doctor; besides, 'the body' was still in his charge; therefore, to the very end he went on caring for it – cleaning his teeth as he had always done three or four times a day, even the roof of his mouth as well as his tongue; doing his daily Bates's eye exercises; putting into his left eye the drops against glaucoma. When Dr Deutsch told him that blowing into a surgical glove would help clear the fluid that had collected in the base of his lung as a result of lying in bed, he inflated the glove every hour until he no longer had the strength to blow.

Every afternoon now, at Dr Deutsch's suggestion, he was taken in the wheelchair into the large living room where he sat watching the flames of a great log fire. The first time he went in there he asked to be left alone but allowed Scott to stand behind him in case he tipped backwards. Scott wrote afterwards: 'He did something to the room. One could see him doing it, and the room was not the same afterwards. He had all the power and magnificence he had always had. Though he was sitting in his wheeled walker, covered up in blankets, being fed intravenously from these bottles, yet he was immense and majestic, and he absolutely filled the room and made the whole thing vibrate. And he glowed.' When, after half an hour, he wanted to return to bed, he amazed everyone by walking back unaided to his room.

On the 10th, the answer came from Pandit Jagannath Upadhyaya to K's enquiry about the traditional Indian treatment of the body of a religious man after death. On hearing it, K said that he did not want any of it. He did not want anyone to see his body after death and there should be as few people as possible at his cremation.

When he became too weak to get into the wheelchair, he was carried to the living-room sofa in a hammock of his bedclothes. On the 14th the pain returned and he was given morphine again. During the ten minutes it took to work, he said to Mary, 'Too good to be true – sorrow I thought I had lost you.' Mary is quite sure that what he meant by this was, 'I thought I had lost suffering but that was too good to be true.' Next day he started talking to Scott about the state of the world, and asked, 'Do you think Dr Deutsch knows all about this? Do you think he sees it? I will have to talk to him about it.' This he did when the doctor came that afternoon. Scott recorded:

What Krishnaji said to Dr Deutsch on that occasion was an extraordinary ten- or fifteen-minute encapsulation of so much of what he says about the nature of the world. It was eloquent and concise and complete, and I stood there astonished and impressed, listening at the foot of the bed with Dr Deutsch sitting next to him by the side of the bed. The one thing I do remember Krishnaji saying to Dr Deutsch was, 'I am not afraid of dying because I have lived with death all my life. I have never carried any memories.' Later the doctor was to say, 'I feel like I was Krishnaji's last pupil.' It was really lovely. It was also extraordinarily impressive that Krishnaji, as weak as he was and also as close to death as he was, could have summoned up the strength to make that encapsulation that he did, and it's also an indication of the affection he felt for the doctor.

K died in his sleep at just after midnight on 17 February. The end comes in Mary's words:

Parchure, Scott and I were there as usual and as usual K was thinking of others' welfare. He urged me, 'Go to bed, good-night, go to bed, go to sleep.' I said I would but that I would be close by. He fell asleep and when I moved to sit on his left and hold his hand it did not disturb him. The upper part of his bed was raised as he had been more comfortable with it that way and his eyes were half open. We sat with him, Scott on his right and I on his left, Dr Parchure quietly keeping watch and coming and going, the male nurse, Patrick Linville, in the next room. Slowly Krishnaji's sleep deepened into a coma, his breath slowed. Dr Deutsch suddenly and quietly arrived around eleven. Somewhere in the night one's desperate wanting him to be better had to change to wanting him to be free at last of his suffering. Dr Deutsch, Scott and I were there when Krishnaji's heart stopped beating at ten minutes past midnight.

In accordance with his wishes, only a few people saw him after death, and only a handful of friends were present at his cremation which took place at Ventura at eight o'clock that same morning.

23

'*The brain can't understand*'

Krishnamurti's death was in some ways as mysterious as his life. It was ironical that, having felt for a great part of his life that it was easier to 'slip away' than to stay alive, he should go on living when he longed to 'slip away'. He had believed that he knew when he was going to die, yet his death came as a surprise to him. When, in his last recording at Ojai, he had spoken of 'damned Indian superstitions', he had, of course, meant the traditional belief in India that a holy man can *will* himself to die. K could have died by asking to be detached from the tube that fed him, but that, he felt, would be suicide, a violation of the body consigned to his charge – a sacred trust. But was not *willing* oneself to die, if successful, also a form of suicide?

K expressed surprise that 'the other' should want to inhabit a sick body; why did it not let him go? He wondered whether his illness had been caused by something he had done wrong. One may ask, did 'the other' allow him to die because his body had become useless, or did it allow him to develop a fatal illness because there was nothing left for him to say, because his teaching was complete? In either case, 'the other' did not, apparently, desert him at the end.

K believed that 'something' was deciding what should happen to K, something which he was not allowed to talk about; yet, at the same time, he was saying how extraordinary it would be if there *were* something deciding everything that happened to K. Surely there is a contradiction here? But then there are several other anomalies in his statements about himself.

K never doubted that he had always been protected by something. He was convinced that nothing could happen to him while he was on an aeroplane or travelling in any way in order to speak, and that that protection was extended to anyone travelling with him. It was his duty, though, not to expose himself to any danger merely for pleasure, such as gliding. He never doubted either the importance of the teaching or of the body entrusted to his care. He went so far as to say that it had taken many centuries to produce such a body.(It was always 'the teaching', 'the body'; never 'my teaching', 'my body'.) He seemed to be both inside and outside his own mystery. He did not want to make a mystery; nevertheless, a mystery existed which he seemed quite incapable of solving himself, thinking it was not his business to do so, although he was eager that others should solve it, in which case he would be able to corroborate their solution.

K had said that the teaching came as 'a revelation', that if he sat down to think about it, it would not come to him, and yet it evidently came every day while he was writing his *Notebook*. What prompted him suddenly to write the *Notebook*? Apart from its content, it is an extraordinary manuscript, 323 pages without a single erasure.

From K's own words one is forced to the conclusion that he was a 'vehicle' for something and that it was from this something that the teaching came to him. He was, however, for the most part so imbued with this something that it *was* him and, even when it withdrew, it would return if he talked seriously about it or left himself open to it, especially in his meditations at night – *never* inviting it. Sometimes he was surprised that it should be there, as when he described in the *Notebook* how he had arrived from the peace of Gstaad to an eighth-floor apartment in Paris to find that 'sitting quietly in the afternoon, looking over the roof-tops ... most unexpectedly, that benediction, that strength, that otherness came with gentle clarity; it filled the room and remained. It is here as this is being written.'

I have heard it argued that K's inspiration was no different from that of any other artist, particularly any musician; that one might just as well try to find out where Mozart's genius came from. If the teaching had come through K's brain that argument would hold water, but no other genius I have heard of has ever had to undergo anything like 'the process'.

The mystery of Krishnamurti would disappear at once if one could accept the theory of the Lord Maitreya taking over the body prepared for him. Everything about 'the process' would then fall into place – all those messages 'brought through' at Ojai, Ehrwald and Pergine, and K's own conviction that the pain was something that had to be endured without any attempt to prevent or alleviate it. The unique quality of the phenomenon would be explained by that message to Nitya 'brought through' at Ojai: 'The work being done now is of gravest importance and exceedingly delicate. It is the first time this experiment is being carried out in the world.'

K himself did not altogether dismiss this theory, any more than he denied being the World Teacher. He merely said that it was 'too concrete', 'not simple enough', and, indeed, one does feel this about it. In 1972, when speaking to the group at Ojai who had questioned him about who he was, he had answered: 'I feel we are delving into something which the conscious mind can never understand... There is something, a tremendous reservoir as it were, which, if the mind can touch, reveals something which no intellectual mythology – invention, supposition, dogma – can ever reveal. There is something but the brain can't understand it.' Yet, when I questioned him two years later, he said that although he could not find out himself ('water cannot know what water is'), he was 'absolutely sure' that Mary Zimbalist and I and others could discover the truth if we sat down and said: 'Let us enquire', but, he added, 'you have to have your brain empty'.

This brings us to the 'vacant mind'. K kept on returning during my enquiry to 'the boy's' vacant mind – a vacancy which, he said, he had never lost. What had kept it vacant? he asked. What had always protected the vacancy? If he himself were writing about the mystery he would begin with the vacant mind. Those words he had uttered nine days before his death are as haunting to me as anything he ever said: 'If you all only knew what you had missed – that vast emptiness.'

K maintained that the Theosophy on which he had been nurtured had never conditioned him. Is it not possible, though, that subconsciously he had been conditioned by it (although he did not acknowledge that there was such a thing as the subconscious), and that when he was away from his body all that he had been told about the Lord Maitreya, the Masters, etc. surfaced? But that would not explain why he left the body, why 'the process' ever took place.

Another aspect to consider is the energy that so frequently entered him or passed through him. When he was talking seriously about who he was, he would say, 'You can feel it in the room now – a throbbing.' In the last tape he ever recorded, he said, 'I don't think people realize what tremendous energy and intelligence went through this body....' When I heard those words on a cassette I at once thought of the power, the force, that had rushed out at me through the drawing-room door at Brockwood that afternoon when I was least expecting it. If that force, that 'tremendous energy', had been using K's body since 'the process' first began in 1922, it was amazing that he had lived so long. Was that energy 'the other'? Was it energy that caused the pain of 'the process'? Did the energy, 'the process', continue from 1922 for the rest of his life with a gradual diminution of pain only because his body had been slowly opened up to create more emptiness? Would the energy that went through him when he was old have killed him with its force if it had entered him all at once before his body had been attuned to receive it?

Now I think one must ask: did K know more about who and what he was than he ever revealed? When he told Mary Zimbalist and me that if we could find out the truth he would be able to corroborate it and that we would be able to find words for it, was he really saying, 'I must not tell you but if you can find out for yourselves then I can say, "Yes, that is it"'? Perhaps the most significant thing he ever said was to Mary, when she asked him before he left Brockwood for Delhi at the end of October 1985 whether she would ever see him again: 'I won't die all of a sudden . . . it is all decided by someone else. I can't talk about it. I'm not allowed to, do you understand? It is much more serious. There are things you don't know. Enormous, and I can't tell you.' (All decided by 'someone else', note, not 'something else'.)

So there were things K knew about himself which he never told, although he did lift a corner of the curtain in that last cassette.

Many people will feel that any attempt to solve the mystery of Krishnamurti is not only a waste of time but wholly unimportant; it is the teaching that matters, not the man. But for anyone who knew the young Krishna and participated in some of those early events and cannot accept that the teaching developed in his own brain, a tantalising enigma will remain unless, perhaps, one can succeed in emptying one's own brain. K had said, 'That thing in the room. If you ask it what it is it wouldn't answer. It would say, "You are too small".' Yes, that is the humble feeling one is left with; one is too small, too petty, with an ever-chattering brain.

In much the same way, K had said in that last tape: 'They'll all pretend or try to imagine they can get in touch with that. Perhaps they will somewhat *if* [my italics] they live the teachings.'

But, quite apart from its origin, Krishnamurti's teaching has come at a critical moment in the world's history. As he once said to a reporter in Washington: 'If man doesn't radically change, fundamentally bring about a mutation in himself, we will destroy ourselves. A psychological revolution is possible now, not a thousand years later. We've already had thousands of years and we're still barbarians. So if we don't change now we'll still be barbarians tomorrow or a thousand tomorrows.' If one then asks: how can one person's transformation affect the world?, there is only K's own answer to give: 'Change and see what happens.'

Notes

Sources for Notes

AA   Adyar Archives, Theosophical Society, Adyar, Madras, India
BA   Brockwood Archives, Brockwood Park, Hampshire, England
EFB   English Foundation *Bulletin*
Herald   *The Herald of the Star*
ISB   *International Star Bulletin*
KFAA   Krishnamurti Foundation of America Archives, Ojai, California
SPT   Star Publishing Trust
TPH   Theosophical Publishing House, Adyar, Madras, India

All correspondence between Mrs Besant and C. W. Leadbeater are in AA. They are quoted here from copies sent to me by B. Shiva Rao at Krishnamurti's request.
    Krishnamurti's letters to Lady Emily Lutyens are in BA. Lady Emily's letters to Mrs Besant are in AA.

Page	*Note*	
2	1	*Blavatsky and her Teachers*, Jean Overton Fuller, pp. 24–7 (East–West Publications, 1988).
2	2	According to tradition, the Buddha was a position in the hierarchy. Gautama had been the last Buddha. The Lord Maitreya, it was said, was to be the next Buddha after he had fulfilled his mission on earth, hence the title of Bodhisattva. Madame Blavatsky made no mention in any of her writings of the coming of the Lord Maitreya, but she evidently said something to her followers, even if it was misunderstood, because Mrs Besant reminded her

215

Page	Note	

critics when she founded the Order of the Star in the East that Madame Blavatsky had 'regarded it as the mission of the Theosophical Society to prepare the world for the coming of the next great Teacher, though she put that event perhaps half a century later than I do'.

3 3 *The Masters and the Path*, C. W. Leadbeater (TPH, 1925).

4 4 *Krishnamurti*, Pupul Jayakar, p. 16 (Harper & Row, 1986).

8 5 AA. From an essay Krishna was set to write in 1913 at Varengeville in Normandy on 'Fifty Years of my Life'. Krishna intended to add to it year by year but all that was actually written was some 3,500 words, giving a sketch of his life up to 1911.

8 6 *Clairvoyant Investigations by C. W. Leadbeater and the Lives of Alcyone*, Ernest Wood (privately printed, Adyar, 1947). See also *Theosophical Journal*, England, January–February 1965.

10 7 Mrs Besant's and Leadbeater's communications with each other in this chapter were published by C. Jinarajadasa in *The Theosophist*, June 1932.

11 8 Clarke's account of the Initiation in *Australian Theosophist*, September 1928.

11 9 AA. This letter is quoted in full in *The Years of Awakening*, pp. 35–8.

12 10 Quoted in *The Man and his Message*, Lily Heber, p. 49 (Allen & Unwin, 1931).

15 11 *Candles in the Sun*, Lady Emily Lutyens, p. 32 (Hart-Davis, 1957).

17 12 An account of the trial is given in Leadbeater's letters to Lady Emily (BA).

19 13 *Candles in the Sun*, pp. 59–60.

24 14 *Occult Investigations*, C. Jinarajadasa (TPH, 1938).

33 15 *Herald*, June 1922.

42 16 Nitya's and Krishna's accounts are quoted from the copies sent to Lady Emily, now in BA.

43 17 AA. Signed by Nitya and dated 17 February 1923. Quoted from copy of original by kind permission of Mrs Radha Burnier. First quoted in Pupul Jayakar's *Krishnamurti*, pp. 49–57.

45 18 This article, a prose-poem running to 9,000 words, was published in the *Herald* under the title *The Path* in three monthly parts from October 1923. In 1981 *The Path* was included in *Poems and Parables*, J. Krishnamurti (Gollancz, Harper & Row, 1981).

Page	Note	
52	19	From Lady Emily's diary, 1925 (BA).
56	20	For an account of life in Leadbeater's community at The Manor see *To be Young*, Mary Lutyens (reprinted Corgi, 1989).
58	21	*Herald*, September 1925. The other 'occult' events recorded in this chapter come from Lady Emily's diary (BA).
61	22	*Herald*, February 1926.
61	23	*Ibid*, June 1926.
61	24	*Ibid*, March 1926.
61	25	*Candles in the Sun*, p. 144.
65	26	Letter from Maria-Luisa Kirby to R. G. Macbean, 31 July 1926 (*Theosophist*, 19 July 1948).
65	27	*The Pool of Wisdom* (SPT, 1928).
69	28	KFAA.
70	29	*Who brings the Truth* (SPT, 1928).
71	30	*The Last Four Lives of Annie Besant*, A. H. Nethercote, p. 193n (Hart-Davis, 1961).
71	31	Interview with Bourdelle in *L'Intransigéant*, March 1928, quoted in English translation in *ISB*, April 1928.
75	32	*Let Understanding be the Law* (SPT, 1928).
76	33	KFAA.
77	34	*Bernard Shaw*, Hesketh Pearson, p. 115 (Collins, 1942).
78	35	*ISB*, July 1929.
80	36	*Ibid*, September 1929.
81	37	These pronouncements were made in: *Theosophist*, June 1931; *ibid*, December 1931; *Theosophy in India*, 1931, and Wedgwood to Lady Emily, October 1929.
83	38	*ISB*, June 1931.
85	39	Lady Emily's letters to Krishnamurti are in KFAA with copies in BA.
85	40	*ISB*, June 1931.
85	41	Communication from Krishnamurti to the author.
88	42	Authentic reports of Krishnamurti's talks in Latin America and Mexico, revised by himself, were published by SPT in 1936.
92	43	MS by Krishnamurti, 1976 (BA),
96	44	*Commentaries on Living*, pp. 15, 16 and 44. Two further volumes of *Commentaries on Living* were published in 1959 and 1960. All three volumes were edited by Rajagopal.
99	45	*Krishnamurti*, Pupul Jayakar, p. 57. Passages from Krishnamurti's beautiful letters to Nandini Mehta, written between 1948 and 1960 are quoted in this book (pp. 251–73).

217

Page	Note	
100	46	*Trial of Mr Gandhi*, Francis Watson (1969).
102	47	From a copy of Pupul Jayakar's notes, first published in *The Years of Fulfilment*. The account is also given in her *Krishnamurti*, pp. 125–30, with some slight differences.
108	48	*Ibid*, pp. 202–3.
111	49	Letters to and from Doris Pratt (BA).
113	50	*Krishnamurti*, Pupul Jayakar, p. 242.
118	51	From a copy of Vanda Scaravelli's notes.
119	52	*Aldous Huxley*, Sybille Bedford, II, p. 71 (Chatto & Windus, 1973).
132	53	EFB, no. 2, Spring 1969.
134	54	*The Urgency of Change*. This book, bound with an earlier publication, *The Only Revolution*, makes up the *Second Penguin Krishnamurti Reader* (1973).
137	55	January and March, 1972 (KFAA).
143	56	From transcripts (BA).
148	57	These video tapes, available from all three Foundations, have remained extremely popular.
148	58	*Freedom from the Known*, p. 116.
149	59	*Golden Jubilee Souvenir Book* (Krishnamurti Foundation India, 1979).
156	60	*Letters to the Schools* (Krishnamurti Foundation England, 1981). A further eighteen *Letters to the Schools*, dated between 15 November 1981 and 15 November 1983, were published by the Foundation in 1985.
157	61	*Exploration into Insight*, Pupul Jayakar and Sunanda Patwardhan (eds), p. 77 (Gollancz, Harper & Row, 1979).
157	62	EFB, no. 42, 1982.
170	63	*The Future of Humanity* (Mirananda, Holland, 1986). Mary Cadogan edited *The Ending of Time* anonymously.
173	64	*The Network of Thought*, pp. 99–110 (Mirananda, Holland, 1983).
174	65	*The Flame of Attention* (Mirananda, Holland, 1983).
175	66	Available from KFAA and BA.
176	67	Many of these discussions are given at length in Pupul Jayakar's book *Krishnamurti*.
178	68	*Krishnamurti to Himself* (Gollancz, Harper & Row, 1987).
182	69	*Los Alamos* (a booklet) (Krishnamurti Foundation England, 1985).
182	70	UN *Secretarial News*, 16 May 1984, and ESB, no. 47, 1984.
186	71	*Washington D.C. Talks 1985* (Mirananda, Holland, 1988).
187	72	Seventy of these excellent photographs were published in *Last Talks at Saanen* (Gollancz, Harper & Row, 1986).

Page	Note	
191	73	BA.
192	74	*Ibid.*
192	75	When talking about the Centre with Mary Zimbalist and Scott Forbes at Schönried in August 1984.
196	76	*The Future is Now*, Radhika Herzberger (ed.) (Gollancz, 1988).
197	77	From a long account of K's illness written by Scott Forbes after K's death.
197	78	From a letter from Stephen Smith to the author, written after K's death.
198	79	Indian Foundation Archives and BA.
199	80	A video of this film is available from BA.
199	81	EFB, special edition, 1986, and *The Future is Now* (Gollancz, Harper & Row, 1988).
199	82	Indian Foundation Bulletin, 1986/3.
204	83	From tape recording (BA).
205	84	*Ibid.*
206	85	*Ibid* (verbatim transcription).

Books by Krishnamurti

PUBLISHED BY GOLLANCZ AND HARPER & ROW
The First and Last Freedom (1954)
Education and the Significance of Life (1955)
Commentaries on Living (1956)
Commentaries on Living, Second Series (1959)
Commentaries on Living, Third Series (1960)
This Matter of Culture (1964)
Freedom from the Known (1969)
The Only Revolution (1970)
The Urgency of Change (1971)
The Impossible Question (1972)
Beyond Violence, paperback (1973)
The Awakening of Intelligence, illustrated (1973)
The Beginnings of Learning, illustrated (1975)
Krishnamurti's Notebook (1976)
Truth and Actuality, paperback (1977)
The Wholeness of Life (1978)
Exploration into Insight (1979)
Meditations (1979)
Poems and Parables (1981) (American title: *From Darkness to Light*)
Krishnamurti's Journal (1982)
The Ending of Time (1985)
Last Talks at Saanen, illustrated (1986)
Krishnamurti to Himself (1987)
The Future is Now (1988)

Index